GOVERNMENT PROCEDURES AND OPERATIONS

THE SANCTIONS WAY

ISSUES AND USE BY THE UNITED STATES

GOVERNMENT PROCEDURES AND OPERATIONS

Additional books in this series can be found on Nova's website under the Series tab.

Additional e-books in this series can be found on Nova's website under the e-book tab.

GOVERNMENT PROCEDURES AND OPERATIONS

THE SANCTIONS WAY

ISSUES AND USE BY THE UNITED STATES

BRIAN FIELDS
EDITOR

nova publishers
New York

Library of Congress Cataloging-in-Publication Data

ISBN: 978-1-63482-679-2

Published by Nova Science Publishers, Inc. † New York

CONTENTS

PREFACE

Economic sanctions on Russian individuals, entities, and sectors have been a key part of the U.S. response to Russia's annexation of the Crimean region of Ukraine and Russia's efforts to destabilize eastern Ukraine. This book discusses the economic implications of the U.S. sanctions on Russia. The book continues by examining U.S. sanctions in several other countries including Cuba, Iran, North Korea, and Burma.

Chapter 1 – In response to Russia's annexation of the Crimean region of Ukraine and ongoing military intervention in eastern Ukraine, the United States has imposed a number of economic sanctions on Russian individuals, entities, and sectors. The United States coordinated its sanctions with other countries, particularly the European Union (EU). Russia has retaliated against sanctions by banning imports of certain agricultural products from countries imposing sanctions, including the United States, for one year.

Many Members of Congress have been strong proponents of economic sanctions on Russia. In December 2014, Congress unanimously passed the Ukraine Freedom Support Act of 2014 (P.L. 113-272), which authorizes the President to impose sanctions on specific Russian individuals and entities. The President signed the bill but also stated that he would not impose additional sanctions on Russia at this time. As the conflict in Ukraine continues, some Members of Congress are calling for tighter economic sanctions on Russia, in addition to other measures.

Analysts have debated the potential effects of current U.S. sanctions on Russia and Russia's retaliatory measures. Russia is a major player in the international economy; it has the world's ninth-largest economy and it is a major producer and exporter of natural gas and oil. However, there is relatively little overall trade and investment between the United States and Russia, although ties at the firm-level are significant in some instances.

Economic conditions in Russia have deteriorated at a faster rate in recent months. Capital flight from Russia has accelerated, the ruble has depreciated by more than 50%, inflation has increased, and the Russian economy is projected to contract by 3.0% in 2015. It is difficult to assess whether, and if so how much, targeted U.S. sanctions on Russian individuals and entities have contributed to worsening economic conditions in Russia, since other factors are likely contributing to Russia's economic challenges. In particular, oil prices have fallen by 50% in the past six months, and oil is a major Russian export and source of revenue for the government. However, many analysts, including senior officials at the International Monetary Fund, have argued that sanctions are at least one factor contributing to the increasingly difficult economic situation in Russia.

U.S. business groups have raised concerns that sanctions will harm American manufacturers, jeopardize American jobs, and cede business opportunities to firms from other countries. However, there are questions about the extent to which the sanctions and retaliatory measures will affect U.S. economic interests. Russia is a relatively minor trading and investment partner for the United States overall. U.S. sanctions target a specific subset of Russian individuals and entities and, in some cases, restrict only specific types of economic transactions.

The full economic impact on U.S. firms and the U.S. economy remains to be seen. To date, news reports have cited a number of U.S. firms have been adversely affected by U.S. sanctions on Russia and Russia's retaliatory measures. Russia is taking steps to develop alternative economic partners, particularly in emerging markets. Some analysts argue that the impact on U.S. firms should not be overstated; some firms were able to prepare for the disruptions, and the impact could be minimized as alternative markets are located. More broadly, U.S. exports to Russia have remained relatively robust but a weaker ruble and a contraction of the Russian economy may provide additional challenges to U.S. exports to Russia.

Chapter 2 – In December 2014, President Obama announced major changes in U.S. policy toward Cuba, including the restoration of diplomatic relations (relations were severed in January 1961), a review by the Department of State of Cuba's designation as a state sponsor of terrorism (Cuba was designated in 1982), and an increase in travel, trade, and the free flow of information to Cuba. This third step required the Departments of Commerce and the Treasury to amend the embargo regulations, which were announced on January 15, 2015.

When the President announced his policy change on Cuba, he acknowledged that he does not have authority to lift the embargo because it is codified in legislation. While the embargo was first imposed in the early 1960s under the authority of the Foreign Assistance Act of 1961 and the Trading with the Enemy Act, Congress enacted additional laws over the years that strengthened the embargo on Cuba, including the Cuban Democracy Act of 1992, the Cuban Liberty and Democratic Solidarity Act (LIBERTAD) Act of 1996 (which codified the embargo regulations), and the Trade Sanctions Reform and Export Enhancement Act of 2000. Congress also has enacted numerous other provisions of law that impose sanctions on Cuba, including restrictions on trade, foreign aid, and support from the international financial institutions.

This report provides information on legislative provisions restricting relations with Cuba. It lists the various provisions of law comprising economic sanctions on Cuba, including key laws that are the statutory basis of the embargo, and provides information on the authority to lift or waive these restrictions.

Chapter 3 – International sanctions on Iran's key energy and financial sectors harmed Iran's economy and arguably contributed to Iran's acceptance of restrictions on expanding its nuclear program in exchange for modest sanctions relief. The interim nuclear "standstill" agreement (Joint Plan of Action, JPA) has been in effect since January 20, 2014, and extended twice (now until July 6, 2015) to allow time to translate it into a comprehensive nuclear agreement. The economic pressure of sanctions included the following:

- Iran's crude oil exports are about 1.1 million barrels per day (mbd) at the end of 2013—far below the 2.5 million barrels per day Iran exported during 2011.
- Iran's economy shrank by about 5% in 2013 as Iran's private sector reduced operations and many of its loans became delinquent, and has rebounded only modestly since the JPA sanctions relief went into effect.

Sanctions have constricted Iran's ability to procure equipment for its nuclear and missile programs and to import advanced conventional weaponry. However, the sanctions have not halted Iran's provision of arms to the Assad government in Syria, the Iraqi government and related Shiite militias, Houthi rebels in Yemen, or other pro-Iranian factions in the Middle East. Nor have sanctions altered Iran's repression of dissent or monitoring of the Internet.

Under the JPA, the United States has provided Iran with some sanctions relief through presidential waivers of several U.S. sanctions laws and authority under several executive orders. The core of the sanctions relief is $700 million per month in access to hard currency from oil sales, plus about $65 million per month in additional hard currency provided to educational institutions for Iranians studying abroad. The JPA caps Iran's oil exports at about 1mbd but does not cap exports to its crude oil customers of oil products such as condensates, and Iran appears to be increasing exports of condensates to partly compensate for the limitations on crude oil sales. The JPA suspends sanctions on Iran's auto manufacturing sector and on its sales of petrochemicals, although available data indicate activity in these sectors does not appear to be producing nearly as much revenue as was estimated. And, the fall in oil prices since June 2014 has introduced additional uncertainty to Iran's economy, to the point where many experts assess that Iranian leaders urgently need a comprehensive nuclear deal to achieve the economic improvement demanded by the population.

By all accounts, a comprehensive nuclear agreement, if reached, will entail significant easing of U.S. and third country sanctions on Iran—particularly those sanctions that reduced Iran's oil exports and limit its access to the international financial system. The Administration has said that substantial sanctions relief under a comprehensive deal would be provided, but would be implemented stepwise as Iran fulfills the terms of an agreement. The Administration has asserted that, in the event of an agreement, it will act on its own authority to suspend most sanctions on Iran and, after testing Iran's compliance over a period of time, work with Congress on long-term sanctions relief. Some in Congress are proposing additional sanctions if diplomacy fails, but the Administration strongly opposes enacting additional sanctions while talks are ongoing. The Administration asserts that doing so will fracture the coalition negotiating with Iran and cause Iran to walk away from the talks.

Chapter 4 – U.S. economic sanctions imposed on North Korea are instigated by that country's activities related to weapons proliferation; regional disruptions; terrorism; narcotics trafficking; undemocratic governance; and illicit activities in international markets, including money laundering, counterfeiting of goods and currency, and bulk cash smuggling. The sanctions have the following consequences for U.S.-North Korea relations:

- *Trade is minimal* and mostly limited to food, medicine, and other humanitarian-related goods. North Korea has no advantageous trade status and is outright denied certain goods—including luxury goods—and trade financing, primarily due to its proliferation activities. The Department of Commerce places North Korea in the two most restricted country groups for exports; imports require a license from the Treasury Department's Office of Foreign Assets Control; using a North Korea-flagged vessel for any transaction is prohibited.
- *Foreign aid is minimal* and mostly limited to refugees fleeing North Korea; broadcasting into the country; nongovernmental organization programs dedicated to democracy promotion, human rights, and governance; emergency food aid; and aid related to disabling and dismantling the country's nuclear weapons program. By law, U.S. representatives in the international financial institutions (IFI) are required to vote against any support for North Korea due to its nuclear weapons ambitions. Human rights and environmental activities would also likely result in U.S. objections to North Korea's participation in the IFI.
- *Arms sales and arms transfers* are fully denied.
- *Assets are blocked* for certain individuals and entities, should such assets come under U.S. jurisdiction.

Since the outbreak of the Korean War in 1950, the United States had imposed fairly comprehensive economic, diplomatic, and political restrictions on North Korea. In 1999, however, President Clinton announced he would lift many restrictions on U.S. exports to and imports from North Korea in areas other than those controlled for national security concerns; the Departments of Commerce, Treasury, and Transportation issued new regulations a year later that implemented the new policy. On June 26, 2008, President George W. Bush removed restrictions based on authorities in the Trading With the Enemy Act and the terrorism designation, replacing them with more circumscribed economic restrictions related to proliferation concerns.

The U.S. sanctions in place are a result both of requirements incorporated into U.S. law by Congress and decisions made in the executive branch to exercise discretionary authorities. Though the President, in accordance with the Constitution, leads the way in conducting foreign policy, Congress holds substantial power to shape foreign policy by authorizing and funding programs, advising on appointments, and specifically defining the terms of engagement in accordance with U.S. political and strategic interests. This report presents the legislative basis for U.S. sanctions policy toward North Korea. These sanctions are a critical tenet of the larger bilateral relationship, and this report highlights Congress's role and responsibility in determining the nature of U.S.-North Korea relations.

Chapter 5 – The release of all Burma's political prisoners is one of the fundamental goals of U.S. policy. Several of the laws imposing sanctions on Burma—including the Burmese Freedom and Democracy Act of 2003 (P.L. 108-61) and the Tom Lantos Block Burmese JADE (Junta's Anti-Democratic Efforts) Act of 2008 (P.L. 110-286)—require the release of all political prisoners before the sanctions can be terminated. The Consolidated Appropriations Act of 2014 (P.L. 113- 76) requires the Department of State and the U.S. Agency for International Development (USAID) to "support programs for former political prisoners" in Burma, as well as "monitor the number of political prisoners in Burma."

Burma's President Thein Sein pledged during a July 2013 trip to the United Kingdom to release all "prisoners of conscience" in his country by the end of the year. Since his announcement, he granted amnesties or pardons on seven occasions. While President Thein Sein has asserted that all political prisoners have been freed, several Burmese organizations maintain that dozens of political prisoners remain in jail and that new political prisoners continue to be arrested and sentenced.

Hopes for a democratic government and national reconciliation in Burma depend on the release of prisoners, including those associated with the country's ethnic groups. Several ethnic-based political parties have stated they will not participate in parliamentary elections until their members are released. Also, prospects for stable ceasefires and lasting peace with various ethnic-based militias may depend on the release of their members currently in detention.

Estimates of how many political prisoners are being detained in Burma vary. According to the Assistance Association for Political Prisoners (Burma), or AAPP(B), a nonprofit organization dedicated to identifying and locating political prisoners in Burma, the Burmese government was incarcerating 84 political prisoners as of the end of August.

Differences in estimates of the number of political prisoners in Burma can be attributed to two main factors. First, Burma's prison and judicial system is not transparent, making it difficult to obtain accurate information. Second, there is no consensus on the definition of a "political prisoner." Some limit the definition of "political prisoner" to "prisoners of conscience"; others include members of the ethnic militias as political prisoners. President Thein Sein established the Political Prisoner Review Committee (PPRC) in February 2013 to identify all political prisoners in Burma, but the committee reportedly has been unable to agree on a common definition.

The State Department is actively discussing the political prisoner issue with the Burmese government, opposition political parties, and representatives of some ethnic groups. In these discussions, U.S. officials emphasize the importance of the release of all political prisoners for the further easing or removal of U.S. sanctions on Burma.

The status of Burma's political prisoners is likely to figure prominently in any future congressional consideration of U.S. policy in Burma. Congress may choose to examine the political prisoner issue in Burma either separately or as part of a broader review of U.S. policy towards Burma. Congress may also consider inserting in legislation—such as the FY2015 appropriations bills for the State Department (H.R. 5013 and S. 2499)—language pertaining to the political prisoner issue in Burma.

In: The Sanctions Way
Editor: Brian Fields

ISBN: 978-1-63482-679-2

Chapter 1

U.S. SANCTIONS ON RUSSIA: ECONOMIC IMPLICATIONS*

Rebecca M. Nelson

SUMMARY

In response to Russia's annexation of the Crimean region of Ukraine and ongoing military intervention in eastern Ukraine, the United States has imposed a number of economic sanctions on Russian individuals, entities, and sectors. The United States coordinated its sanctions with other countries, particularly the European Union (EU). Russia has retaliated against sanctions by banning imports of certain agricultural products from countries imposing sanctions, including the United States, for one year.

Many Members of Congress have been strong proponents of economic sanctions on Russia. In December 2014, Congress unanimously passed the Ukraine Freedom Support Act of 2014 (P.L. 113-272), which authorizes the President to impose sanctions on specific Russian individuals and entities. The President signed the bill but also stated that he would not impose additional sanctions on Russia at this time. As the conflict in Ukraine continues, some Members of Congress are calling for tighter economic sanctions on Russia, in addition to other measures.

---

* This is an edited, reformatted and augmented version of a Congressional Research Service publication R43895 , prepared for Members and Committees of Congress dated February 4, 2015.

Analysts have debated the potential effects of current U.S. sanctions on Russia and Russia's retaliatory measures. Russia is a major player in the international economy; it has the world's ninth-largest economy and it is a major producer and exporter of natural gas and oil. However, there is relatively little overall trade and investment between the United States and Russia, although ties at the firm-level are significant in some instances.

Economic conditions in Russia have deteriorated at a faster rate in recent months. Capital flight from Russia has accelerated, the ruble has depreciated by more than 50%, inflation has increased, and the Russian economy is projected to contract by 3.0% in 2015. It is difficult to assess whether, and if so how much, targeted U.S. sanctions on Russian individuals and entities have contributed to worsening economic conditions in Russia, since other factors are likely contributing to Russia's economic challenges. In particular, oil prices have fallen by 50% in the past six months, and oil is a major Russian export and source of revenue for the government. However, many analysts, including senior officials at the International Monetary Fund, have argued that sanctions are at least one factor contributing to the increasingly difficult economic situation in Russia.

U.S. business groups have raised concerns that sanctions will harm American manufacturers, jeopardize American jobs, and cede business opportunities to firms from other countries. However, there are questions about the extent to which the sanctions and retaliatory measures will affect U.S. economic interests. Russia is a relatively minor trading and investment partner for the United States overall. U.S. sanctions target a specific subset of Russian individuals and entities and, in some cases, restrict only specific types of economic transactions.

The full economic impact on U.S. firms and the U.S. economy remains to be seen. To date, news reports have cited a number of U.S. firms have been adversely affected by U.S. sanctions on Russia and Russia's retaliatory measures. Russia is taking steps to develop alternative economic partners, particularly in emerging markets. Some analysts argue that the impact on U.S. firms should not be overstated; some firms were able to prepare for the disruptions, and the impact could be minimized as alternative markets are located. More broadly, U.S. exports to Russia have remained relatively robust but a weaker ruble and a contraction of the Russian economy may provide additional challenges to U.S. exports to Russia.

INTRODUCTION

Economic sanctions on Russian individuals, entities, and sectors have been a key part of the U.S. response to Russia's annexation of the Crimean region of Ukraine and Russia's efforts to destabilize eastern Ukraine.[1] For example, the United States has frozen the assets of a number of Russian individuals and entities with close ties to Russia's political leadership; restricted financial transactions with firms operating in key sectors in the Russian economy (finance, energy, and defense); and restricted oil-related exports from the United States to Russia, among other measures.[2]

The United States has been a leader in advocating that other countries also take action against Russia. Currently the European Union (EU) and several other countries have also imposed economic sanctions on Russia. Russia has retaliated against Western sanctions, primarily by imposing a one-year ban on the import of certain agricultural goods and products from the United States and other countries imposing sanctions.[3]

Many Members of Congress have been strong proponents of economic sanctions against Russia. At the end of the 113th Congress, Congress unanimously passed the Ukraine Freedom Support Act of 2014 (P.L. 113-272), which authorizes the President to impose sanctions on specific Russian individuals and entities. The President signed the bill but also stated that he would not impose additional sanctions on Russia at this time. As the conflict in Ukraine continues, some Members of Congress are calling for tighter economic sanctions on Russia, in addition to other options.[4]

Economic sanctions on Russia raise a host of policy questions. One set of questions focuses on the economic impact of the sanctions. Specifically, are the economic sanctions increasing pressure on Russia's government? Additionally, how do the sanctions impact U.S. economic interests? The subsequent discussion of U.S-Russia economic ties, recent economic trends in Russia, and U.S. economic interests in Russia may provide some insight into these questions.

U.S.-RUSSIA ECONOMIC TIES

Overall U.S.-Russia Trade and Investment

Russia is a major player in the international economy: it has the world's ninth-largest economy, is home to a population of more than 140 million, and is a major producer and exporter of natural gas and oil.[5] Despite Russia's size, however, there is relatively little overall direct trade and investment between the United States and Russia.

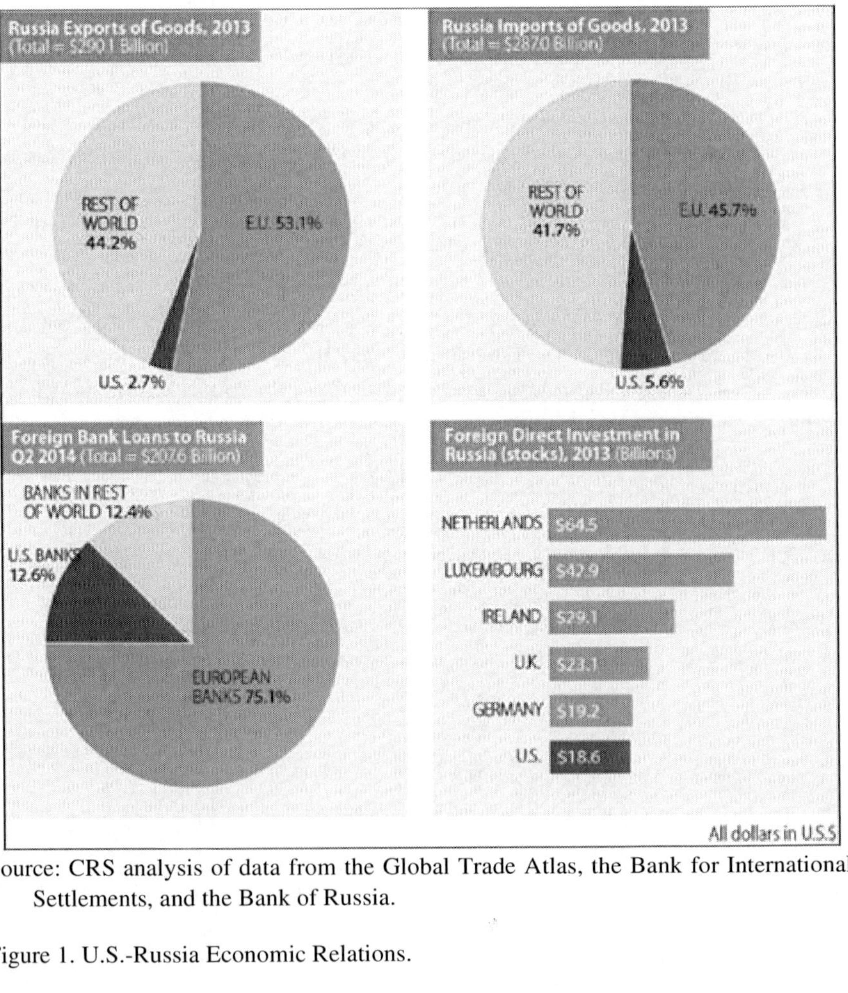

Source: CRS analysis of data from the Global Trade Atlas, the Bank for International Settlements, and the Bank of Russia.

Figure 1. U.S.-Russia Economic Relations.

The United States accounts for a small share of Russia's total trade and inflows of investment (*Figure 1*). In 2013, Russia imported 5.6% of its goods from the United States and exported 2.7% of its goods to the United States.[6] Of the more than $550 billion in foreign direct investment in Russia at the end of 2013, less than 3% was from the United States.[7] Direct financial exposures are also relatively low; U.S. banks accounted for less than 13% of foreign bank loans to Russia in the second quarter of 2014.[8]

Likewise, Russia accounts for a small portion of U.S. international economic activity. In 2013, just 0.71% of U.S. exports of goods went to Russia and 1.19% of U.S. imports of goods came from Russia. In terms of investment, less than 0.4% of U.S. overseas investment was in Russia in 2013.[9] In the second quarter of 2014, Russia accounted for 0.8% of outstanding U.S. bank loans overseas.[10]

EU-Russian Economic Ties

Russia has a much stronger economic relationship with Europe than with the United States (Figure 1). In 2013, more than 50% of Russia's exports of goods went to EU countries, and Russia purchased 46% of its imports of goods from EU countries. In the financial sector, European banks accounted for about 75% of Russia's total foreign bank loans in the second quarter of 2014. Similarly, Russia is important to Europe. Among other factors, Russia supplies the EU with about a third of its oil and natural gas imports. The close economic relationship between Russia and the EU is one reason why some analysts argued that U.S.-EU cooperation on sanctions with Russia would be critical for their success. At the same time, Europe's imports of oil and natural gas from Europe are one reason why it was initially difficult for European leaders to reach a consensus on Russia sanctions.

Firm- and Sector-Level Activity

Even though overall trade and investment flows between the United States and Russia are relatively small, economic ties at the firm- and sector-level are in some cases substantial. Several large U.S. companies have been actively engaged with Russia: exporting to Russia, entering joint ventures with Russian partners, and relying on Russian suppliers for inputs. A notable example is ExxonMobil, which in 2011 signed a strategic cooperation agreement with Rosneft to drill in the Russian Arctic, among other activities; initial investments were expected to be worth tens of billions of dollars.[11] Other examples include PepsiCo, the largest food and beverage company in Russia; Ford Motor Co., which recently announced a partnership with Sollers, a Russian car company; General Electric, which has joint ventures with Russian firms to manufacture gas turbines; Boeing, among the top U.S. exporters to Russia; Visa and MasterCard, which provide payment services to 90% of the Russian market; and United Launch Alliance, a Lockheed Martin and Boeing joint venture, which imports Russian rocket engines.[12] Russia is also an important market for Philip Morris and Avon Products.[13] The U.S.-Russia Business Council, a Washington-based trade association that provides services to U.S. and Russian member companies, has a membership of 230 U.S. companies conducting business in Russia.[14]

The U.S. Commercial Service identifies a number of key sectors for U.S. exports and investment in Russia.[15] In its 2013 *Country Commercial Guide*, the key sectors it identifies include: agricultural equipment; apparel; auto parts and service equipment/accessories; aviation; chemicals/plastics; construction; consumer electronics; electrical power generation and transmission equipment; energy efficiency; medical equipment; refinery equipment; safety and security equipment; and travel and tourism services. For example, in recent years Russia has focused on developing and modernizing Russian oil and gas refining operations, including upgrading domestic refining capacities, which are generally below European standards. In this initiative, the United States has been a major supplier of refinery equipment to Russia. The U.S. Commercial Service estimates that 30% (about $900 million) of Russia's imports of refinery equipment in 2013 were from the United States.

Russia is also a major supplier of some specific U.S. imports. For example, the United States has relied on a Russian rocket engine in key civilian and military space launch programs.[16] Russia is also a major supplier of certain types of metals. For example, Boeing buys about 35% of the titanium it uses for commercial jetliners from VSMPO, a Russian titanium producer.[17] Russia is also a top global producer of palladium, which is used in catalytic converters in cars, and accounted for a third of U.S. imports of palladium in 2013.[18] Other U.S. imports from Russia include non-crude oil products; iron and steel, particularly semi-finished steel products; enriched uranium; fertilizers; fish and crustaceans; and certain synthetic rubbers, among other products. *Table 1* shows the top U.S. exports to and imports from Russia.

Russia may be particularly reliant on access to the U.S. financial system, which, together with access to the U.S. dollar, has been important for Russia's cross-border trade and investment.[19] Russia has relied on other countries, including the United States, for financing and access to the international payments system. Russia's reliance on the U.S. dollar ties into the importance of the energy sector to Russia's economy. The dollar has traditionally been used to settle oil transactions, and oil is a key export for Russia.

Table 1. Major U.S. Exports to and Imports from Russia

Commodity (HS Code)	Amount (Million US$)
Top 5 U.S. Exports to Russia	
Nuclear Reactors, Boilers, Machinery Etc.; Parts (84)	2,313
Vehicles, Except Railway Or Tramway, And Parts Etc. (87)	1,999
Aircraft, Spacecraft, And Parts Thereof (88)	1,961
Electric Machinery Etc.; Sound Equip; TV Equipment; Parts (85)	675
Optic, Photo Etc., Medic Or Surgical Instruments Etc. (90)	659
Top 5 U.S. Imports from Russia	
Mineral Fuel, Oil, Etc. (27)	19,458
Iron And Steel (72)	1,640
Inorganic Chemicals; Precious & Rare-Earth Met & Radioactive	
Compounds (28)	1,354
Precious Metals, Etc. (71)	813
Fertilizers (31)	796

Source: Data from the U.S. Census Bureau, as accessed from Global Trade Atlas.

U.S. Sanctions and Russia's Retaliatory Measures

The Obama Administration first imposed U.S. sanctions relating to the events in Ukraine in March 2014, and announced additional measures in subsequent months. The Obama Administration has targeted the sanctions on specific individuals, firms, and sectors, and explained that the sanctions "aim to increase Russia's political isolation as well as the economic costs to Russia, especially in areas of importance to President Putin and those close to him."[20]

In December 2014, Congress passed and the President signed into law the Ukraine Freedom Support Act of 2014 (P.L. 113-272; 22 U.S.C. 8921 *et seq.*), which, among other measures, authorizes the President to impose sanctions on specific Russian individuals and entities. The President stated that he did not intend at this time to impose sanctions under this law, but could at a later date if circumstances warrant.[21]

Examples of current U.S. sanctions on Russia include:

- *Asset freezes for specific individuals.* The U.S. government has frozen assets of a number of individuals in Russian President Vladimir Putin's "inner circle," including presidential aides, key figures in Russia's legislature, and businesspersons with close ties to the Kremlin. U.S. individuals and entities are prohibited from conducting economic transactions with them.
- *Asset freezes for specific entities.* Some Russian companies are also subject to U.S. asset freezes and are prohibited from engaging in economic transactions with U.S. individuals and entities. Examples include Bank Rossiya, which has been called the "personal bank of Putin," and the Volga Group, a holding company owned by a close ally of Putin.[22]
- *Restrictions on financial transactions with Russian firms operating in key sectors.* Sanctions also target key sectors in the Russian economy, including finance, energy, and defense. As a result, U.S. individuals and entities face restrictions on dealings in some types of new debt, and in some cases new equity, with several major Russian companies. Examples include Rosneft, a state-owned oil company and the world's largest publicly-traded oil producer; Rostec, a major Russian defense conglomerate; and Sberbank, the largest bank in Russia.
- *Restrictions on oil-related exports.* The United States restricts U.S. individuals and entities from exporting goods, services, or technology in support of projects that have the potential to produce oil in Russia.
- *Restrictions on dual-use exports.* The United States has tightened restrictions on U.S. exports of dual-use and military items to Russia.

Economists generally agree that sanctions are more likely to be effective foreign policy tools when they are applied multilaterally, rather than unilaterally.[23] The United States has taken a lead in urging other countries to impose sanctions on Russia. Currently the European Union (EU), Australia, Canada, Japan, Norway, and Switzerland, among others, have also imposed sanctions on Russia.[24]

The United States and other countries have also taken cooperative actions to increase economic pressure on Russia. For example, several countries, including the United States, are opposing new World Bank and European Bank for Reconstruction and Development (EBRD) projects in Russia.[25] Canada, France, Germany, Italy, Japan, the United Kingdom, and the United

States have suspended participation in the G-8 and instead have convened as the G-7, of which Russia is not a member, for the first time since the late 1990s.

In response to sanctions, Russia has pursued retaliatory measures. Most notably, in August 2014, Russia announced a one-year ban on the import of certain foods from the United States, the EU, Australia, Canada, and Norway.[26] The Russian government also cracked down on McDonald's restaurants operating in Russia, although restrictions may be loosening.[27] Additionally, in May 2014, Russia's Deputy Prime Minister, Dmitry Rogozin, threatened to ban exports of rocket engines to the United States.[28] The Russian government did not ultimately impose the ban, but in December 2014, Congress passed and the President signed legislation that could restrict the military's use of rocket engines designed or manufactured in Russia (Section 1608 of P.L. 113-291).

Sanctions, Retaliatory Measures, and the World Trade Organization (WTO)

Some Russian officials have argued that Western sanctions are a breach of the rules and principles of the World Trade Organization (WTO).[29] Similarly, some U.S. and European officials have questioned whether Russia's ban on agricultural imports from the United States, the EU, and other countries are a violation of WTO rules. To date, neither side has initiated any formal proceedings under the WTO dispute settlement process with regards to the sanctions or retaliatory measures. Some argue that the U.S. measures are permitted under the WTO's national security exemption.[30]

ECONOMIC TRENDS IN RUSSIA

Economic sanctions on Russia come at a time when Russia's economy is still struggling to recover from the global financial crisis of 2008-2009. In the 2000s, Russia's economy benefited from rising oil prices. Its economy was hit hard by the global financial crisis and ensuing global economic downturn, as demand for its exports fell, particularly in Europe. Russia's economy sharply contracted by 7.8% in 2009.[31] The economy rebounded the following year, growing by 4.5%. Since 2010, however, the rate of economic growth has slowed in Russia every year. Economists argue that the financial crisis and weak economic performance in recent years have highlighted fundamental problems in Russia's economy. These problems include the economy's dependence on the production and export of oil and gas, as well as the need for reform in a number of areas, including governance, corruption, administrative barriers, regulation, privatization, competition, the banking sector, and utility pricing.[32]

In recent months, economic conditions in Russia have started deteriorating at a faster rate. As discussed in greater detail below, capital flight from Russia has accelerated, the ruble has depreciated, inflation has increased, the economy is contracting, and public finances are strained. It is difficult to assess the extent to which, if at all, U.S. sanctions on Russian individuals and entities directly or indirectly contributed to worsening economic conditions in Russia, since other factors are likely contributing to Russia's economic challenges. In particular, oil prices have fallen by 50% in six months. Russia is a major oil producer and exporter, and oil and gas account for about half of the government's revenues.[33]Additionally, domestic economic policy decisions, the general political crisis in Ukraine, corruption, and an economic slowdown in Europe could be among the contributing factors. However, many policy makers and analysts, including senior officials at the IMF, have argued that sanctions are at least one factor contributing to the increasingly difficult economic situation in Russia.[34]

Recent Economic Challenges

The economic challenges facing Russia have intensified in recent months. Some of these challenges are discussed in greater detail below and depicted in *Figure 2*.

Capital flight. Investors have become more uncertain about doing business in Russia and have started pulling capital out of Russia. In 2014, net private capital outflows from Russia totaled $152 billion, compared to net outflows of $54 billion in 2012 and $61 billion in 2013.[35] U.S., European, and other countries' financial institutions have reportedly cut off many major borrowers in Russia, even those not subject to sanctions.[36] In July 2014, no Russian companies received loans in U.S. dollars, Swiss francs, or euros, for the first time since the global financial crisis.[37] Some analysts have suggested that the Russian central bank could impose capital controls to stop money from leaving the country, but there are questions about the effectiveness and longterm consequences of capital controls. Russian officials have denied any plans to use capital controls.

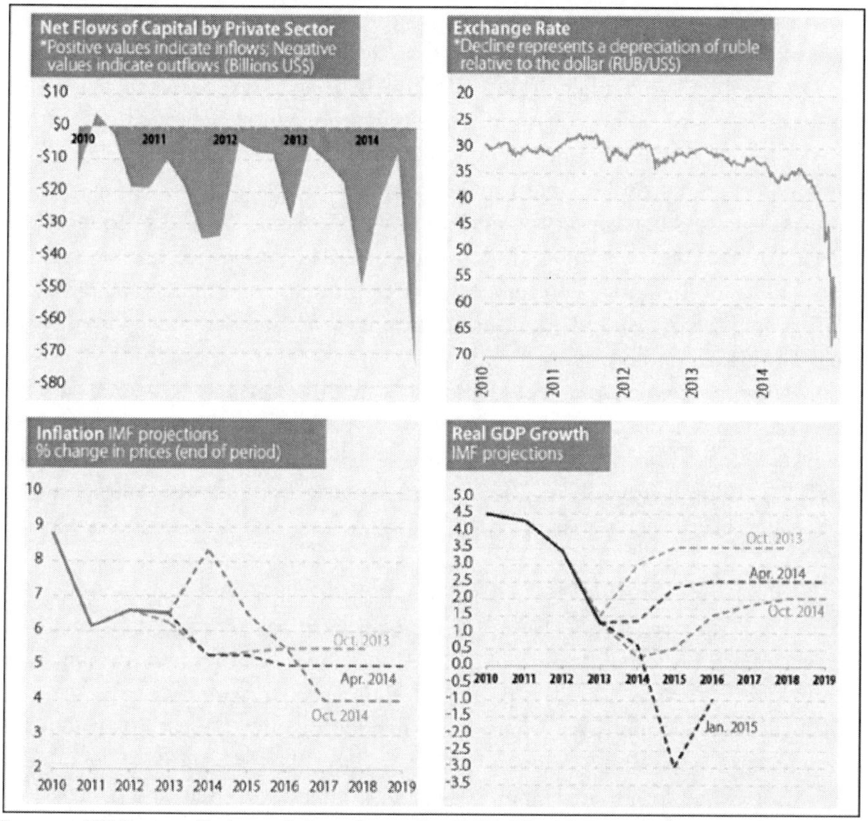

Source: CRS compilation of data from the IMF World Economic Outlook and the Bank of Russia.

Figure 2. Economic Trends in Russia.

Depreciation of the ruble. Capital flight from Russia contributed to downward pressure on the ruble, which depreciated against the dollar by more than 50% between July 2014 and early December 2014. On December 15, 2014, investors started a massive sell-off of the ruble. In order to stem its further depreciation, the Bank of Russia (Russia's central bank) announced its biggest interest rate hike since 1998, raising a key interest rate from 10.5% to 17%, at an emergency meeting on December 16. Despite this measure, the ruble continued to sharply depreciate. In early January 2015, the ruble was trading at 63 rubles per dollar, compared to 33 rubles per dollar a year earlier. The central bank is periodically intervening in foreign exchange markets (meaning it is selling foreign currencies and purchasing rubles) to support the value of the ruble. It sold $11.9 billion U.S. dollars in December 2014.[38]

Inflation. In November 2014, inflation in Russia increased to 9.1%, the fastest acceleration since 2011 and well above the central bank's target rate of 5% to 6%. One factor driving higher rates of inflation has been the depreciation of the ruble, which makes imports in Russia more expensive. In addition, Russia's ban on certain agricultural imports has caused food prices in Russia to rise. For example, in November 2014, the price of buckwheat increased more than 50% and the cost of fresh tomatoes jumped nearly 35%.[39] The ban has also resulted in limited shortages and/or decline in quality of certain kinds of food products.[40]

Economic contraction. The IMF has steadily lowered its forecasts for economic growth in Russia over the past several months. In its most recent forecast, released in January 2015, the IMF downgraded its forecast for Russia's economic growth in 2015, from growing by 0.5% to contracting by 3.0%. The IMF projects that, in 2016, Russia's economy will also contract by 1.0%.[41]

Strain on public finances. Russia entered the current period of economic challenges with a relatively strong fiscal position: it had large foreign currency reserves ($339 billion at the end of 2014) and relatively little debt (projected to be only 16% of gross domestic product (GDP) in 2014, compared to 120% of GDP for the G-7 countries).[42] Russia's financial resources have given it some leverage to provide direct financial assistance to selected Russian firms under stress. For example, in December 2014, Putin announced that one of Russia's sovereign wealth funds, the National Welfare Fund, would be used to recapitalize Russian banks.[43] However, some analysts question how liquid Russia's foreign exchange reserves actually are, and how long they will last in the current economic environment.[44] The Russian government, reliant on oil and natural gas sales for its revenue, is planning a 10% budget cut for 2015 and to use reserves to cover some of the expected budget shortfall.[45]

U.S. Economic Interests

U.S. business groups, including the Chamber of Commerce, the National Association of Manufacturers, and USA*Engage, have raised concerns that U.S. sanctions on Russia could disrupt the operations of U.S. firms in Russia, thereby harming American manufacturers, jeopardizing American jobs, and ceding business opportunities to firms from other countries.[46] However, there may be questions about the extent to which the sanctions and retaliatory measures are affecting, or will affect, U.S. firms and the U.S. economy. As discussed above, Russia is a relatively minor trading and investment partner for the United States as a whole. Additionally, U.S. sanctions do not prohibit all economic transactions between the United States and Russia. They target specific Russian individuals and entities and, in some cases, only restrict specific types of economic transactions.

In many ways, it is still too early to gauge the full economic effect of the sanctions. Some initial trends and indicators are discussed below:

Some U.S. firms and industries have been adversely impacted by the sanctions. News reports have cited a number of examples of U.S. firms whose operations have been, or are starting to be, disrupted by the sanctions. For example, sanctions forced ExxonMobil to suspend its $700 million exploration in Russia's Kara Sea (a joint venture with Rosneft).[47] Oilfield service companies, including Halliburton and National Oilwell Varco, have reported that sanctions are restricting their operations in Russia and expressed concern that sanctions will limit their profits in the second half of 2014.[48] Likewise, John Deere, which makes heavy farm equipment and has two factories in Russia, has attributed weaker sales to the sanctions.[49] U.S. gun dealers also face restrictions on imports of specific Russian-made rifles, of which they have reportedly sold tens of thousands in previous years.[50]

It is difficult to extrapolate the full impact of sanctions on U.S. firms from these examples. One reason is that Russia may not be a critical economic partner for some U.S. firms and industries affected by the sanctions. This may be the case, for example, with Visa and MasterCard. In response to the sanctions, Russia announced plans to accelerate the development of its own national payments system, which would undermine MasterCard and Visa's dominance in the Russian market.[51] However, Russia only accounts for a small portion (2%) of their profits.[52]

Another factor is that the implementation of sanctions in phases or "rounds" has given U.S. companies some time to prepare for disruptions in economic transactions with Russia. According to news reports, many multinational companies have developed contingency plans that would allow them to adjust to suppliers and banks outside of Russia and minimize the impact of sanctions on their operations.[53] There is likely less press coverage of U.S. firms that have been able to minimize the impact of the sanctions on Russia or the effects of Russian retaliation.

Some U.S. agricultural producers have been affected by Russia's retaliatory ban on agricultural imports. The overall economic impact of

Russia's ban on certain U.S. agricultural exports is expected to be relatively small; Russia accounts for about 1% of the United States' total food and agricultural exports.[54] However, specific producers within the United States have been or could be adversely affected. For example, the congressional delegation from Alaska has expressed concerns about the impact on Alaska's seafood industry.[55] Another example is Washington state apple and pear producers, who sold $23 million worth of pears and apples to Russia last year and had to locate new purchasers at the start of the new harvest season.[56] According to one private sector estimate, the ban could result in 12,000 job losses in the United States.[57] Over the longer-term, however, the impact of the sanctions could be mitigated in part as alternative markets for U.S. agricultural exports are located.

U.S. exports of goods to Russia are up slightly. To date, U.S. exports to Russia have remained relatively robust since sanctions on Russia were announced. U.S. exports of goods to Russia were 1.3% higher in the first three quarters of 2014 than in the first three quarters of 2013. However, U.S. imports of goods from Russia were 10% lower over the same time period.[58] It is not clear how U.S.-Russian trade flows will evolve in coming months. A weaker ruble relative to the U.S. dollar may make U.S. exports to Russia less competitive and may increase the competitiveness of U.S. imports from Russia. Additionally, if Russia's economy contracts, as many economists are projecting, Russian demand for U.S. exports could decline.

The U.S. economy overall has strengthened in recent months. To date, U.S. economic growth has remained relatively strong since sanctions on Russia were announced. In January 2015, the IMF estimated that U.S. growth will be 3.6% in 2015 and 3.3% in 2016, up from its forecast for the United States in October 2014.[59] IMF projections for U.S. economic growth are also higher than the average growth rate for other advanced economies (2.4% in 2015 and 2.4% in 2016). Additionally, the U.S. unemployment rate fell to 5.6% in December 2014, its lowest rate since June 2008.[60] However, it is difficult to know whether these macroeconomic indicators would have been even stronger in the absence of sanctions. It is also difficult to predict the impact of sanctions on U.S. growth and employment going forward. For example, an economic crisis in Russia could cause growth in the EU to slow. Slower growth in Europe could have spillover effects for the United States, given their strong economic links.

Russia is seeking alternative economic partners. Some analysts are concerned that sanctions will cause Russia to turn away from U.S. companies and seek out alternative economic partners, particularly in emerging markets (which have not imposed sanctions on Russia).[61] There is some evidence to support this concern. For example, in October 2014, Russia and China completed approximately 40 agreements related to finance and technology.[62] Russia is also reportedly turning to Brazil and other Latin American countries for food imports to compensate for losses resulting from its ban on agricultural imports from other countries.[63] However, it is not clear whether and to what extent these relationships would continue in the absence of U.S. sanctions on Russia.

CONCLUSION

The United States has imposed sanctions on a number of Russian individuals and entities in response to Russia's government's annexation of Crimea and involvement in the Ukraine crisis. U.S. sanctions include, for example, targeting officials in Putin's inner circle, placing restrictions on new debt to key sectors in Russia's economy, and opposing new multilateral development projects in Russia. The United States has worked to coordinate its sanctions with a number of other countries, particularly those in the EU. As Congress considers additional economic sanctions on Russia, it may consider the impact of current economic sanctions on Russia's economy and foreign policy, in addition to their impact on U.S. economic interests.

Russia's economy has deteriorated rapidly in recent months, marked by capital flight, depreciation of the ruble, rising inflation, weaker growth prospects, and budgetary pressures. Many experts believe that sanctions are contributing to Russia's economic challenges. However, it is difficult to assess the impact of sanctions separate from other domestic and international factors, particularly low oil prices. Longer-term, the economic impact of the sanctions will depend on a number of factors, including whether any new sanctions on Russia are imposed. The effectiveness of the sanctions in inducing a change in the behavior of the Russian government remains to be seen.

Some U.S. business groups have raised concerns about the economic costs of sanctions on Russia to the United States. Economic growth in the United States has remained strong since the sanctions were imposed. However, news reports indicate that some U.S. firms and industries have been adversely affected. Longer-term, the impact of the sanctions may depend on a number of factors, such as the ability of U.S. firms to find alternative markets, potential spillover effects from a slowdown in Russia, and whether Russia implements additional retaliatory measures against the United States.

End Notes

[1] For more information about the crisis in Ukraine, see CRS Report RL33460, *Ukraine: Current Issues and U.S. Policy*, by Steven Woehrel.

[2] For more information on U.S. sanctions on Russia, see CRS Insight IN10048, U.S. Sanctions on Russia in Response to Events in Ukraine, coordinated by Dianne E. Rennack. For information on economic sanctions as a foreign policy tool more broadly, see CRS Report 97-949, *Economic Sanctions to Achieve U.S. Foreign Policy Goals: Discussion and Guide to Current Law*, by Dianne E. Rennack and Robert D. Shuey.

[3] For more information on Russia's agricultural ban, see CRS Insight IN10133, *Russia's Ban on Certain Imported Food and Agricultural Goods*, by Joel L. Greene.

[4] For more on other legislative proposals for additional sanctions on Russia considered in the 113th Congress, see CRS Insight IN10117, Russia Sanctions: Options, by Dianne E. Rennack.

[5] The relative ranking of Russia's economy is based on one conventional measure: nominal gross domestic product (GDP) measured in current prices. Alternative measures of GDP, such as adjusted for differences in price levels across countries, may produce different orderings.

[6] Unless otherwise noted, trade data from the U.S. Census Bureau, the Customs Committee of Russia, and Eurostat, as accessed from *Global Trade Atlas.*

[7] Bank of Russia, "Inward Foreign Direct Investment Positions by Instruments and Geographical Allocation in 2009-2013," http://www.cbr.ru/eng/statistics/print.aspx?file=credit_statistics/dir-inv_in_country_e. htm&pid=svs&sid=ITM_14544.

[8] Bank for International Settlements. Data is for consolidated international bank claims on an ultimate risk basis.

[9] U.S. Bureau of Economic Analysis. Data is U.S. direct investment position abroad on a historical-cost basis.

[10] Bank for International Settlements. Data is for consolidated international bank claims on an ultimate risk basis.

[11] Andrew E. Kramer, "Exxon Reaches Arctic Oil Deal with Russians," *New York Times*, August 30, 2011; Rosneft, "Rosneft and ExxonMobil to Join Forces in the Artic and Black Sea Offshore, Enhance Co-operation through Technology Sharing and Joint International Projects," Press Release, August 30, 2011, http://www.rosneft.com/news/pressrelease/30082011.html.

[12] Howard Schneider and Holly Yeager, "As Talk of Russia Sanctions Heats Up, Business Draws a Cautionary Line," *Washington Post*, March 7, 2014; "Visa, MasterCard Will Continue to Work in Russia," *Wall Street Journal*, May 20, 2014; Robert Wright, "Satellite Pinpoints US's Russian Space Dependence," *Financial Times*, May 16, 2014.

[13] Myles Udland, "Here's a List of Stocks with Lots of Exposure to Russia," *Business Insider*, July 17, 2014.

[14] U.S.-Russia Business Council, https://www.usrbc.org/membership/.

[15] The U.S. Commercial Service is the trade promotion arm of the Department of Commerce's International Trade Administration. U.S. Commercial Service, "Doing Business in Russia: Country Commercial Guide for U.S. Companies," 2013, http://www.buyusainfo.net/docs/x_5396902.pdf.

[16] Stuart Clark, "Russia Halts Rocket Exports to US, Hitting Space and Military Programmes," *The Guardian*, May 15, 2014. For more information, see CRS Insight IN10069, *Russian Sanctions*

Reprisal Against the RD-180 Rocket Engine: Paths Ahead for U.S. National Security Space Launch, by Steven A. Hildreth.

[17] Jon Ostrower and Andy Pasztor, "Boeing, United Technologies Stockpile Titanium Parts," *Wall Street Journal*, August 7, 2014.

[18] U.S. Geological Survey, "Mineral Commodity Summaries 2014," http://minerals.usgs.gov /minerals/pubs/ mcs/2014/mcs2014.pdf.

[19] Robert Kahn, "Putin's Lehman Moment: Why Sanctions Will Work in Russia," *Foreign Affairs*, April 10, 2014.

[20] White House, "Statement by the President on New Sanctions Related to Russia," Office of the Press Secretary, September 11, 2014, http://www.whitehouse.gov/the-press-office/2014/09/11/ statement-president-new-sanctionsrelated-russia.

[21] White House, "Statement by the President on the Ukraine Freedom Support Act," Office of the Press Secretary, December 18, 2014, http://www.whitehouse.gov/the-press-office/2014/12/18/ statement-president-ukraine-freedomsupport-act.

[22] Steven Lee Myers, "Private Bank Fuels Fortunes of Putin's Inner Circle," *New York Times*, September 27, 2014; Carol Matlack, "Why the U.S. is Targeting the Business Empire of a Putin Ally," *Bloomberg Businessweek*, April 28, 2014.

[23] For example, see "Economic Sanctions: Effectiveness as Tools of Foreign Policy," Government Accountability Office (GAO), February 19, 1992, http://www.gao.gov/products/NSIAD-92-106.

[24] For more on EU sanctions, see CRS Insight IN10129, U.S.-EU Cooperation on Ukraine and Russia, by Kristin Archick and Derek E. Mix.

[25] Sandrine Rastello and Helene Fouquet, "G-7 Nations Said to Oppose New World Bank Russia Projects," *Bloomberg*, August 1, 2014; EBRD, "EBRD Statement on Operation Approach in Russia," EBRD Press Release, July 23, 2014, http://www.ebrd.com/english/pages/ news/press/2014/140723b.shtml.

[26] For more information, see CRS Insight IN10133, *Russia's Ban on Certain Imported Food and Agricultural Goods*, by Joel L. Greene.

[27] In August 2014, Russia closed 12 McDonald's restaurants. Although officials cite health reasons for the closures, critics argue that the closures were a response to the sanctions. In October 2014, more than 200 McDonald's restaurants, out of 440 in Russia, were under investigation by the Russian government. In December 2014, the closed McDonald's were allowed to re-open. See Justin Worland, "McDonald's Objects to Russia Restaurant Closures," *Time*, August 29, 2014; Carol Matlack, "Putin's Latest Target: More than 200 Russian McDonald's," *Bloomberg Businessweek*, October 20, 2014; Jessica Wohl, "Most McDonald's in Russia Reopen," *Chicago Tribune*, December 9, 2014.

[28] Stuart Clark, "Russia Halts Rocket Exports to US, Hitting Space and Military Programmes," *The Guardian*, May 15, 2014.

[29] For example, see Alexander Kolyandr, "Russia's Putin Slams Sanctions as Breach of WTO Rules," *Wall Street Journal*, September 18, 2014.

[30] For example, see Kathrin Hille and Shawn Donnan, "Russia Threatens US with WTO Action over Crimea Sanctions," *Financial Times*, April 16, 2014; "USTR Signals Russia Ag Ban Violates WTO Rules; Faults Procurement Policies," *Inside U.S. Trade*, January 8, 2015.

[31] Unless otherwise noted, macroeconomic data (for example, on growth, inflation, and debt levels) is from the IMF, *World Economic Outlook*, October 2014.

[32] "Geopolitical Risks Cloud Future of Russian Economy," *IMF Survey*, June 30, 2014.

[33] "Russia: Analysis," U.S. Energy Information Administration, March 12, 2014, http:// www . eia . gov / countries/cab.cfm?fips=rs.

[34] This includes the top two officials at the IMF: Managing Director Christine Lagarde and First Managing Director David Lipton. See Justin Sculletti, "IMF Head Lagarde: Russia Feeling the Effects of U.S., European Sanctions," *PBS*, April 2, 2014; William Mauldin, "U.S. Increases Pressure on Russia over Ukraine as Europe Holds Back," *Wall Street Journal*, April 13, 2014. For

other examples of policymakers and analysts attributing sanctions to contributing to Russia's economic challenges, see Paul Feinberg, "Head of U.S. Treasury Tells Students Sanctions against Russia are Having Impact," *UCLA Newsroom*, September 18, 2014; Robert Khan, "October Monthly: Breaking the Sanctions Code," *Council on Foreign Relations Macro and Markets*, October 17, 2014; Menzie Chinn, "Russia Under Pressure," *Econbrowser*, October 9, 2014.

[35] Bank of Russia, "Net Inflows/Outflows of Capital by Private Sector for 2005-20014," http://www.cbr.ru /eng/statistics/print.aspx?file=credit_statistics/capital_new_e.htm.

[36] Alexander Kolyandr and Andrey Ostroukh, "Russia Plans Emergency Fund for Companies Hurt by Ukraine Sanctions," *Wall Street Journal*, September 15, 2014.

[37] Sally Bakewell and Stephen Morris, "Putin Sanctions Drive Away Banks as Loans Dry Up: Russia Credit," *Bloomberg*, August 4, 2014.

[38] Bank of Russia, "Data on the Bank of Russia Currency Interventions (Monthly)," http://www.cbr.ru /eng/ hd_base/?PrtId=valint.

[39] "Ruble's Fall and Food Import Bands Send Inflation Even Higher," *Moscow Times*, October 6, 2014; Rob Wile, "Food Prices Have Begun Skyrocketing in Parts of Russia," *Business Insider*, September 1, 2014.

[40] Mark Adomanis, "Russian Inflation is Increasing and That Could Be A Huge Problem for the Kremlin," *Forbes*, September 16, 2014.

[41] IMF, *World Economic Outlook Update*, January 2015, http://www.imf. org/external/pubs /ft/weo /2015 /update/01/pdf/0115.pdf.

[42] Bank of Russia, "International Reserves of the Russian Federation," http://cbr.ru /eng/hd _base / default.aspx?Prtid=mrrf_m; IMF, *World Economic Outlook*, October 2014.

[43] Frances Coppola, "The Great Russian Bank Bailout," *Forbes*, December 26, 2014.

[44] For example, see "Not Quite All there?," *Economist*, November 22, 2014.

[45] Matthew Cowley, "Russia to Cut 2015 Budget by Around 10% Following Decline in Oil Price," *Wall Street Journal*, January 21, 2015.

[46] For example, the U.S. Chamber of Commerce and the National Association of Manufacturers ran ads in the *New York Times*, the *Wall Street Journal*, and the *Washington Post*, warning about the potential implications of sanctions on Russia for the United States. See Mike Dorning, "Business at Odds with Obama Over Russia Sanctions Threat," *Bloomberg News*, June 24, 2014. In September 2014, USA*Engage, a coalition of manufacturing, agricultural, and services producers sponsored by the National Foreign Trade Council, cautioned that "U.S. sanctions are exacting substantial collateral damage to U.S. investments and operations in Russia across sectors." See "USA*Engage Opposes S. 2828, 'Ukraine Freedom Support Act of 2014,'" *USA*Engage*, September 18, 2014.

[47] Clifford Krauss, "Exxon Halts Oil Drilling in Waters of Russia," *New York Times*, September 16, 2014.

[48] Ryan Holeywell, "Russia Sanctions May Squeeze Oil Services Profits," *Houston Chronicle*, August 12, 2014.

[49] Adam Shell, "U.S. Companies Get Hurt by Sanctions Targeting Russia," *USA Today*, May 14, 2014.

[50] However, the restriction resulted in a run these types of rifles already in the United States (and thus not subject to the restriction), providing a short-term boost to U.S. gun dealers. Joshua Green, "Banned by U.S. Sanctions, AK-47s are Going, Going, Gone," *Bloomberg Businessweek*, September 4, 2014.

[51] Natalia Kaurova and Anastasia Nesvetailova, "Making a Non-Western Payment Card System, in Russia," *FT Alphaville*, April 25, 2014.

[52] Elizabeth Dexheimer, "MasterCard CEO Sees Russia Having Small Impact on Profit," *Bloomberg*, May 1, 2014; Elizabeth Dexheimer, "Visa Profit Beats Estimates as Card Spending Climbs," *Bloomberg*, July 25, 2014.

[53] "Too Smart by Half?: Effective Sanctions Have Always Been Hard to Craft," *Economist*, September 6, 2014.

[54] CRS Insight IN10133, Russia's Ban on Certain Imported Food and Agricultural Goods, by Joel L. Greene.

[55] For example, see Lisa Murkowski, "Alaska Delegation: U.S. Should Push Back Against Russian Seafood Boycott," press release, August 26, 2014, http://www.murkowski. senate.gov/ public/index. cfm/ pressreleases?ID=532b03cb-182a46b2-b3e0-4e41f1e12199.

[56] Ross Courtney, "Russia Sanctions Affect Washington Apples, Pears," Yakima Herald, August 8, 2014.

[57] ING, "Russian Sanctions: 130,000 European Jobs at Stake," ING International Trade Special Report, August 2014.

[58] U.S. Census Bureau, as accessed from Global Trade Atlas.

[59] IMF, World Economic Outlook Update, January 2015, http://www.imf.org/ external/pubs/ft/weo/2015 /update/01/pdf/0115.pdf.

[60] U.S. Department of Labor, Bureau of Labor Statistics.

[61] "International Producers Risk Losing Russian Market over Sanctions," RT, November 13, 2014.

[62] Olga Razumovskaya, "An Isolated Russia Signs Business, Finance Pacts with China," Wall Street Journal, October 13, 2014.

[63] "Russia's Import Ban Means Big Business for Latin America," RT, August 7, 2014.

In: The Sanctions Way
Editor: Brian Fields

ISBN: 978-1-63482-679-2

Chapter 2

Cuba Sanctions: Legislative Restrictions Limiting the Normalization of Relations*

Dianne E. Rennack and Mark P. Sullivan

Summary

In December 2014, President Obama announced major changes in U.S. policy toward Cuba, including the restoration of diplomatic relations (relations were severed in January 1961), a review by the Department of State of Cuba's designation as a state sponsor of terrorism (Cuba was designated in 1982), and an increase in travel, trade, and the free flow of information to Cuba. This third step required the Departments of Commerce and the Treasury to amend the embargo regulations, which were announced on January 15, 2015.

When the President announced his policy change on Cuba, he acknowledged that he does not have authority to lift the embargo because it is codified in legislation. While the embargo was first imposed in the early 1960s under the authority of the Foreign Assistance Act of 1961 and the Trading with the Enemy Act, Congress enacted additional laws over the years that strengthened the embargo on Cuba, including the Cuban Democracy Act of 1992, the Cuban Liberty and Democratic Solidarity

---

* This is an edited, reformatted and augmented version of a Congressional Research Service publication R43888, prepared for Members and Committees of Congress, dated February 13, 2015.

Act (LIBERTAD) Act of 1996 (which codified the embargo regulations), and the Trade Sanctions Reform and Export Enhancement Act of 2000. Congress also has enacted numerous other provisions of law that impose sanctions on Cuba, including restrictions on trade, foreign aid, and support from the international financial institutions.

This report provides information on legislative provisions restricting relations with Cuba. It lists the various provisions of law comprising economic sanctions on Cuba, including key laws that are the statutory basis of the embargo, and provides information on the authority to lift or waive these restrictions.

INTRODUCTION

Since the early 1960s, U.S. policy toward Cuba has consisted largely of isolating the island nation through comprehensive economic sanctions, including an embargo on trade and financial transactions. President John F. Kennedy proclaimed an embargo on trade between the United States and Cuba in February 1962,[1] citing Section 620(a) of the Foreign Assistance Act of 1961 (FAA), which authorizes the President "to establish and maintain a total embargo upon all trade between the United States and Cuba."[2] At the same time, the Department of the Treasury issued the Cuban Import Regulations to deny the importation into the United States of all goods imported from or through Cuba.[3] The authority for the embargo was later expanded in March 1962 to include the Trading with the Enemy Act (TWEA).[4]

In July 1963, the Treasury Department revoked the Cuban Import Regulations and replaced them with the more comprehensive Cuban Assets Control Regulations (CACR)—31 C.F.R. Part 515 under the authority of TWEA and Section 620(a) of the FAA.[5] The CACR, which include a prohibition on most financial transactions with Cuba and a freeze of Cuban government assets in the United States, remain the main body of Cuba embargo regulations, and have been amended many times over the years to reflect changes in policy. They are administered by the Treasury Department's Office of Foreign Assets Control (OFAC), and prohibit financial transactions as well as trade transactions with Cuba. The CACR also require that all exports to Cuba be licensed by the Department of Commerce, Bureau of Industry and Security, under the provisions of the Export Administration Act of 1979, as amended.[6] The Export Administration Regulations (EAR) are found at 15 C.F.R. Sections 730-774.[7]

Congress subsequently strengthened sanctions on Cuba through provisions in such legislation as the Cuban Democracy Act of 1992 (CDA, P.L. 102-484, Title XVII), the Cuban Liberty and Democratic Solidarity (LIBERTAD) Act of 1996 (P.L. 104-114), and the Trade Sanctions Reform and Export Enhancement Act of 2000 (TSRA, P.L. 106-387, Title IX).

- Among its sanctions, the CDA prohibits U.S. subsidiaries from engaging in trade with Cuba and prohibits entry into the United States for any sea-borne vessel to load or unload freight if it has been involved in trade with Cuba within the previous 180 days.
- The LIBERTAD Act codified the economic embargo, including all restrictions under the CACR, although the President retains broad authority to amend the regulations. Nevertheless, as set forth in the LIBERTAD Act, the President cannot eliminate the embargo regulations without making a determination that a transition government is in power in Cuba. The LIBERTAD Act also requires the President to end the embargo if he determines that a democratically elected government is in power.
- While TSRA authorizes U.S. commercial exports to Cuba, it also includes prohibitions on U.S. assistance and financing and requires "payment of cash in advance" or third-country financing for the exports. The act also prohibits tourist travel to Cuba.

In addition to these key acts that constitute the economic embargo, there are numerous other provisions of law that impose sanctions on Cuba, including restrictions on trade, foreign aid, and support from international financial institutions. The government of Cuba also was designated by the State Department as a state sponsor of international terrorism in 1982 under Section 6(j) of the Export Administration Act and other laws because of its alleged ties to international terrorism.[8]

On December 17, 2014, President Barack Obama announced major changes in policy toward Cuba, including the intention to reestablish diplomatic relations that were severed in 1961, a review of Cuba's designation as a state sponsor of international terrorism, and numerous policy measures to increase travel, commerce, and the free flow of information to Cuba. To implement this last step, the Departments of the Treasury and Commerce issued amendments to the CACR[9] and EAR to enter into effect on January 16, 2015, that significantly eased the embargo in such areas as travel, remittances, trade (including consumer communication devices and certain goods and services for the private sector), and financial services (permitting U.S. correspondent bank accounts in Cuban financial institutions).[10]

When announcing the policy changes, the President acknowledged that he does not have the authority to lift the embargo, but maintained that he looks forward to engaging Congress in a debate about doing so. Without a presidential determination required by the LIBERTAD Act that Cuba has a democratically elected government in place, congressional action would be required to end the embargo by amending or repealing the LIBERTAD and other embargo-related statutes.[11]

This report provides information on legislative provisions restricting relations with Cuba. *Table 1* lists the various provisions of law comprising economic sanctions on Cuba, including key laws that are the statutory basis of the embargo, and provides information on the authority to lift or waive the restrictions.

Table 1. Legislative Restrictions Limiting the Normalization of U.S.-Cuban Relations

Statutory Basis	Restriction	Authority to Lift or Waive
Key Restrictions that Form the Core of the U.S. Economic Sanctions Regime on Cuba: The Embargo		
Sec. 620(a)(1), Foreign Assistance Act of 1961 (22 U.S.C. 2370(a)(1))	Prohibits foreign aid "to the present government of Cuba." Authorizes the President "to establish and maintain a total embargo upon all trade between the United States and Cuba."	The prohibition on aid has no waiver, though could be overridden by appropriations language that provides aid "notwithstanding any other provision of law." As set forth in the law, the total embargo is a discretionary authorization. Sec. 204, Cuban Liberty and Democratic Solidarity (LIBERTAD) Act (22 U.S.C. 6064), however, authorizes the President to suspend the enforcement of sec. 620(a) only if he determines "a transition government is in power in Cuba." Sec. 204 of that Act, furthermore, requires the President to terminate sanctions under sec. 620(a) and other measures if he determines

Statutory Basis	Restriction	Authority to Lift or Waive
		that "a democratically elected government in Cuba is in power." Sec. 204(d)(1) of that Act repeals sec. 620(a) on President making such a determination.
Sec. 620(a)(2), Foreign Assistance Act of 1961 (22U.S.C. 2370(a)(2))	Authorizes the President to prohibit foreign aid to "any government of Cuba." Denies Cuba a quota for sugar trade, "or to receive any other benefit under any law of the United States....	As set forth in the law, the prohibitions on aid and sugar imports are discretionary, "except as may be deemed necessary by the President in the interests of the United States." Sec. 204, Cuban Liberty and Democratic Solidarity (LIBERTAD) Act (22 U.S.C. 6064), however, authorizes the President to suspend the enforcement of sec. 620(a) only if he determines "a transition government is in power in Cuba." Sec. 204, furthermore, requires the President to terminate sanctions under sec. 620(a) and other measures if he determines that "a democratically elected government in Cuba is in power." Sec. 204(d)(1) of that Act repeals sec. 620(a) on President making such a determination.
Sec. 5(b), Trading With the Enemy Act (50 U.S.C. App. 5(b))	Authorizes the President to restrict or prohibit trade, transactions, and access to assets and property.	The Cuban Assets Control Regulations, 31 CFR Part 515, were issued in July 1963 under the authority of TWEA. Pursuant to the law, the President may terminate the national emergency and restrictions under TWEA at any time. Sec. 204, Cuban Liberty and Democratic Solidarity (LIBERTAD) Act (22 U.S.C. 6064), however, authorizes the President to suspend the enforcement of 31 CFR Part 515 only if he determines that "a transition government is in power

Table 1. (Continued)

Statutory Basis	Restriction	Authority to Lift or Waive
		in Cuba." Sec. 204, furthermore, requires the President to terminate the economic embargo of Cuba, including the restrictions under 31 CFR Part 515 if he determines that "a democratically elected government in Cuba is in power." Nevertheless, the Secretary of the Treasury retains authority to amend regulations therein, in accordance with 31 CFR Part 515. 201, which, in part, provides: "All of the following transactions are prohibited, except as specifically authorized by the Secretary of the Treasury.... "
Sec. 1704, Cuban Democracy Act of 1992 (22 U.S.C. 6003)	Authorizes the President to prohibit foreign aid under the Foreign Assistance Act of 1961, transactions under the Arms Export Control Act, or debt forgiveness, to any third country providing assistance to Cuba.	As set forth in the law, the prohibitions are at the President's discretion. Sec. 204, Cuban Liberty and Democratic Solidarity (LIBERTAD) Act (22 U.S.C. 6064), however, authorizes the President to suspend the enforcement of sec. 1704 only if he determines that "a transition government is in power in Cuba." Sec. 204, furthermore, requires the President to terminate sanctions under sec. 1704 and other measures if he determines that "a democratically elected government in Cuba is in power." Sec. 204(d)(1) of that Act repeals sec. 1704 on President making such a determination.
Sec. 1705(d), Cuban Democracy Act of 1992 (22 U.S.C. 6004(d))	Requires on-site verification for the export of medicines and medical supplies (unless the recipient is a nongovernmental	The President is required to determine that the U.S. government can verify the end use of such exports.

Statutory Basis	Restriction	Authority to Lift or Waive
	organization receiving donations).	Sec. 204, Cuban Liberty and Democratic Solidarity (LIBERTAD) Act (22 U.S.C. 6064) authorizes the President to suspend the enforcement of sec. 1705(d) only if he determines that "a transition government is in power in Cuba." Sec. 204, furthermore, requires the President to terminate sanctions under sec. 1705 and other measures if he determines that "a democratically elected government in Cuba is in power." Sec. 204(d)(1) of that Act repeals sec. 1705(d) on President making such a determination.
Sec. 1705(e)(5), Cuban Democracy Act of 1992 (22 U.S.C. 6004(e)(5))	Sec. 1705, overall, authorizes "support for the Cuban people," including allowing telecommunications services between the United States and Cuba. Sec. 1705(e)(5), however, clarifies that this allowance does not authorize a U.S. person to invest in Cuba's domestic telecommunications network.	
Sec. 1706(a), Cuban Democracy Act of 1992 (22 U.S.C. 6005(a))	Prohibits specific licenses for transactions relating to trade between Cuba and U.S.-owned or -controlled companies in third countries "in appropriate cases," codifying requirements stated in 31 CFR Part 515.559 as of July 1, 1989 (effective October 23, 1992).	Sec. 1708 provides that the President may waive if he determines that the government of Cuba (1) has held free and fair elections, (2) permits opposition parties to participate, (3) respects "basic civil liberties and human rights of the citizens of Cuba," (4) is moving toward a free market economy, and (5) is committed to constitutional change that ensures regular free and fair elections. Sec. 204, Cuban Liberty and Democratic Solidarity (LIBERTAD) Act (22 U.S.C.

Table 1. (Continued)

Statutory Basis	Restriction	Authority to Lift or Waive
		6064), however, authorizes the President to suspend the enforcement of sec. 1706 only if he determines that "a transition government is in power in Cuba." Sec. 204, furthermore, requires the President to terminate sanctions under sec. 1706 and other measures if he determines that "a democratically elected government in Cuba is in power." Sec. 204(d)(1) of that Act repeals sec. 1706 on President making such a determination.
Sec. 1706(b), Cuban Democracy Act of 1992 (22 U.S.C. 6005(b))	Prohibits entry into U.S. ports by any vessel that has entered a Cuban port in the previous 180 days. Prohibits entry into U.S. ports by any vessel carrying goods or passengers to or from Cuba in which Cuba or a Cuban national has any interest. Prohibits the use of a general license for ship stores for any vessel carrying goods or passengers to or from Cuba in which Cuba or a Cuban national has any interes	Licenses may be issued at the discretion of the Secretary of the Treasury. Sec. 1708 provides that the President may waive if he determines that the government of Cuba (1) has held free and fair elections, (2) permits opposition parties to participate, (3) respects "basic civil liberties and human rights of the citizens of Cuba," (4) is moving toward a free market economy, and (5) is committed to constitutional change that ensures regular free and fair elections. Sec. 204, Cuban Liberty and Democratic Solidarity (LIBERTAD) Act (22 U.S.C. 6064), however, authorizes the President to suspend the enforcement of sec. 1706 only if he determines that "a transition government is in power in Cuba." Sec. 204, furthermore, requires the President to terminate sanctions under sec. 1706 and other measures if he determines that "a democratically elected government

Statutory Basis	Restriction	Authority to Lift or Waive
		in Cuba is in power." Sec. 204(d)(1) of that Act repeals sec. 1706 on President making such a determination.
Sec. 1706(c), Cuban Democracy Act of 1992 (22 U.S.C. 6005(c))	Requires the President to "establish strict limits on remittances to Cuba by United States persons for the purpose of financing the travel of Cubans to the United States.... "	The term "strict limits" is undefined, so left to the discretion of the President. Sec. 1708 provides that the President may waive if he determines that the government of Cuba (1) has held free and fair elections, (2) permits opposition parties to participate, (3) respects "basic civil liberties and human rights of the citizens of Cuba," (4) is moving toward a free market economy, and (5) is committed to constitutional change that ensures regular free and fair elections. Sec. 204, Cuban Liberty and Democratic Solidarity (LIBERTAD) Act (22 U.S.C. 6064), however, authorizes the President to suspend the enforcement of sec. 1706 only if he determines that "a transition government is in power in Cuba." Sec. 204, furthermore, requires the President to terminate sanctions under sec. 1706 and other measures if he determines that "a democratically elected government in Cuba is in power." Sec. 204(d)(1) of that Act repeals sec. 1706 on President making such a determination.
Sec. 102(h), Cuban Liberty and Democratic Solidarity (LIBERTAD) Act of 1996 (22 U.S.C. 6032(h))	Codifies the economic embargo as in effect on March 1, 1996, including restrictions stated in regulations at 31 CFR Part 515.	Within 31 CFR Part 515, the Secretary of the Treasury retains authority to amend regulations therein, in accordance with 31 CFR Part 515. 201, which, in part, provides: "All of the following transactions are prohibited, except as specifically authorized by the

Table 1. (Continued)

Statutory Basis	Restriction	Authority to Lift or Waive
		Secretary of the Treasury.... " Sec. 204, Cuban Liberty and Democratic Solidarity (LIBERTAD) Act (22 U.S.C. 6064) authorizes the President to suspend the enforcement of 31 CFR Part 515 only if he determines that "a transition government is in power in Cuba." Sec. 204, furthermore, requires the President to terminate the economic embargo of Cuba, including the restrictions under 31 CFR Part 515, if he determines that "a democratically elected government in Cuba is in power."
Sec. 103(a), Cuban Liberty and Democratic Solidarity (LIBERTAD) Act of 1996 (22 U.S.C. 6033(a))	Prohibits a U.S. person or entity from financing any transaction that involves confiscated property in Cuba where the claim is owned by a U.S. national.	Sec. 103(b) provides that the President may suspend if he determines a transition government is in power; he may terminate if the transition to democracy is met as stated in secs. 203 and 204.
Sec. 104(a), Cuban Liberty and Democratic Solidarity (LIBERTAD) Act of 1996 (22 U.S.C. 6034(a))	Requires the Secretary of the Treasury to instruct U.S. executive directors to the international financial institutions to oppose Cuba's admission to such institution.	The President may suspend if he determines a democratically elected government is in power. The President may encourage membership, and the Secretary of the Treasury may encourage loans and assistance, when a transition government is in power, "to contribute to a stable foundation for a democratically elected government in Cuba."
Sec. 104(b), Cuban Liberty and Democratic Solidarity (LIBERTAD) Act of 1996 (22 U.S.C. 6034(b))	Requires the Secretary of the Treasury to withhold U.S. payment to any international financial institution in an amount equal to that institution's loan or assistance to Cuba if that loan is opposed by the United States.	The statute requires the United States to oppose Cuba's membership (in sec. 104(a)); it does not require opposing any loan or program of an international financial institution. If the United States supports a program or abstains from a vote, this

Statutory Basis	Restriction	Authority to Lift or Waive
		requirement would be inapplicable. Only if the United States opposes a loan would proportionate withholding be required.
Sec. 111(b), Cuban Liberty and Democratic Solidarity (LIBERTAD) Act of 1996 (22 U.S.C. 6041(b))	Requires withholding some foreign aid to any third country in amounts equal to that country's aid to Cuba to complete its nuclear facility at Juragua.	No waiver; however the statute allows aid to continue for humanitarian needs, disaster relief, refugee relief, democracy, rule of law, private sector and NGO development, free market economy development, nonproliferation, and secondary school exchanges.
Title III, Cuban Liberty and Democratic Solidarity (LIBERTAD) Act of 1996 (22 U.S.C. 6081-6085)	Allow U.S. nationals whose property was confiscated by the Cuban government a right of action to seek compensation in U.S. federal court from those who "traffic" in such property.	The President may suspend the right of action for successive 6-month periods if he determines that such suspension is in the U.S. national interest and will expedite Cuba's transition to democracy. The President has exercised this suspension since the law's enactment. Sec. 204 of the Act also authorizes the President, once he determines that a transition government is in power, to suspend the right of action under title III to the extent that it contributes to a stable foundation for a democratically elected government in Cuba.
Title IV, Cuban Liberty and Democratic Solidarity (LIBERTAD) Act of 1996 (22 U.S.C. 6091)	Requires the Secretary of State and Attorney General to deny entry into the United States to any person (or family member of that person) who has confiscated property, or has been involved in a related transaction, to which a U.S. person has a claim.	Secretary of State may, case-by-case, allow entry into the United States for medical purposes or to attend to litigation actions under title III of the Act (relating to protection of property rights of U.S. nationals).
Sec. 906, Trade Sanctions and Export Enhancement Act of	Exports of agricultural commodities, medicine, and medical supplies to Cuba	No waiver.

Table 1. (Continued)

Statutory Basis	Restriction	Authority to Lift or Waive
2000 (22 U.S.C. 7205)	require a 1-year license and 1-year contract.	
Sec. 908, Trade Sanctions and Export Enhancement Act of 2000 (22 U.S.C. 7207)	Prohibits U.S. aid for exports to Cuba. Limits the means by which a U.S. person may finance the sale of agricultural products to Cuba to cash in advance or third-country financing.	No waiver.
Sec. 910(b), Trade Sanctions and Export Enhancement Act of 2000 (22 U.S.C. 7208(b))	The Secretary of the Treasury may not authorize travel-related transactions listed in paragraph (c) of section 515.560 of title 31, Code of Federal Regulations, either by a general license or on a case-by-case basis by a specific license for travel to, from, or within Cuba for tourist activities.	No waiver.
Sec. 620A, Foreign Assistance Act of 1961 (22 U.S.C. 2371)	Prohibits funding under the Foreign Assistance Act of 1961, Agricultural Trade Development and Assistance Act of 1954, Peace Corps Act, and Export-Import Bank Act of 1945, to any country the government of which the Secretary of State finds "has repeatedly provided support for acts of international terrorism."	President may lift restrictions if he determines (1) "there has been a fundamental change in the leadership and policies of the government," (2) the government does not support acts of international terrorism, and (3) the government provides assurances that it will not support international terrorism in the future. Alternatively, the President may lift restrictions if he determines that the government has not supported terrorism in the preceding six months, and has provided assurances that it will not support international terrorism in the future. The President may waive if he determines it is in U.S. national security interests or that

Statutory Basis	Restriction	Authority to Lift or Waive
		humanitarian reasons (for non-lethal aid) justify a waiver.
Sec. 40, Arms Export Control Act (22 U.S.C. 2780)	Prohibits transactions relating to providing, directly or indirectly, any munitions acquisition to any country the government of which the Secretary of State finds "has repeatedly provided support for acts of international terrorism." U.S. persons are prohibited from exporting, selling, leasing, loaning, granting, providing, or facilitating the acquisition of any munitions item to/by Cuba.	The Secretary of State may waive some prohibitions if he determines, after consulting Congress, that "unusual and compelling circumstances require" it. President may lift restrictions if he determines that (1) "there has been a fundamental change in the leadership and policies of the government," (2) the government does not support acts of international terrorism, and (3) the government provides assurances that it will not support international terrorism in the future. Alternatively, the President may lift restrictions if he determines that the government has not supported terrorism in the preceding six months, and has provided assurances that it will not support international terrorism in the future. The President may waive for a specific transaction if he determines it is "essential to the national security of the United States" and consults with and reports to Congress. Congress may block lifting this restriction by passing a joint resolution.
Sec. 6(j), Export Administration Act of 1979 (50 U.S.C. App. 2405(j))	Requires a validated export license, with a presumption of denial for such issuance, to any country the government of which has repeatedly provided support for acts of international terrorism.	The Secretary of State may issue licenses with prior notification to Congress. President may lift restrictions if he determines that (1) "there has been a fundamental change in the leadership and policies of the government," (2) the government

Table 1. (Continued)

Statutory Basis	Restriction	Authority to Lift or Waive
		does not support acts of international terrorism, and (3) the government provides assurances that it will not support international terrorism in the future. Alternatively, the President may lift restrictions if he determines that the government has not supported terrorism in the preceding six months, and has provided assurances that it will not support international terrorism in the future.
Sec. 40A, Arms Export Control Act (22 U.S.C. 2781)	Prohibits the selling or leasing of defense articles or defense services to any country that "is not cooperating fully with United States antiterrorism efforts." Determined annually to apply only to that fiscal year.	President could delist (list comes out annually by May 15). President may waive for a specific transaction if he finds it "important to the national interests of the United States."
Sec. 6, Bretton Woods Agreements Act Amendments, 1978 (22 U.S.C. 286e-11)	Requires the Secretary of the Treasury to instruct U.S. executive directors to the International Monetary Fund "to work in opposition to" loans to any state that permits entry to any person who has committed an act of international terrorism, or otherwise harbors such person.	No waiver. A determination pursuant to sec. 6(j), Export Administration Act of 1979 to remove Cuba from the list of state sponsors of terrorism, however, could indirectly remove this restriction.
Additional Restrictions: Foreign Aid, Trade, and International Financial Institutions Programs		
Sec. 307, Foreign Assistance Act of 1961 (22 U.S.C. 2227)	Withholds a proportion of U.S. contributions to the United Nations and other international programs operating in Cuba (except UNICEF and some International Atomic Energy	No waiver.

Statutory Basis	Restriction	Authority to Lift or Waive
	Agency programs).	
Sec. 498A(b), (c), Foreign Assistance Act of 1961 (22 U.S.C. 2295a)	Prohibits some foreign aid to any government of an independent state of the former Soviet Union that the President determines is providing assistance for, or engaging in nonmarket trade with, the Cuban government.	President may waive if he determines that (1) "it is important to the national interest of the United States" to do so; (2) aid will foster respect for internationally recognized human rights, rule of law, development of democratic governance institutions; (3) aid alleviates results of a disaster; (4) aid is for secondary school programs run by the U.S. Information Agency (USIA).
Sec. 498A(d), Foreign Assistance Act of 1961 (22 U.S.C. 2295a)	Reduces aid to any government of an independent state of the former Soviet Union in proportion with that country's aid to Cuba's intelligence facilities.	President may waive if he determines that it is important to U.S. national security. In the case of Russia, must further determine Russia is not sharing intelligence data with the Cuban government.
Sec. 620(f), Foreign Assistance Act of 1961 (22U.S.C. 2370(f))	Prohibits foreign aid to any Communist country, explicitly naming Cuba.	President may waive if he finds it is vital to the security of the United States, the recipient is not controlled by the "international Communist conspiracy," and aid will promote the independence of the recipient. President may also remove Cuba from the stated list of communist countries for any period of time if he finds it important to U.S. national interests to do so.
Sec. 620(t), Foreign Assistance Act of 1961 (22U.S.C. 2370(t))	Prohibits foreign aid and sales under the Food for Peace Act to any government that has, or with which the United States has, severed diplomatic relations.	Aid and sales may resume when diplomatic relations resume.
Sec. 620(y), Foreign Assistance Act of 1961 (22U.S.C. 2370(y))	Prohibits foreign aid to a third country in amounts equal to that country's providing nuclear fuel and related assistance to Cuba the	Prohibition is lifted when Cuba signs and complies with the Treaty on the Non-proliferation of Nuclear Weapons and the Treaty of Tlatelelco, negotiates full-scope

Table 1. (Continued)

Statutory Basis	Restriction	Authority to Lift or Waive
	previous fiscal year.	safeguards, and is found in compliance with the treaties.
Sec. 2(b)(2), Export-Import Bank Act of 1945 (12 U.S.C. 635(2)(b)(2))	Prohibits Ex-Im Bank funding for Marxist-Leninist states, explicitly naming Cuba.	President may determine Cuba has ceased to be a Marxist-Leninist country. President may determine that a specific transaction, or a transaction of a certain kind, is in the national interest.
Sec. 110, Trafficking Victims Protection Act of 2000 (22 U.S.C. 7107)	Prohibits nonhumanitarian, nontrade-related aid to Cuba for its failure to comply with minimum standards or make significant efforts related to trafficking in persons.	Determination made annually: Secretary of State could find Cuba in compliance the next fiscal year. Secretary of State could make a determination of compliance outside the annual cycle of reporting. The President may continue nonhumanitarian, non-trade-related aid if he finds it would "promote the purposes" of the act or is otherwise in the U.S. national interest.
Sec. 7007, 7015(f), Department of State, Foreign Operations, and Related Programs Appropriations Act, 2015 (Division J, P.L. 113-235)	Sec. 7007: Prohibits direct funding to Cuba. Sec. 7015(f): prohibits aid to Cuba without regular notification procedures of the Committees on Appropriations.	No waivers. The two sections apply only to the current fiscal year.
Sec. 12, International Development Association Act (22 U.S.C. 284j) Sec. 21, Inter-American Development Bank Act (22 U.S.C. 283r)	Requires the President to instruct U.S. executive directors to the relevant international financial institution to oppose loans to any state that has nationalized, expropriated, or seized property owned by a U.S. citizen; canceled contracts with a U.S. citizen; imposed discriminatory taxes that have the result of property seizure.	The President may determine that (1) arrangements for compensation have been made; (2) the issue has been submitted to arbitration; or (3) good faith negotiations are underway.

Statutory Basis	Restriction	Authority to Lift or Waive
Sec. 401, Tariff Classification Act of 1962 (19 U.S.C. 1351 note)	Requires Cuba to be treated as a nation "dominated or controlled by the foreign government or foreign organization controlling the world Communist movement," resulting in denying articles that are "the growth, produce, or manufacture of Cuba" favorable trade terms. The U.S. Harmonized Tariff Schedule (HTS) designates Cuba in the most restricted trade category ("Column 2") pursuant to this provision and other trade laws as follows: "b) Rate of Duty Column 2. Notwithstanding any of the foregoing provisions of this note, the rates of duty shown in column 2 shall apply to products, whether imported directly or indirectly, of the following countries and areas pursuant to section 401 of the Tariff Classification Act of 1962, to section 231 or 257(e)(2) of the Trade Expansion Act of 1962, to section 404(a) of the Trade Act of 1974 or to any other applicable section of law, or to action taken by the President thereunder: Cuba, North Korea."	The restrictions ceases to apply "on or after the date on which the President proclaims that he has determined that Cuba is no longer dominated or controlled" by such a foreign power.
Sec. 401, Trade Act of 1974 (19 U.S.C. 2431)	Continues to deny nondiscriminatory trade treatment for countries that were so denied prior to enactment of this title.	The President may temporarily waive or lift by entering into a bilateral commercial agreement (sec. 405; 19 U.S.C. 2435), and may temporarily extend nondiscriminatory terms (sec. 404; 19 U.S.C. 2434). Granting permanent

Table 1. (Continued)

Statutory Basis	Restriction	Authority to Lift or Waive
		nondiscriminatory trade treatment (Normal Trade Relations, or NTR), however, requires an act of Congress (sec. 151; 19 U.S.C. 2191).
Sec. 402, Trade Act of 1974 (Jackson-Vanik Amendment; 19 U.S.C. 2432)	Continues to deny nondiscriminatory trade treatment for countries that were so denied prior to enactment of this title, including countries under sec. 401, communist countries, or non-market economies (as defined in the Senate report accompanying H.R. 10710, 93rd Congress, enacted as the Trade Act of 1974).	President may suspend temporarily, and may renew the suspension semiannually (by June 30 and December 31) if he determines and notifies Congress that the government of Cuba does not (1) deny its citizens the right or opportunity to emigrate; (2) impose more than a nominal tax on emigration and documents required to emigrate or travel; or (3) impose more than a nominal tax on a citizen as a result of that citizen's desire to emigrate. President may suspend temporarily, with annual renewal, by issuing an executive order stating that (1) waiving will promote the objectives of Jackson-Vanik; and (2) "he has received assurances that the emigration practices of that country will henceforth lead substantially to the achievements of the objectives of the section." Congress may block the President's initial determinations (sec. 152; 19 U.S.C. 2192), or extension of waiver (sec. 153; 19 U.S.C. 2193). Granting permanent nondiscriminatory trade treatment however, requires an act of Congress (sec. 151; 19 U.S.C. 2191). Removal of Jackson-Vanik

Statutory Basis	Restriction	Authority to Lift or Waive
		restrictions, however, does not require NTR status (the President may exercise the above-described waiver authority).
Sec. 502(b), Trade Act of 1974 (19 U.S.C. 2462(b))	A country is denied "beneficiary developing country" status under the Generalized System of Preferences if it is a Communist country, and if it has expropriated property of a U.S. citizen.	President may waive if he finds it in the national economic interest of the United States to do so.
Sec. 212, Caribbean Basin Economic Recovery Act (19 U.S.C. 2702)	Cuba is not eligible for CBERA benefits because it is not listed in sec. 212(b). In addition, a country is denied "beneficiary country" status under the CBERA if it is a Communist country; has nationalized, expropriated, or seized property owned by a U.S. citizen; canceled contracts with a U.S. citizen; imposed discriminatory taxes that have the result of property seizure; fails to recognize certain arbitral awards in favor of a U.S. citizen, corporation, partnership, or corporation; affords preferential treatment to products of a developed country other than the United States (unless there is no significant adverse effect on U.S. commerce); if a government-owned entity engages in the broadcast of U.S.-owned copyrighted material without express consent; is not a signatory to an agreement regarding the extradition of U.S. citizens; and has not or is not taking	Congress would have to amend sec. 212(b) to add Cuba to the list of countries eligible for CBERA designation. Once listed, the President could designate Cuba as beneficiary country, despite other restrictions, if he finds it in the national economic interest of the United States to do so, except if the country affords preferential treatment to products of a developed country other than the United States (unless there is no significant adverse effect on U.S. commerce), and is a signatory to an agreement regarding the extradition of U.S. citizens.

Table 1. (Continued)

Statutory Basis	Restriction	Authority to Lift or Waive
	steps to afford internationally recognized worker rights.	
Sec. 902, Food Security Act of 1985 (7 U.S.C. 1446 note)	Sec. 902, Food Security Act of 1985 (7 U.S.C. 1446 note)	Sec. 204, Cuban Liberty and Democratic Solidarity (LIBERTAD) Act (22 U.S.C. 6064) authorizes the President to suspend the enforcement of sec. 902 if he determines "a transition government is in power in Cuba." Sec. 204, furthermore, requires the President to terminate sanctions under sec. 902 and other measures if he determines that "a democratically elected government in Cuba is in power." Sec. 204(d)(1) of that Act repeals sec. 902 on President making such a determination.
Sec. 211, Omnibus Consolidated and Emergency Supplemental Appropriations Act, 1999 (Division A, Title II, P.L. 105-277)	Prohibits a transaction or payment with respect to a mark, trade, name or commercial name that is the same as or substantially similar to a mark, trade name, or commercial name used in connection with a business or assets that were confiscated. Prohibits U.S. courts from considering or enforcing trademark claims of a Cuba national, or their successor in interest, regarding property confiscated by the Cuban government.	No waiver.

End Notes

[1] 27 Federal Register 1085, February 7, 1962 (Proclamation 3447, Embargo on All Trade with Cuba, February 3, 1962).

[2] Previously, in October 1960 under the Eisenhower Administration, exports to Cuba were placed under strict export controls under the authority of the Export Control Act of 1949 in response to the expropriation of U.S. properties. This in effect amounted to an embargo on exports of all products with the exception of certain foods, medicines, and medical supplies.

[3] 27 Federal Register 1116, February 7, 1962.

[4] 27 Federal Register 2765-2766, March 24, 1962.

[5] 28 Federal Register 6974-6985, July 9, 1963.

[6] 31 C.F.R. §515.533.

[8] Cuba's designation on the state sponsor of terrorism list has allowed U.S. nationals injured by an act of international terrorism to file lawsuits against Cuba in the United States for damages. For more information, see CRS Report WSLG254, Can Victims of Terrorism in the United States Sue Foreign Governments? by Jennifer K. Elsea.

[9] CRS has prepared a memorandum for general distribution on Cuban Assets Control Regulations, with Final Rule of January 16, 2015 Incorporated in Ramseyer Form, available on request from the authors.

[10] 80 Federal Register 2286-2302, January 16, 2015.

[11] U.S. Government Accountability Office, U.S. Embargo On Cuba: Recent Regulatory Changes and Potential Presidential or Congressional Actions, GAO-09-0951R, September 17, 2009.

In: The Sanctions Way
Editor: Brian Fields
ISBN: 978-1-63482-679-2

Chapter 3

IRAN SANCTIONS*

Kenneth Katzman

SUMMARY

International sanctions on Iran's key energy and financial sectors harmed Iran's economy and arguably contributed to Iran's acceptance of restrictions on expanding its nuclear program in exchange for modest sanctions relief. The interim nuclear "standstill" agreement (Joint Plan of Action, JPA) has been in effect since January 20, 2014, and extended twice (now until July 6, 2015) to allow time to translate it into a comprehensive nuclear agreement. The economic pressure of sanctions included the following:

- Iran's crude oil exports are about 1.1 million barrels per day (mbd) at the end of 2013—far below the 2.5 million barrels per day Iran exported during 2011.
- Iran's economy shrank by about 5% in 2013 as Iran's private sector reduced operations and many of its loans became delinquent, and has rebounded only modestly since the JPA sanctions relief went into effect.

Sanctions have constricted Iran's ability to procure equipment for its nuclear and missile programs and to import advanced conventional weaponry. However, the sanctions have not halted Iran's provision of

* This is an edited, reformatted and augmented version of a Congressional Research Service publication, No. RS20871, dated January 28, 2015.

arms to the Assad government in Syria, the Iraqi government and related Shiite militias, Houthi rebels in Yemen, or other pro-Iranian factions in the Middle East. Nor have sanctions altered Iran's repression of dissent or monitoring of the Internet.

Under the JPA, the United States has provided Iran with some sanctions relief through presidential waivers of several U.S. sanctions laws and authority under several executive orders. The core of the sanctions relief is $700 million per month in access to hard currency from oil sales, plus about $65 million per month in additional hard currency provided to educational institutions for Iranians studying abroad. The JPA caps Iran's oil exports at about 1mbd but does not cap exports to its crude oil customers of oil products such as condensates, and Iran appears to be increasing exports of condensates to partly compensate for the limitations on crude oil sales. The JPA suspends sanctions on Iran's auto manufacturing sector and on its sales of petrochemicals, although available data indicate activity in these sectors does not appear to be producing nearly as much revenue as was estimated. And, the fall in oil prices since June 2014 has introduced additional uncertainty to Iran's economy, to the point where many experts assess that Iranian leaders urgently need a comprehensive nuclear deal to achieve the economic improvement demanded by the population.

By all accounts, a comprehensive nuclear agreement, if reached, will entail significant easing of U.S. and third country sanctions on Iran—particularly those sanctions that reduced Iran's oil exports and limit its access to the international financial system. The Administration has said that substantial sanctions relief under a comprehensive deal would be provided, but would be implemented stepwise as Iran fulfills the terms of an agreement. The Administration has asserted that, in the event of an agreement, it will act on its own authority to suspend most sanctions on Iran and, after testing Iran's compliance over a period of time, work with Congress on long-term sanctions relief. Some in Congress are proposing additional sanctions if diplomacy fails, but the Administration strongly opposes enacting additional sanctions while talks are ongoing. The Administration asserts that doing so will fracture the coalition negotiating with Iran and cause Iran to walk away from the talks.

Overview and Objectives

U.S. sanctions have been a major feature of U.S. Iran policy since Iran's 1979 Islamic revolution, but U.N. and worldwide bilateral sanctions on Iran are a relatively recent (post-2006) development. Many of the U.S. sanctions reinforce U.N. and multilateral sanctions put in place in recent years by

European and some Asian countries. Successive Administrations have sought to ensure that U.S. sanctions do not hamper cooperation with key international partners whose support is needed to isolate Iran.

The objectives of U.S. sanctions have evolved over time. In the 1980s and 1990s, U.S. sanctions were intended to try to compel Iran to cease supporting acts of terrorism and to limit Iran's strategic power in the Middle East more generally. Since the mid-2000s, U.S. sanctions have focused intently on compelling Iran to limit the scope of its nuclear program to ensure purely civilian use. Particularly since 2010, the international community has joined U.S. sanctions in pursuit of that goal. However, most sanctions against Iran have multiple objectives and address different perceived threats from Iran at the same time.

This report analyzes U.S. and international sanctions against Iran and, in so doing, provides examples, based on a wide range of open source reporting, of companies and countries that conduct business with Iran. CRS has no way to independently corroborate any of the reporting on which these examples are based and no mandate to assess whether any entity is complying with U.S. or international sanctions against Iran. The sections below are grouped according to functional theme, in the chronological order in which these themes have emerged in U.S. sanctions policy toward Iran. It is so indicated if a certain sanctions provision is suspended to implement the JPA.

Implementation of some of the sanctions is subject to interpretation. On November 13, 2012, the Administration published in the *Federal Register* (Volume 77, Number 219) "Policy Guidance" explaining how it implements many of the sanctions.[1] The guidance provides examples of specific products and chemicals that are included in the definitions of such terms as "petroleum," "petroleum products," and "petrochemical products" that are used in the laws and executive orders discussed below.

BLOCKED IRANIAN PROPERTY AND ASSETS

Some U.S. sanctions began at the time of the U.S.-Iran hostage crisis of 1979-1981 in the form of Carter Administration executive orders blocking Iranian assets held in the United States. The assets were unblocked by subsequent Orders when the crisis was resolved in early 1981 under the "Algiers Accords." The Accords established a "U.S.-Iran Claims Tribunal" at the Hague continues to arbitrate cases resulting from the 1980 break in relations and freezing of some of Iran's assets. Major cases yet to be decided center on hundreds of Foreign Military Sales (FMS) cases between the United States and the Shah's regime, which Iran claims it paid for but were unfulfilled. A reported $400 million in proceeds from the resale of that equipment was placed in a DOD FMS account and may remain in this escrow account, although DOD has not provided CRS with a precise balance. In addition, about $50 million in Iranian diplomatic property and accounts remains blocked—this amount includes proceeds from rents received on the former Iranian embassy in Washington, DC, and 10 other properties in several states, along with related bank accounts.[2] Including Iranian assets blocked under Executive Order 1399 of February 2010, discussed below, about $1.95 billion in Iranian assets is blocked, according to the 2013 "Terrorist Assets Report."

Other past financial disputes include the mistaken U.S. shoot-down on July 3, 1988, of an Iranian Airbus passenger jet (Iran Air flight 655), for which the United States paid Iran $61.8 million in compensation ($300,000 per wage earning victim, $150,000 per nonwage earner) for the 248 Iranians killed. The United States did not compensate Iran for the airplane itself, although officials involved in the negotiations told CRS in November 2012 that the United States later arranged to provide a substitute, used aircraft to Iran.

In late 2009, the U.S. Attorney for the Southern District of New York seized the assets of the Assa Company, a UK-chartered entity. Assa allegedly was maintaining the interests of Bank Melli in an office building in New York City. An Iranian foundation, the Alavi Foundation, allegedly is an investor in the building.

Some of Iran's assets have been held against legal judgments ordering Iran to compensate U.S. victims of Iranian-backed terrorism. Recent terrorism-related judgments include those in favor of the families of the 241 U.S. soldiers killed in the October 23, 1983, bombing of the U.S. Marine barracks in Beirut. About $8.8 billion has been awarded in eight judgments against Iran for that bombing, which was perpetrated by elements that formed Lebanese Hezbollah.

The Algiers Accords appears to have precluded compensation for the 52 U.S. diplomats held hostage by Iran from November 1979 until January 1981.

Executive Order 13599 Impounding Iran-Owned Assets

Several Executive Orders discussed in this report direct the blocking of U.S.-based assets of designated Iranian entities. Executive Order 13599, issued February 5, 2012, imposes sanctions on the Central Bank and on other entities determined to be owned or controlled by the Iranian government ("government of Iran"). The order requires that any U.S.-based assets of the Central Bank of Iran, or of any Iranian government-controlled entity, be impounded by U.S. financial institutions. U.S. persons are prohibited from any dealings with such entities. U.S. financial institutions previously were required to merely refuse such transactions with the Central Bank, or return funds to it. Several designations have been made under order, as shown in **Table 5**; on June 21, 2013, OFAC published the names of 38 entities, mostly including oil, petrochemical, and investment companies, determined to meet the definition of "government of Iran."[3] Executive Orders 13224 and 13382 are discussed later in this report because they block assets of persons involved in support of terrorism or proliferation, respectively.

SANCTIONS AGAINST IRAN'S SUPPORT FOR INTERNATIONAL TERRORISM AND REGIONAL ACTIVITIES

The United States began imposing sanctions again Iran again in the mid-1980s. The Secretary of State designated Iran a "state sponsor of terrorism" on January 23, 1984, following the October 1983 bombing of the U.S. Marine barracks in Lebanon perpetrated by elements that later became Hezbollah. This designation triggers substantial sanctions on any nation so designated.

Sanctions Triggered by Terrorism List Designation: Ban on U.S. Aid, Arms Sales, Dual-Use Exports, and Certain Programs for Iran

The U.S. naming of Iran as a "state sponsor of terrorism"—commonly referred to as Iran's placement on the U.S. "terrorism list"—triggers several sanctions. The designation is made under the authority of Section 6(j) of the Export Administration Act of 1979 (P.L. 96-72, as amended), sanctioning countries determined to have provided repeated support for acts of international terrorism. The sanctions triggered by Iran's state sponsor of terrorism designation are:

- *Restrictions on sales of U.S. dual use items.* The restriction is required by the Export Administration Act, as continued through presidential authorities under the International Emergency Economic Powers Act, IEEPA, as implemented by executive orders).
- *Ban on direct U.S. financial assistance and arms sales to Iran.* Section 620A of the Foreign Assistance Act, FAA (P.L. 87-95) and Section 40 of the Arms Export Control Act (P.L. 95-92, as amended), respectively, bar these benefits to terrorism list countries. In addition, successive foreign aid appropriations laws since the late 1980s have banned direct assistance to Iran (loans, credits, insurance, Ex-Im Bank credits) without providing for a waiver.
- *Requirement that the United States vote to oppose multilateral lending.* U.S. officials are required to vote against multilateral lending to any terrorism list country by Section 1621 of the International Financial Institutions Act (P.L. 95- 118, as amended, which was added by Section 327 of the Anti-Terrorism and Effective Death Penalty Act of 1996 (P.L. 104-132). These laws provide waiver authority.
- *Withholding of U.S. foreign assistance to Suppliers of Terrorism List Countries.* Under Section 620G and 620H of the Foreign Assistance Act, as added by the Anti-Terrorism and Effective Death Penalty Act (sections 325 and 326 of P.L. 104-132), the President is required to withhold foreign aid from any country that provides to a terrorism list country financial assistance or arms. Waivers are provided. Section 321 of that act also makes it a criminal offense for U.S. persons to conduct financial transactions with terrorism list governments.
- *Withholding of U.S. Aid to Organizations that Assist Iran.* Section 307 of the FAA (added in 1985) names Iran as unable to benefit from U.S. contributions to international organizations, and require proportionate cuts if these institutions work in Iran. For example, if an international organization spends 3% of its budget for programs in Iran, then the United States is required to withhold 3% of its contribution to that international organization. No waiver is provided for.

No Ban on U.S. Humanitarian Aid

The terrorism list designation, and other U.S. sanctions laws, do not bar disaster aid. The United States donated $125,000, through relief agencies, to help victims of two earthquakes in Iran (February and May 1997); $350,000 worth of aid to the victims of a June 22, 2002, earthquake; and $5.7 million in assistance (out of total governmental pledges of about $32 million) for the victims of the December 2003 earthquake in Bam, Iran, which killed as many as 40,000 people. The U.S. military flew in 68,000 kilograms of supplies to Bam.

Removal from Terrorism List/Sanctions Termination

Terminating the sanctions triggered by Iran's terrorism list designation would require Iran's removal from the terrorism list. The Arms Export Control Act spells out two different requirements for a President to remove a country from the list, depending on whether the country's regime has changed.

If the regime has changed, the President can remove a country from the list immediately by certifying that change in a report to Congress.

If the country's regime has not changed, the President must report to Congress 45 days in advance of the effective date of removal. The President must certify that (1) the country has not supported international terrorism within the preceding six months, and (2) the country has provided assurances it will not do so in the future. In this latter circumstance, Congress has the opportunity to block the removal by enacting a joint resolution to that effect. The President has the option of vetoing the joint resolution, in which case blocking the removal would require a congressional veto override vote.

Executive Order 13224 Sanctioning Terrorism- Supporting Entities

In signing Executive Order 13324 (September 23, 2001), the President ordered the freezing of the U.S.-based assets of and a ban on U.S. transactions with entities determined to be supporting international terrorism. This order was issued two weeks after the September 11, 2001, attacks on the United States, under the authority of the IEEPA, the National Emergencies Act, the

U.N. Participation Act of 1945, and Section 301 of the U.S. Code, and initially targeted Al Qaedarelated entities. The Order is therefore not specific to Iran.

Implementation: Iran-related entities designated under the order for terrorism-related activities are listed in the table at the end of this report.

Sanctioning Iranian Involvement in the Region

Some sanctions have been imposed to try to curtail Iran's influence in the region:

- *Executive Order 13438.* On July 7, 2007, President Bush issued Executive Order 13438. The Order sanctions Iranian persons who are posing a threat to Iraqi stability, presumably by providing arms or funds to Shiite militias there. Persons sanctioned under the order, including Qods Force officers, Iraqi Shiite militia-linked figures, and other some entities sanctioned under the Order are shown in the tables at the end of this report.
- *Executive Order 13572.* Issued on April 29, 2011, the Order targets those responsible for human rights abuses and repression of the Syrian people. The IRGC-Qods Force, Qods Force officers including overall commander Qasem Soleimani, and others sanctioned under this and related Orders are shown in the tables at the end of the report.

BAN ON U.S. TRADE AND INVESTMENT WITH IRAN

The next major sanction imposed on Iran after those required by the terrorism list designation was a ban on U.S. trade with and investment in Iran. It was imposed on May 6, 1995, by President Clinton, through Executive Order 12959, under the authority primarily of the International Emergency Economic Powers Act (IEEPA, 50 U.S.C. 1701 et seq.).[4] IEEPA gives the President wide powers to regulate commerce with a foreign country when a state of emergency is declared in relations with that country. Executive Order 12959 followed and superseded an earlier (March 15, 1995) Executive Order (12957) barring U.S. investment in Iran's energy sector, which accompanied President Clinton's declaration that a "state of emergency" exists with respect to Iran. A subsequent Executive Order, 13059 (August 19, 1997), added a prohibition on U.S. companies' knowingly exporting goods to a third country for incorporation into products destined for Iran. Each March since 1995, the U.S. Administration has renewed a declaration of a state of emergency that triggers the President's trade regulation authority under IEEPA. The operation of the trade regulations is stipulated in Section 560 of the Code of Federal Regulations (Iranian Transactions Regulations, ITRs). *The U.S. trade and investment ban is unaffected by the JPA— with selected exceptions, U.S. firms remain generally banned from the Iran market.*

Codification of the Ban and U.S.-Iran Trade Figures

Section 103 of the Comprehensive Iran Sanctions, Accountability, and Divestment Act of 2010 (CISADA, P.L. 111-195) codified the ban on U.S trade with Iran. In so doing, it reinstated the full ban on imports that had been relaxed by executive order in April 2000 to allow U.S. importation of Iranian nuts, fruit products (such as pomegranate juice), carpets, and caviar. The relaxations to the trade ban from then until CISADA's effective date of September 29, 2010, account for the fact that U.S. trade with Iran expanded during that period. The restoration of the full import ban explains why U.S. imports from Iran since that time have been negligible (a total of about $2.2 million for all of 2013 and nil for 2014). U.S. imports from Iran consist primarily of artwork for exhibitions around the United States (and count as imports even though the works return to Iran after the exhibitions conclude). For all of 2013, U.S. exporters sold about $312 million in goods to Iran, mostly grain sales, but dropped to about half that for 2014. CISADA also specifies exemptions to the trade ban, including: (1) exports not only of food and medical goods; (2) information technology to support personal communications among the Iranian people; (3) goods to allow civilian aircraft to fly safely; and (4) goods for supporting democracy in Iran.

Section 101 of the Iran Freedom Support Act (P.L. 109-293) separately codified the ban on U.S. investment in Iran. Section 101 of that law gives the President the authority to terminate sanctions under the Iran Freedom Support Act if he notifies Congress 15 days in advance (or 3 days in advance if there are "exigent circumstances").

What U.S.-Iran Trade Is Allowed or Prohibited?

The following provisions apply to the U.S. trade ban on Iran as specified in regulations ("Iran Transaction Regulations," ITRs) written pursuant to the executive orders and laws discussed above. The regulations are administered by the Office of Foreign Assets Control (OFAC) of the Treasury Department.

- *Oil Dealings.* The 1995 trade ban greatly expanded a 1987 ban on imports from Iran under Executive Order 12613 (October 29, 1987). That 1987 ban was imposed under authorities provided in Section 505 of the International Security and Development Cooperation Act of 1985 (22 U.S.C. 2349aa-9). The import ban barred U.S. oil companies from importing Iranian oil but did not ban them from buying Iranian oil and trading it overseas. The 1995 ban prohibits such trading of Iranian oil overseas. The 1995 trade ban does allow U.S. companies to apply for licenses to conduct "swaps" of Caspian Sea oil with Iran. However, these swaps have been prohibited in practice; a Mobil Corporation application to do so was denied in April 1999, and no known applications have been submitted since.
- Regulations pursuant to the 1995 trade ban *do not ban the importation, from foreign refiners, of gasoline or other energy products in which Iranian oil is contained and mixed with oil from other producers.* The product of a refinery— for example major refineries in the EU countries—is considered a product of the country where that refinery is located and can be imported into the United States, even if the refined product has some Iran-origin crude oil. No EU refineries have imported Iranian oil since July 1, 2012, and only a few other refineries worldwide both continue to receive Iranian oil and export gasoline to the United States. U.S. gasoline imports from those refineries are minor.
- *Transshipment and Brokering.* The regulations that implement the trade ban prohibit transshipment of goods across Iran. They also ban any activities by U.S. persons to broker commercial transactions involving Iran.
- *Civilian Airline Parts.* Under the original 1995 Executive order banning U.S. trade with Iran, goods related to the safe operation of civilian aircraft may, on a case-by-case basis, be licensed for export to Iran (§560.528 of Title 31, C.F.R.). Some spare parts sales were licensed occasionally since that time. However, on June 23, 2011, the Administration sanctioned Iran Air under Executive Order 13382 (see below), rendering licensing of parts or repairs for that airline impermissible. Other Iranian airlines have been sanctioned under that and Executive Order 13224, as discussed below. The JPA provides for

provision of spare civilian airline parts to Iran, specifically including Iran Air (notwithstanding its designation), and relevant provisions of E.O. 13382 have been suspended to enable Iran Air to benefit from this commitment. Boeing and GE have received export licenses to sell aircraft equipment and aircraft manuals to Iran since the JPA began implementation.[5]

- *Personal Communications, Remittances, and Publishing.* There are no applicable restrictions on personal communications (phone calls, e-mails) between the U.S. and Iran or on personal remittances. In December 2004, the trade regulations were modified to allow Americans to engage in ordinary publishing activities with entities in Iran (and Cuba and Sudan). On May 30, 2013, OFAC issued a general license for the exportation to Iran of goods (such as cellphones) and services, on a fee basis, that enhance the ability of the Iranian people to access communication technology. However, sanctions on banking transactions make processing payments for many of these transactions difficult, in practice.
- *Food and Medical Exports.* Since April 1999, commercial sales of food and medical products to Iran have been allowed, on a case-by-case basis and subject to OFAC licensing. Among earlier relaxations, on October 22, 2012, OFAC attempted to facilitate medical sales by issuing a list of medical products, such as scalpels, prosthetics, canes, burn dressings, and other products that could be sold to Iran under "general license"—no export license requirement. That list was updated on July 25, 2013, to include electrocardiogram, electroencephalogram, and dialysis machines and other medical products. According to OFAC, licenses for exports of medical products not on the list are routinely expedited for sale to Iran, and the U.S. government has been informing foreign banks that financing such transactions is not sanctionable. The JPA commits the United States and its partners to facilitate humanitarian sales to Iran. Implementing that commitment did not require modifications to U.S. trade regulations on that issue.

Regulations have a specific definition of "food" that can be licensed for sale to Iran, and that definition excludes alcohol, cigarettes, gum, or fertilizer.[6] This definition addresses information in a December 24, 2010,[7] article that said that OFAC had approved exports to Iran of such condiments as ice cream sprinkles, chewing gum, food additives, hot sauces, body-building supplements, and other goods that have uses other than purely nutritive. Some of the licensed U.S. goods were sold through a Revolutionary Guard-owned chain of stores in Iran called Qods, as well as a government-owned Shahrvand store.

- *Humanitarian and Related Services*. Private non-financial donations by U.S. residents to Iranian victims of natural disasters (such as mailed packages of food, toys, clothes, etc.) are not prohibited, but donations to relief organizations require a specific OFAC license, because such transfers generally require use of the international banking system. Prior to September 2013, all NGOs that sought to perform relief efforts in Iran required a specific license to do so, which apparently made work in Iran impractical. On September 10, 2013, the Treasury Department eliminated licensing requirements for the provision to Iran of services for health projects, disaster relief, wildlife conservation, human rights projects, and activities related to sports matches and events. The amended regulation also allows importation from Iran of services related to sporting activities, including sponsorship of players, coaching, referees, and training. In some cases, such as the earthquake in Bam in 2003 and the earthquake in northwestern Iran in August 2012, OFAC has issued blanket temporary general licensing for relief organizations to perform relief efforts in Iran. The licensing requirements in the latter case allowed an NGO to transfer up to $300,000 without requiring a specific license.
- *Export Financing*. As far as financing of approved U.S. sales to Iran, private letters of credit (from non-Iranian banks) can be used to finance approved transactions. Title IX of the Trade Sanctions Reform and Export Enhancement Act of 2000 (P.L. 106-387) bans the use of official credit guarantees for food and medical sales to Iran and other countries on the U.S. terrorism list, except Cuba, although allowing for a presidential waiver to permit such credit guarantees. No U.S. Administration has authorized credit guarantees for any U.S. exports to Iran.

Application to Foreign Subsidiaries of U.S. Firms

The U.S. trade ban does not bar subsidiaries of U.S. firms from dealing with Iran, as long as the subsidiary has no operational relationship to—or control by—the parent company. For legal and policy purposes, foreign subsidiaries are considered foreign persons and are subject to the laws of the country in which the subsidiaries are incorporated. Section 218 of the Iran

Threat Reduction and Syrian Human Rights Act (P.L. 112-158) applies the U.S. trade ban to foreign subsidiaries if (1) the subsidiary is more than 50% owned by the U.S. parent; (2) the parent firm holds a majority on the Board of Directors; or (3) the parent firm directs the operations of the subsidiary. However, many subsidiaries might not meet the criteria for sanctioning stipulated in that law.

Trade Ban Easing and Termination

Termination: Section 401 of CISADA provides for the President to terminate the trade ban (Section 103) if the Administration certifies to Congress that Iran has no longer satisfies the requirements to be designated as a state sponsor of terrorism and that Iran has ceased pursuing and has dismantled its nuclear, biological, and chemical weapons and ballistic missiles and related launch technology. Alternatively, the trade ban provision in CISADA could be repealed outright by congressional action.

Waiver Authority: Section 103(b)(vi) of CISADA allows the President to license exports to Iran if he determines that doing so is in the national interest of the United States. This gives the President flexibility to ease the ban on U.S. exports through executive action. There is no similar provision in CISADA to ease the ban on U.S. imports from Iran.

The JPA did not require the United States to ease or lift the ban on U.S. trade with or investment in Iran. There are no indications that Iran will demand this sanction ban be lifted or suspended part of a comprehensive nuclear deal.

ENERGY AND OTHER SECTOR SANCTIONS: IRAN SANCTIONS ACT (ISA) AND RELATED LAWS AND EXECUTIVE ORDERS

Since 1996, Congress and successive Administrations have put in place steps to try to force foreign firms to choose between participating in the U.S. market and continuing to conduct various energy-related transactions with Iran. The intent of energy sanctions has been to put pressure on Iran's economy and its leadership calculations, and to deny Iran the financial resources to further its nuclear and WMD programs and support terrorist organizations. Iran's petroleum sector is vital to the Iran state and economy—prior to the imposition of oil export-related sanctions in 2012 it generated about 20% of Iran's GDP, about 80% of its foreign exchange earnings, and about 50% of its government revenue.

Iran's oil sector is as old as the petroleum industry itself (early 20th century), and Iran's onshore oil fields are past peak production and in need of substantial investment. Iran has 136.3 billion barrels of proven oil reserves, the third largest after Saudi Arabia and Canada. With the exception of relatively small swap and barter arrangements with neighboring countries, virtually all of Iran's oil exports flow through the Strait of Hormuz, which carries about one-third of all internationally traded oil. Iran's large natural gas resources (940 trillion cubic feet, exceeded only by Russia) were virtually undeveloped when ISA was first enacted. Its small gas exports are mainly to Armenia and Turkey; most of its gas is injected into its oil fields to boost their production.

The Iran Sanctions Act, Amendments, and Related Applications

The Iran Sanctions Act (ISA) has been a key component of U.S. sanctions against Iran's energy sector, and it has been expanded to sanction dealings with other Iranian economic sectors. As initially enacted, ISA sought to thwart Iran's opening of the sector to foreign investment in late 1995. Iran uses a "buy-back" foreign investment program in which foreign firms gradually recoup their investments as oil and gas is discovered and then produced. In September 1995, Senator Alfonse D'Amato introduced a bill to sanction foreign firms' exports to Iran of energy technology. A revised version instead sanctioning *investment* in Iran's energy sector, and also applying all provisions to Libya passed the Senate. The Iran and Libya Sanctions Act (ILSA) was signed on August 5, 1996 (H.R. 3107, P.L. 104-172). It was later retitled the Iran Sanctions Act after it terminated with respect to Libya in 2006. ISA was the first major "extra-territorial sanction" on Iran—a sanction that authorizes U.S. penalties against third country firms. ISA's application has been further expanded by several laws enacted since 2010 that amend its provisions.

Key "Triggers"

ISA consists of a number of "triggers"—transactions with Iran that would be considered violations of ISA and could cause a firm or entity to be sanctioned under ISA's provisions. When triggered, ISA provides for a number of different sanctions that could harm a foreign firm's business opportunities in the United States.

"Investment" to Develop Iran's Oil and Gas Fields

ISA requires the President to sanction companies (entities, persons) that make an "investment"[8] of more than $20 million[9] in one year in Iran's energy sector.[10] The definition of "investment" in ISA (§14 (9)) includes not only equity and royalty arrangements but any contract that includes "responsibility for the development of petroleum resources" of Iran. The definition includes additions to existing investment (added by P.L. 107-24) and pipelines to or through Iran and contracts to lead the construction, upgrading, or expansions of energy projects (added by the Comprehensive Iran Sanctions, Accountability, and Divestment Act of 2010 [CISADA; P.L. 111- 195]).

Implementation: Several firms have been sanctioned under ISA for investing in Iran's oil and gas fields, as discussed below.

Sales of Weapons Related Technology and Uranium Mining Ventures

The Iran Freedom Support Act (P.L. 109-293, signed September 30, 2006) amended ISA by adding Section 5(b)(1) subjecting to ISA sanctions firms or persons determined to have sold to Iran (1) technology useful for weapons of mass destruction (WMD) or (2) "destabilizing numbers and types" of advanced conventional weapons. (Sanctions apply if the exporter knew or had cause to know that the final destination of the items sold would be Iran.)

Entities determined by the Administration to participate in a joint venture with Iran relating to the mining, production, or transportation of uranium are sanctionable under ISA. Under *Section 5(b)(2)* added by the Iran Threat Reduction and Syria Human Rights Act (P.L. 112-158, signed August 10, 2012).

Implementation: No ISA sanctions have been imposed on any entities under these provisions.

Sales of Gasoline and Related Equipment and Services

Section 102(a) of the Comprehensive Iran Sanctions, Accountability, and Divestment Act of 2010 (CISADA, signed on July 1, 2010, P.L. 111-195) amended Section 5 of ISA to exploit Iran's dependency on imported gasoline (40% dependency at that time). It followed legislation such as H.R. 2880 (110th Congress, not enacted); P.L. 111-85 that prohibited the use of U.S. funds to fill the Strategic Petroleum Reserve with products from firms that sell gasoline to Iran; and P.L. 111- 117 that denied Ex-Im Bank credits to any firm that sold gasoline or related equipment and services to Iran—initiatives that prompted Reliance Industries Ltd. of India to cease new sales of gasoline to Iran as of December 2008. (The Ex-Im Bank, in August 2008, had extended $900 million in financing guarantees to Reliance.) The provision made sanctionable:

- sales to Iran of over $1 million worth (or $5 million in a one year period) of gasoline and related aviation and other fuels. (Fuel oil, a petroleum by-product, is not included in the definition of refined petroleum.)
- sales to Iran of equipment or services (same dollar threshold as above) which would help Iran make or import gasoline. Examples of such sales include equipment and services that Iran can use to construct or maintain its oil refineries, or provision of related services such as shipping or port operations.

Implementation: Several firms, as discussed below, have been sanctioned under ISA for selling or shipping gasoline to Iran.

Sales of Energy Sector Equipment, Services, and Petrochemicals

An Executive Order, 13590 (November 21, 2011), was codified by Section 201 of the Iran Threat Reduction and Syria Human Rights Act of 2012 (ITRSHA, P.L. 112-158). The ITRSHA provision added Section 5(a)(5 and 6) to ISA sanctioning firms that:

- provide to Iran $1 million or more (or $5 million in a one year period) worth of goods or services that Iran could use to maintain or enhance its oil and gas sector. This made sanctionable, for example, transactions with Iran by global oil services firms and the sale to Iran of energy industry gear such as drills, pumps, vacuums, oil rigs, and the like.
- provide to Iran $250,000 (or $1 million in a one year period) worth of goods or services that Iran could use to maintain or expand its production of petrochemical products.[11] *This provision was not required to be waived as a consequence of the JPA.*

Implementation: No firms have been sanctioned under these provisions.

Purchasing of Iranian Crude Oil and Petrochemical Products

Executive Order 13622 (July 30, 2012) applies virtually all of the same sanctions as ISA—as well as restrictions on foreign banks (see below)—to entities that the Administration determines have:

- purchased oil or other petroleum products from Iran.[12] The part of this provision pertaining to petrochemical purchases will need to be waived as a consequence of the interim nuclear deal.
- conducted transactions with the National Iranian Oil Company (NIOC) or Naftiran Intertrade Company (NICO).

Under the Order, sanctions do not apply if the parent country of the entity has received an exemption under Section 1245 of P.L. 112-81—an exemption earned for "significantly reducing" oil purchases from Iran. (See below for more information on the exemption process.) *A law cannot be amended by executive order and E.O. 13622 does not amend ISA.*

Implementation: Several firms were sanctioned under this order on May 31, 2013, for petrochemical sales to Iran.

Sanctions on transactions related to purchasing Iranian crude oil were codified by Section 201 of the Iran Threat Reduction and Syria Human Rights Act (P.L. 112-158, signed August 10, 2012). It amends ISA by applying ISA sanctions to entities determined by the Administration to have:

- Owned a vessel that was used to transport Iranian crude oil. This sanction does not apply in cases of transporting oil to countries that have received exemptions under P.L. 112-81, discussed below. The section also *authorizes but does not require* the President, subject to regulations, to prohibit a ship from putting to port in the United States for two years, if it is owned by a person sanctioned under this provision. *(Adds Section 5(a)(7) to ISA.)*
- Participated in a joint oil and gas development venture with Iran, outside Iran, if that venture was established after January 1, 2002. The effective date exempts energy ventures in the Caspian Sea, such as the Shah Deniz oil field there. *(Adds Section 5(a)(4 to ISA).)*

Implementation. Some firms have been sanctioned for providing vessels for the shipment of crude oil to Iran.

Insurance for Iranian Oil Entities and Purchases of Iranian Bonds

Separate provisions of the Iran Threat Reduction and Syria Human Rights Act (Sections 212, 213, and 302) *do not specifically amend ISA*, but require the application of 5 out of 12 ISA sanctions on any company:

- that provides insurance or re-insurance for the National Iranian Oil Company (NIOC) or the National Iranian Tanker Company (NITC); or
- that purchases or facilitates the issuance of sovereign debt of the government of Iran, including Iranian government bonds.

Dealings with Iran's Energy, Shipbuilding, and Shipping Sector

The National Defense Authorization Act for FY2013 (H.R. 4310, P.L. 112-239, signed January 2, 2013) Subtitle D, "The Iran Freedom and Counter-Proliferation Act" (IFCA), *does not amend ISA* but imposes at least 5 out the 12 ISA sanctions (as of July 1, 2013, 180 days after enactment) on entities determined to have:

- provided goods or services to the energy, shipbuilding, and shipping sectors of Iran, or to port operations there—or which provide insurance for such transactions. This is under Section 1244 of IFCA, which also blocks U.S.-based property and U.S.-based banking activity on violators. *The sanctions do not apply when such transactions involve purchases of Iranian oil by countries that have active exemptions under P.L. 112-81 or to the purchase of natural gas from Iran (or most transactions related to such gas purchases).*
- provided underwriting services, insurance, or reinsurance for a broad range of transactions with Iran, including those related to shipping oil, gasoline, or other goods for the energy, shipping, or shipbuilding sectors in Iran. This is under Section 1246 of IFCA. *There is no exception to this sanction for countries exempted under P.L. 112-81.*
- Section 1248 of IFCA sanctions Iran's state broadcasting establishment (Islamic Republic of Iran Broadcasting) as a human rights abuser, triggering sanctions under Section 105 of CISADA.
- *Dealings in Precious Metals.* Section 1245 of IFCA imposes at least 5 out of 12 ISA sanctions on entities that provide precious metals to Iran (including gold) or semi-finished metals or software for integrating industrial processes. The section therefore affects foreign firms that transfer gold or other precious metals to Iran in exchange

for oil or any other product. *There is no exception to this sanction for countries exempted under P.L. 112-81. The provision does not amend ISA.* This essentially codifies Section 5 of Executive Order 13622 that blocks U.S.- based property of individuals or firms determined to have helped Iran purchase U.S. bank notes or precious metals or to have provided financial support to NIOC, NICO, or the Central Bank of Iran. Executive Order 13645 of June 3, 2013, (Section 16), applies the restriction to transfers of stones or jewels.

Waiver authority is discussed in the box on ISA waivers below.

Sanctions Imposed Under IFCA: On August 29, 2014, the State Department sanctioned UAEbased Goldentex FZE in accordance with IFCA for providing support to Iran's shipping sector.

The Automotive Sector and Rial Trading

Executive Order 13645 of June 3, 2013, (effective July 1, 2013):

- imposes ISA sanctions on firms that supply goods or services to Iran's automotive (cars, trucks, buses, motorcycles, and related parts) sector, and blocks foreign banks from the U.S. market if they finance transactions with Iran's automotive sector. (An executive order cannot amend a law, so the order does not amend ISA.) *This provision was suspended to implement the November 24, 2013, interim nuclear deal with Iran.*
- blocks U.S.-based property and prohibits U.S. bank accounts for foreign banks that conduct transactions in Iran's currency, the rial, or hold rial accounts. This provision most likely will affect banks in countries bordering or nearby Iran that sometimes have dealt in the rial.
- blocks U.S.-based property of any person that conducts transactions with any Iranian entity on the list of Specially Designated Nationals (SDNs) or Blocked Persons.

Mandate and Time Frame to Investigate ISA Violations

In the original version of ISA, there was no firm requirement, and no time limit, for the Administration to investigate potential violations and determine that a firm has violated ISA's provisions. The "Iran Freedom Support Act" (P.L. 109-293, signed September 30, 2006) added a provision calling for, *but not requiring*, a 180-day time limit for a violation determination.[13] CISADA

(Section 102(g)(5)) mandated that the Administration begin an investigation of potential ISA violations when there is “credible information” about a potential violation, and made mandatory the 180-day time limit for a determination of violation.

A subsequent law, the Iran Threat Reduction and Syria Human Rights Act (P.L. 112-158), contains a provision to define “credible information” to begin an investigation of a violation. The law defines credible information to include a corporate announcement or corporate filing to its shareholders that it has undertaken transactions with Iran that are potentially sanctionable under ISA. It also says the President *may* (not mandatory) use as credible information reports from the Government Accountability Office and the Congressional Research Service.

Oversight Mechanisms: Reports Required

The Iran Threat Reduction and Syria Human Rights Act (P.L. 112-158) sets up several mechanisms for Congress to oversee whether the Administration is investigating ISA violations. Section 223 requires a Government Accountability Office report, within 120 days of enactment, and another such report a year later, on companies that have undertaken specified activities with Iran that might constitute violations of ISA. Section 224 amends a reporting requirement in Section 110(b) of CISADA by requiring an Administration report every 180 days on investment in Iran’s energy sector, joint ventures with Iran, and estimates of Iran’s imports and exports of petroleum products. The GAO reports have been issued; there is no information available on whether the required Administration reports have been issued as well.

Available Sanctions under ISA

Once a firm is determined to be a violator, the original version of ISA required the imposition of *two* of a menu of six sanctions on that firm. CISADA added three new possible sanctions and required the imposition of at least three out of the nine against violators. CISADA added three more sanctions to the ISA menu and required imposition at least *5 out of the 12* sanctions. Executive Orders 13590 and 13622 provide for exactly the same penalties as those in ISA. The 12 available sanctions against the sanctioned entity, from which the Secretary of State or the Treasury can select, are:

1) denial of Export-Import Bank loans, credits, or credit guarantees for U.S. exports to the sanctioned entity (original ISA)
2) denial of licenses for the U.S. export of military or militarily useful technology to the entity (original ISA)
3) denial of U.S. bank loans exceeding $10 million in one year to the entity (original ISA)
4) if the entity is a financial institution, a prohibition on its service as a primary dealer in U.S. government bonds; and/or a prohibition on its serving as a repository for U.S. government funds (each counts as one sanction) (original ISA)
5) prohibition on U.S. government procurement from the entity (original ISA)
6) prohibitions in transactions in foreign exchange by the entity (added by CISADA)
7) prohibition on any credit or payments between the entity and any U.S. financial institution (added by CISADA)
8) prohibition of the sanctioned entity from acquiring, holding, using, or trading any U.S.-based property which the sanctioned entity has a (financial) interest in (added by CISADA)
9) restriction on imports from the sanctioned entity, in accordance with the International Emergency Economic Powers Act (IEEPA; 50 U.S.C. 1701) (original ISA)
10) a ban on a U.S. person from investing in or purchasing significant amounts of equity or debt instruments of a sanctioned person (added by Iran Threat Reduction and Syria Human Rights Act, P.L. 112-158)
11) exclusion from the United States of corporate officers or controlling shareholders of a sanctioned firm (added by P.L. 112-158)
12) imposition of any of the ISA sanctions on principal offices of a sanctioned firm (added by P.L. 112-158). Mandatory Sanction: Prohibition on Contracts with the U.S. Government

There is an additional *mandatory* sanction under ISA. CISADA (§102(b)) added a requirement in ISA that companies, as a condition of obtaining a U.S. government contract, certify to the relevant U.S. government agency that the firm— *and any companies it owns or controls*—are not violating ISA. Regulations to implement this requirement were issued on September 29, 2010.

ISA Waiver, Exemptions, and Sunset Provisions

ISA Waiver Provisions

The President has the authority to waive sanctions on firms determined to have violated ISA provisions. Under the original version of ISA to waive sanctions if he certifies that doing so is *important* to the U.S. national interest (§9(c)). CISADA (§102(c)) changed the 9(c) ISA waiver standard to "*necessary*" to the national interest, and the Iran Threat Reduction Act modified the standard further to "*essential to the national security interests*" of the United States. For sanctionable transactions involving WMD equipment, the waiver standard, as modified by the Iran Threat Reduction Act, is "'*vital to the national security interests of the United States*."

Under the original version of ISA, there was also waiver authority (§4(c)) if the parent country of the violating firm joined a sanctions regime against Iran. This waiver provision was changed by the Iran Freedom Support Act (P.L. 109- 293) to allow for a waiver determination based on U.S. vital national security interests. The Section 4(c) waiver was altered again, by CISADA, to provide for a six month (renewable) waiver if doing so is "*vital to the national interest," and* if the parent country of the violating entity is "closely cooperating" with U.S. efforts against Iran's WMD and advanced conventional weapons program. The criterion of "closely cooperating" is defined in the conference report as implementing all U.N. sanctions against Iran. It could be argued that using a Section 4 waiver, rather than a Section 9 waiver, would support U.S. diplomacy with the parent country of the offending entity.

ISA (§5(f)) also contains several exceptions such that the President is not required to impose sanctions that prevent procurement of defense articles and services under existing contracts, in cases where a firm is the sole source supplier of a particular defense article or service. The President also is not required to prevent procurement of essential spare parts or component parts.

Related IFCA Waiver Authority

Sections 1244 and 1245 of IFCA provide for a waiver of sanctions for 180 days, renewable for 180 day periods, if such a waiver is determined to be vital to U.S. national security. These sections were waived in order to implement the JPA.

In addition, Section 5(a)(7) of ISA was waived to allow for certain transactions with NIOC and NITC.

"Special Rule" Exempting Firms That End Their Business with Iran

Under a provision added by CISADA (§102(g)(5)), ISA provides a means—a so-called "special rule"—for firms to avoid ISA sanctions by pledging to verifiably end their business with Iran and to forgo any sanctionable business with Iran in the future. Under the special rule, the Administration is not required to make a determination of sanctionability against a firm that makes such pledges. The special rule has been invoked on several occasions, as discussed below. However, there is some imprecision in the time frame under which countries can wind down their Iran business, and some firms could work in Iran for several more years under their pledges. Energy firms insist they needed time to wind down their investments in Iran because, under the buy-back program used by Iran, the energy firms are paid back their investment over time, making it highly costly for them to suddenly end operations in Iran.

Termination Process and Requirements

In its entirety, ISA application to Iran would terminate if the Administration certifies that three requirements are met:

(1) that Iran has ceased its efforts to acquire WMD; (2) that Iran has been removed from the U.S. list of state sponsors of terrorism; *and* (3) that Iran no longer "poses a significant threat" to U.S. national security and U.S. allies.[14]

This termination provision, and the sunset provision discussed below, *do not apply to those laws that apply ISA sanctions without specifically amending ISA*. The executive orders and laws that apply ISA sanctions to specified violators *but without amending ISA itself* can be revoked by a superseding executive order or congressional action that amends or repeals the provisions involved.

Sunset Provisions

ISA is currently scheduled to sunset on December 31, 2016, as provided for by CISADA. This followed prior sunset extensions to December 31, 2011, (by P.L. 109-293), and to December 31, 2006 (P.L. 107-24, August 3, 2001).

The original law provided for a sunset date of August 5, 2001. P.L. 107-24 also required an Administration report on ISA's effectiveness within 24 to 30 months of enactment; that report was submitted to Congress in January 2004 and did not recommend that ISA be repealed.

Executive Order 13574 Clarifying the Division of Responsibilities Between the State and Treasury Departments

On May 23, 2011, President Obama issued Executive Order 13574 clarifying that it is the responsibility of the Treasury Department to implement those ISA sanctions that involve the financial sector, including bans on loans, credits, and foreign exchange for, or imports from the sanctioned entity, as well as blockage of property of the sanctioned entity (if these sanctions are selected by the Secretary of State, who makes the decision which penalties to impose on sanctioned entities).

Interpretations and Administration of ISA and Related Laws

The sections below analyze how ISA, as amended by related laws, have been interpreted and implemented through real-world cases and examples.

Application to Energy Pipelines

ISA's definition of sanctionable "investment" has been consistently interpreted by successive Administrations to include construction of energy pipelines to or through Iran. Such pipelines are deemed to help Iran develop its petroleum (oil and natural gas) sector. This interpretation was reinforced by amendments to ISA in CISADA, which specifically included in the definition of petroleum resources "products used to construct or maintain pipelines used to transport oil or liquefied natural gas." In March 2012, then-Secretary of State Clinton made clear that the Obama Administration interprets the provision to be applicable from the beginning of pipeline construction.[15]

Implementation

No gas pipelines built linking Iran to neighboring countries have been sanctioned under ISA. Pipeline projects that are under various stages of construction or consideration are discussed in the international compliance section below.

Application to Crude Oil Purchases

The original version of ISA did not provide for sanctioning purchases of oil from Iran. Executive Order 13622 and P.L. 112-158 essentially authorize sanctions on the purchase of Iranian oil—if the parent country of the energy buyer or shipper has not received an exemption under P.L. 112- 81, which is discussed below. Any new customer for Iranian oil is authorized to be sanctioned under the Order and P.L. 112-81.

Shah Deniz Project Exception

The effective dates of U.S. sanctions laws also excludes long-standing joint natural gas projects that involve some Iranian firms—particularly the Shah Deniz natural gas field and pipeline in the Caspian Sea. The project is run by a consortium in which Iran's Naftiran Intertrade Copmany (NICO) holds a passive 10% share. The other partners in the venture are BP, Azerbaijan's natural gas firm SOCAR, Russia's Lukoil, and other firms. NICO has been sanctioned under ISA, as discussed below. An OFAC factsheet of November 28, 2012, states that the Shah Deniz consortium, as a whole, is not determined to be "a person owned or controlled by" the government of Iran, as defined in Executive Order 13599. The factsheet states that transactions with the consortium would not violate U.S. trade regulations on Iran nor require a license from OFAC. The guidance appears to apply to both the existing pipeline as well as the second phase of the project that is now under way, which also involves NICO and will carry gas to Europe.

Application to Purchases from Iran of Natural Gas Purchases

IFCA, discussed above, authorizes sanctions on any dealings with Iran's energy sector. However, IFCA *specifically excludes from sanctions purchases of natural gas from Iran*. Still, *payments* for the natural gas might be subject to sanctions as discussed elsewhere in this report. *Purchases* of Iranian gas are distinguishable from the *construction of natural gas pipelines* involving Iran which, as discussed, does constitute potentially sanctionable activity.

Application to Iranian Liquefied Natural Gas Development

The original version of ISA did not apply to the development by Iran of a liquefied natural gas (LNG) export capability. Iran has no LNG export terminals, in part because the technology for such terminals is patented by U.S. firms and unavailable for sale to Iran. However, CISADA specifically includes LNG in the definition of petroleum resources and therefore made subject to sanctions LNG investment in Iran or supply of LNG tankers or pipelines to Iran.

Application to Private Financing but Not Official Credit Guarantee Agencies

The definitions of investment and other activity that can be sanctioned under ISA clearly include financing for investment in Iran's energy sector, or for sales of gasoline and refinery-related equipment and services. Therefore, banks and other financial institutions that assist energy investment and refining and gasoline procurement activities could be sanctioned under ISA.

However, the definitions of financial institutions in Iran sanctions laws are interpreted not to apply to official credit guarantee agencies—such as France's COFACE and Germany's Hermes. These credit guarantee agencies are arms of their parent governments, and ISA does not provide for sanctioning governments or their agencies. Early versions of CISADA would have sanctioned such entities but such provisions were not included in the final law, reportedly to avoid a backlash from U.S. allies.

Application to Iranian Energy Institutions/NIOC and NITC

As noted above, provisions of P.L. 112-158 and Executive Order 13622—*although they do not amend ISA*—apply ISA sanctions to dealings with the National Iranian Oil Company (NIOC), which is supervised by the Oil Ministry, the National Iranian Tanker Company (NITC), and a previously sanctioned firm, Naftiran Intertrade Company (NICO), which is a subsidiary of NIOC.

Under Section 302 of the Iran Threat Reduction and Syria Human Rights Act (P.L. 112-158), any person who engages in a significant transaction with NIOC and NITC is subject to the imposition of 5 out of 12 ISA sanctions. Section 312 of that law required an Administration determination, within 45 days of enactment (by September 24, 2012) whether NIOC and NITC are IRGC agents or affiliates. If such a determination is made, financial transactions with NIOC and NITC would be sanctionable under CISADA (prohibition on opening U.S.-based accounts).

Implementation. On September 24, 2012, the Department of the Treasury informed Congress that it had determined that NIOC and NITC are agents or affiliates of the IRGC. As noted below, on November 8, 2012, the Treasury Department named NIOC as a proliferation entity under Executive Order 13382. In accordance with Section 104 of CISADA, that designation bars any foreign bank determined to have dealt directly with NIOC (including with a NIOC bank account in a foreign country) from opening a U.S.-based account.

Some major components of NIOC have not been sanctioned, including the Iranian Offshore Oil Company; the National Iranian Gas Export Co.; and Petroleum Engineering and Development Co. There are also independent Iranian energy firms, such as Pasargad Oil Co, Zagros Petrochem Co, Sazeh Consultants, Qeshm Energy, and Sadid Industrial Group. Their relations with NIOC or the Revolutionary Guard (see below) are unclear, and none of these independent firms has been sanctioned under any U.S. law or executive order.

Sanctions on dealings with NIOC and NITC were waived in accordance with the JPA.

Sanctions Imposed or Waived under ISA

The European Union (EU) opposed ISA as an extraterritorial application of U.S. law. In April 1997, the United States and the EU agreed to avoid a trade confrontation over ISA and a separate Cuba sanctions law (P.L. 104-114). The agreement involved the promise by the EU not to file any complaint with the World Trade Organization (WTO) over this issue, in exchange for the eventual May 18, 1998, announcement by the Clinton Administration to waive ISA sanctions ("national interest"—§9c—waiver) on the first project determined to be in violation—a $2 billion[16] contract, signed in September 1997, for Total SA of France and its partners, Gazprom of Russia and Petronas of Malaysia, to develop phases 2 and 3 of the 25+ phase South Pars gas field. The EU, for its part, pledged to increase cooperation with the United States on nonproliferation and counterterrorism. Then-Secretary of State Albright, in the May 18, 1998, waiver announcement, indicated that similar future such projects by EU firms in Iran would not be sanctioned, provided overall EU cooperation against Iranian terrorism and proliferation continued.[17] The EU sanctions against Iran imposed since 2010 have largely rendered this understanding moot because EU firms are barred from investing in Iran's energy sector.

The Obama Administration has used ISA authorities to discourage companies from continuing their business with Iran. This is a contrast from the first 14 years after ISA's passage, in which successive Administrations hesitated to confront companies of partner countries. State Department reports to Congress on ISA, required every six months, do not specifically state which foreign companies, if any, are still being investigated for ISA violations. No publication of such deals has been placed in the *Federal Register,* as required by Section 5e of ISA.

The companies for which ISA determinations have been announced are listed in the table below.

Table 1. ISA Sanctions Determinations

Date	Companies/Country	Status/Comment
May 18, 1998	Total SA (France); Gazprom (Russia); and Petronas (Malaysia)	Waived. ISA Violation determined but sanctions waived in line with U.S.-EU agreement discussed in text above.
Sept. 30, 2010	Naftiran Intertrade Co. (NICO) Switzerland, Iran	Sanctioned. For activities to develop Iran's energy sector
Sept. 30, 2010	Total (France); Statoil (Norway); ENI (Italy); and Royal Dutch Shell (Britain, Netherlands)	Exempted. Under from sanctions under ISA "special rule" for pledging to wind down work on Iran energy fields.
Nov. 17, 2010	Inpex (Japan)	Exempted. Special rule applied for announcement one month earlier that it divested its remaining 10% stake in Azadegan oil field development.
March 29, 2011	Belarusneft (Belarus, subsidiary of Belneftekhim)	Sanctioned. For $500 million contract with NICO (see above) to develop Jofeir oil field. Other subsidiaries of Belneftekhim were sanctioned in 2007 under E.O. 13405 related to policy on Belarus.
May 24, 2011	Petrochemical Commercial Company International (PCCI) of Bailiwick of Jersey and Iran; Royal Oyster Group (UAE); Tanker Pacific (Singapore); Allvale Maritime (Liberia); Societie Anonyme Monegasque Et Aerienne (SAMAMA, Monaco); Speedy Ship (UAE/Iran); Associated Shipbroking (Monaco); and Petroleos de Venezuela (PDVSA, Venezuela).	Sanctioned. Under CISADA amendment to ISA imposing sanctions for selling gasoline to Iran or helping Iran import gasoline. Allvale Maritime and SAMAMA determinations were issued on September 13, 2011, to "clarify" the May 24 determinations that had named Ofer Brothers Group. The two, as well as Tanker Pacific, are affiliated with a Europe-based trust linked to deceased Ofer brother Sami Ofer, and not Ofer Brothers Group based in Israel. The firms named were subjected primarily to the financial-related sanctions provided in ISA. U.S.-based subsidiaries of PDVSA, such as Citgo, were not sanctioned and U.S. purchases of Venezuelan oil were not affected.

Date	Companies/Country	Status/Comment
Jan. 12, 2012	Zhuhai Zhenrong Co. (China); Kuo Oil Pte Ltd. (Singapore); FAL Oil Co. (UAE)	Sanctioned. For brokering sales or making sales to Iran of gasoline.
Aug. 12, 2012	Sytrol (Syria)	Sanctioned. For sales of gasoline to Iran.
Mar. 14, 2013	Dr. Dimitris Cambis; Impire Shipping; Kish Protection and Indemnity (Iran); and Bimeh Markasi-Central Insurance of Iran (CII, Iran)	Sanctioned. Under amendments to ISA by Iran Threat Reduction Act sanctioning owning vessels that transport Iranian oil or providing insurance for the shipments. Treasury sanctions also imposed on these and eight UAE-based oil graders that concealed the transactions.
April 12, 2013	Tanker Pacific; SAMAMA; and Allvale Maritime	Sanctions lifted. Special rule applied after firms provided to the U.S. "reliable assurances" they will not engage in sanctionable activities in the future.
May 31, 2013	Ferland Co. Ltd. (Cyprus and Ukraine)	Sanctioned. For cooperating with National Iranian Tanker Co. to illicitly sell Iranian crude oil. Sanctions also imposed by Treasury under E.O. 13608.
August 29, 2014	Dettin SPA	Sanctioned. Italy-based company sanctioned for providing goods and services to Iran's petrochemical industry.

Source: State Department announcements.

Sanctions on Transactions with Iran's Central Bank for Oil or Other Goods: Section 1245 of the FY2012 NDAA

In late 2011, some in Congress believed that action was needed to cut off the mechanisms oil importers use to pay Iran hard currency for oil. Legislation to cut off Iran's Central Bank from the international financial system were based largely on that objective, as well as on the view that the Central Bank helps other Iranian banks circumvent the U.S. and U.N. banking sanctions.

The FY2012 national defense authorization bill (H.R. 1540, P.L. 112-81, signed on December 31, 2011, provides for the following:

- Requires the President to prevent a foreign bank from opening an account in the United States—or impose strict limitations on existing U.S. accounts—if that bank processes payments through Iran's Central Bank. The provision applies to a foreign central bank only if the transaction with Iran's Central Bank is for oil purchases. The provision went into effect for *non-oil related* transactions 60 days after enactment (February 29, 2012), and for transactions for *oil purchases* after 180 days (June 28, 2012).
- *Exemption Provision.* The President may grant an exemption for foreign banks— for any transactions with the Central Bank, not just for oil—if the President certifies that the parent country of the bank has *significantly reduced* its purchases of oil from Iran. That determination is reviewed every 180 days; countries must continue to reduce their oil buys from Iran, relative to the previous 180-day period, to retain the exemption. The Iran Threat Reduction Act (P.L. 112-158) amended Section 1245 such that any country that completely ceases purchasing oil from Iran would retain an exemption (since it is not possible to reduce purchases any further from zero).
- Sanctions on transactions for oil apply only if the President certifies to Congress—90 days after enactment (by March 30, 2012), based on a report by the Energy Information Administration to be completed 60 days after enactment (by February 29, 2012)—that the oil market *is* adequately supplied. The EIA report and Administration certification are required every 90 days thereafter. The first required EIA report was issued on February 29, 2012, and, on March 30, 2012, President Obama determined that there was a sufficient supply of oil worldwide to permit countries to reduce oil purchases from Iran. An EIA report of April 27, 2012, and Administration determination of June 11, 2012, made similar findings and certifications, triggering potential sanctions as of June 28, 2012. Subsequent EIA reports and Administration determinations of the state of the oil market have kept the sanctions triggers in place.

Although Treasury Under Secretary David Cohen told the Senate Foreign Relations Committee on December 2, 2011, that the provision could lead to a rise in oil prices that would benefit Iran, the Administration accepted the legislation. In the signing statement on the bill, President Obama indicated he would implement the provision so as not to damage U.S. relations with partner countries.

Waiver and Termination Provisions

The law provides for the President to waive the sanctions for 120 days, renewable for successive 120 day periods, if the President determines that doing so is in the national security interest. Outright repeal or amendment of this law would require congressional action.

This provision was waived on January 20, 2014, in order to implement the JPA, meaning that Iran's oil customers will are not required to further reduce oil purchases from Iran while the JPA is in effect. Iran is demanding that this sanction no longer apply as part of a comprehensive nuclear deal.

Implementation: Exemptions Issued

The lack of precise definition of "significant reduction" in oil purchases gave the Administration flexibility in applying the exemption provision. On January 19, 2012, several Senators wrote to Treasury Secretary Geithner agreeing with outside experts that the Treasury Department should define "significant reduction" as an 18% purchase reduction based on total price paid (not just volumes).[18] Administration officials said they largely adopted that standard. The EU embargo on purchases of Iranian oil, announced January 23, 2012, and which took full effect by July 1, 2012, implied that virtually all EU oil customers of Iran would obtain exemptions. The table below on major Iranian oil customers indicates cuts made by major customers compared to 2011.

Exemptions Issued and Maintained[19]

- Since March 20, 2012, Japan has maintained and exemption for significantly reducing purchases and 10 EU countries have maintained exemptions for ending purchases pursuant to the EU Iran oil purchase embargo of July 1, 2012. The 10 EU countries are Belgium, Czech Republic, France, Germany, Greece, Italy, the Netherlands, Poland, Spain, and Britain. (Seventeen EU countries were not granted exemptions because they were not buying Iran's oil and could not "significantly reduce" buys from Iran.)
- Since June 2012, the following countries have maintained exemptions for significant reductions: China, India, South Korea, Turkey, and Taiwan.

- Also since June 2012, the following countries have maintained exemptions based on their ending oil purchases from Iran: Singapore, Malaysia, South Africa, and Sri Lanka.

Sanctions on Paying Iran with Hard Currency

The ability of Iran to acquire hard currency has been further impeded by a provision of the Iran Threat Reduction Act (P.L. 112-158), which went into effect on February 6, 2013—180 days after enactment. Section 504 of the Iran Threat Reduction Act amended P.L. 112-81 (adding "clause ii" to Paragraph D(1)) by requiring that any funds owed to Iran as a result of exempted transactions (oil purchases, for example) be credited to an account located in the country with primary jurisdiction over the foreign bank making the transaction. This has the net effect of preventing Iran from bringing earned hard currency back to Iran and compelling it to buy the products of the oil customer countries.

Waiver Provision

The waiver provision that applies to the sanctions to be imposed under the FY2012 NDAA (P.L. 112-81) applies to this hard currency "lock-up" provision.

To implement the JPA, a waiver was issued under P.L. 112-81 to allow Iran to receive some hard currency from ongoing oil sales in eight installments during the JPA period. Iran remains unable, even under the JPA, to remove hard currency from existing accounts abroad. Iran is likely to demand that this sanction be lifted as part of a comprehensive nuclear deal so that Iran can access its hard currency accounts abroad unfettered.

Table 2. Top Oil Buyers From Iran and Reductions (amounts in barrels per day, bpd, including condensates)

Country/Bloc	2011 Average	Average At JPA Start (and since)
European Union (particularly Italy, Spain, and Greece)	600,000	Negligible
China	550,000	410,000
Japan	325,000	190,000
India	320,000	190,000

Country/Bloc	2011 Average	Average At JPA Start (and since)
South Korea	230,000	130,000
Turkey	200,000	120,000
South Africa	80,000	Negligible
Malaysia	55,000	Negligible
Sri Lanka	35,000	Negligible
Taiwan	35,000	10,000
Singapore	20,000	Negligible
Other	55,000	Negligible
Total	2.5 mbd	1.057 mbd

Source: International Energy Agency and rough estimates based on CRS conversations with foreign diplomats and press reports.

Note: Actual volumes might differ, and import volumes may fluctuate dramatically over short periods of time as actual tanker deliveries occur. Figures include purchases of condensates, which are light petroleum liquids that are associated with oil and natural gas production. Iran's oil buyers reportedly have increased purchases of condensates since the JPA began by about 200,000 barrel per day equivalent, as discussed later in this paper.

PROLIFERATION-RELATED SANCTIONS

Aside from the "terrorism list sanctions" discussed above, several laws and executive orders seek to bars Iran from obtaining U.S. or other technology that can be used for weapons of mass destruction programs (WMD).

Iran-Iraq Arms Nonproliferation Act and Iraq Sanctions Act

The Iran-Iraq Arms Nonproliferation Act (P.L. 102-484, signed in October 1992) imposes a number of sanctions on foreign entities that supply Iran with WMD technology or "destabilizing numbers and types of advanced conventional weapons." Sanctions imposed on violating entities include a ban, for two years, on U.S. government procurement from that entity, and a two-year ban on licensing U.S. exports to that entity. A sanction to ban imports to the United States from the entity is authorized.

If the violator is determined to be a foreign country, sanctions to be imposed are a one-year ban on U.S. assistance to that country; a one-year requirement that the United States vote against international lending to it; a one-year suspension of U.S. co-production agreements with the country; a one-year suspension of technical exchanges with the country in military or dual use technology; and a one-year ban on sales of U.S. arms to the country. The President is also authorized to deny the country most-favored-nation trade status; and to impose a ban on U.S. trade with the country.

Section 1603 of the act amends an earlier law, the Iraq Sanctions Act of 1990 (Section 586G(a) of P.L. 101-513) also provides for a "presumption of denial" for all dual use exports to Iran (which would include computer software).

Waiver and Termination

Section 1606 of the Act provides a presidential waiver for the provisions of the Act, and for those imposed pursuant to the Iraq Sanctions Act of 1990, if the President determines a waiver is "essential to the national interest."

Terminating this sanction outright would require congressional action. It is not clear whether this sanction will be lifted or waived as part of a comprehensive nuclear deal.

Iran-North Korea-Syria Nonproliferation Act

The Iran Nonproliferation Act (P.L. 106-178, signed in March 2000) is now called the Iran-North Korea-Syria Nonproliferation Act (INKSNA) after amendments applying its provisions to North Korea and to Syria. It authorizes sanctions on foreign *persons* (individuals or corporations, not countries or governments) that are determined by the Administration to have assisted Iran's WMD programs. Sanctions imposed include a prohibition on U.S. exportation of arms and dual use items to the sanctioned entity, and, under Executive Order 12938 (of November 14, 1994), a ban on U.S. government procurement and of imports to the United States from the sanctioned entity. The law also bans U.S. extraordinary payments to the Russian Aviation and Space Agency in connection with the international space station unless the President can certify that the agency or entities under its control had not transferred any WMD or missile technology to Iran within the year prior.[20] (A continuing resolution for FY2009, which funded the U.S. government through March 2009, waived this law to allow NASA to continue to use Russian vehicles to access the International Space Station.)

Implementation: Entities sanctioned under this law are listed in the tables at the end of the report.

Waiver and Termination

Section 4 gives the President the authority to not impose sanctions if the President justifies that decision to Congress. Section 5 provides for exemptions from sanctions if certain conditions are met, particularly that the government with jurisdiction over the entity cooperating to stop future such transfers to Iran.

Termination of this law outright would require congressional action.

Executive Order 13382

Executive Order 13382 (June 28, 2005) allows the President to block the assets of proliferators of weapons of mass destruction (WMD) and their supporters under the authority granted by the International Emergency Economic Powers Act (IEEPA; 50 U.S.C. 1701 et seq.), the National Emergencies Act (50 U.S.C. 1601 et seq.), and Section 301 of Title 3, *United States Code*.

Implementation. The numerous entities sanctioned under the order for dealings with Iran are listed in the tables at the end of this report.

Foreign Aid Restrictions for Suppliers of Iran

Successive foreign aid appropriations have withheld 60% of any U.S. assistance to the Russian Federation unless it terminates technical assistance to Iran's nuclear and ballistic missiles programs. Because U.S. aid to Russia generally goes directly to programs in Russia and not to the Russian government, little or no funding has been withheld as a result of the provision.

Sanctions on "Countries of Diversion Concern"

Title III of CISADA established authorities to sanction countries that allow U.S. technology that Iran could use in its nuclear and WMD programs to be re-exported or diverted to Iran. Section 303 of CISADA authorizes the President to designate a country as a "Destination of Diversion Concern" if that country allows substantial diversion of goods, services, or technologies characterized in Section 302 of that law to Iranian end-users or Iranian intermediaries. The technologies specified include any goods that could contribute to Iran's nuclear or WMD programs, as well as goods listed on various U.S. controlled-technology lists such as the Comerce Control List or Munitions List. For any country designated as a country of diversion concern, there would be prohibition of denial for licenses of U.S. exports to that country of the goods that were being re-exported or diverted to Iran.

Implementation: To date, no country has been designated a "Country of Diversion Concern."

Waiver and Termination

Waiver: The President may waive sanctions on countries designated as of Diversion Concern for 12 months, and additional 12 month periods, pursuant to certification that the country is taking steps to prevent such diversions and re-exports.

Termination: The designation terminates on the date the President certifies to Congress that the country has adequately strengthened its export controls to prevent such diversion and re-exports to Iran in the future.

Sanctions on the Islamic Revolutionary Guard Corps (IRGC)

Numerous sanctions discussed in this report target Iran's Islamic Revolutionary Guard Corps (IRGC), which plays a role in repressing domestic dissent, developing Iran's energy sector, developing Iran's WMD programs particularly by procuring technology abroad, and supporting pro-Iranian militant movements and governments in the Middle East region. Much of the work on Iran's oil and gas fields is done through a series of contractors. Some of them, such as Khatam ol-Anbia and Oriental Kish, have been identified by the U.S. government as controlled by the IRGC and have been sanctioned under various executive orders, discussed below. The 2011 appointment of Khatam ol-Anbia's chief, Rostam Ghasemi, as oil minister, caused the U.S. government and many experts to assess that the IRGC role in Iran's energy sector was large and growing. He was replaced by President Hassan Rouhani with a former Oil Minister and oil industry professional, but the IRGC involvement in Iran's energy sector is not shrinking. The *Wal Street Journal* reported on May 27, 2014, that Khatam ol-Anbia has $50 billion in contracts with the Iranian government, including in the energy sector but also in port and highway construction. It has as many as 40,000 employees. Sanctions targeting the IRGC are discussed below:

- Section 311 of the Iran Threat Reduction Act requires a certification by a contractor to the U.S. government that it is not knowingly engaging in a significant transaction with Iran's Islamic Revolutionary Guard Corps (IRGC), or any of its agents or affiliates that have been sanctioned under several executive orders discussed below. A contract may be terminated if it is determined that the company's certification of compliance was false.
- Section 302 of the Iran Threat Reduction Act imposes at least 5 out of 12 ISA sanctions on persons that materially assist, with financing or technology, the IRGC, or assist or engage in "significant" transactions with any of its affiliates that are sanctioned under Executive Order 13382, 13224, or similar executive orders discussed below—or which are determined to be affiliates of the IRGC. *Section 302 did not amend ISA.*
- Section 301 of the Iran Threat Reduction Act requires the President, within 90 days of enactment (by November 9, 2012), to identify "officials, agents, or affiliates" of the IRGC and to impose sanctions in accordance with Executive Order 13382 or 13224, including blocking any such designee's U.S.-based assets or property. Some of these designations, including of National Iranian Oil Company (NIOC), were made by Treasury Department on November 8, 2012.
- Section 303 of the Iran Threat Reduction Act requires the imposition of sanctions on agencies of foreign governments that provide technical or financial support, or goods and services to sanctioned (under U.S. executive orders or U.N. resolutions)

members or affiliates of the IRGC. Sanctions include a ban on U.S. assistance or credits for that foreign government agency, a ban on defense sales to it, a ban on U.S. arms sales to it, and a ban on exports to it of controlled U.S. technology.

- Section 104 of CISADA sanctions foreign banks that conduct significant transactions with the IRGC or any of its agents or affiliates that are sanctioned under any executive order. It also sanctions any entity that assists Iran's Central Bank efforts to help the IRGC acquire WMD or support international terrorism.
- The IRGC is named as a proliferation supporting entity under Executive Order 13382, and the Qods Force, the unit of the IRGC that assists pro-Iranian movements and countries abroad, is named as a terrorism supporting entity under Executive Order 13324. Several Iranian firms linked to the IRGC are sanctioned, as noted in the tables at the end of this report. Several IRGC commanders are named under other executive orders, discussed below, sanctioning Iranian human rights abusers, abusers of Syrian human rights, and entities undermining stability in Iraq.
- No IRGC-related laws or executive orders were waived or suspended to implement the JPA.

FINANCIAL/BANKING SANCTIONS

U.S. efforts to shut Iran out of the international banking system have gained strength as other countries have joined the effort. These efforts have been implemented primarily by the Treasury Department through progressively strong actions, particularly using the authority in legislation in 2011 to cut off Iran's Central Bank from the international financial system.

Early Efforts: Targeted Financial Measures

Since 2006, the Treasury Department has used existing authorities to persuade foreign banks to cease dealing with Iran by attempting to convince the banks that Iran is using the international financial system to fund terrorist groups and acquire weapons-related technology. According to a GAO report of February 2013, the Treasury Department made overtures to 145 banks in 60 countries, including several visits to banks and officials in the UAE, and convinced at least 80 foreign banks to cease handling financial transactions with Iranian banks. In November 6, 2008, the Treasury Department has barred U.S. banks from handling any indirect transactions ("U-turn transactions," meaning transactions with non-Iranian foreign banks that are handling transactions on behalf of an Iranian bank) with all Iranian banks.[21]

Implementation: The Treasury Department also used punishments against banks that have helped Iran violate U.S. financial restrictions. Among the major fines levied or paid: (1) in 2004, UBS paid a $100 million fine for the unauthorized movement of U.S. dollars to Iran and other sanctioned countries; (2) in December 2005, the Dutch bank ABN Amro paid an $80 million fine for failing to fully report the processing of financial transactions involving Iran's Bank Melli; (3) in December 2009, Credit Suisse paid a $536 million settlement for illicitly processing of Iranian transactions with U.S. banks; (4) in June 2012, Dutch bank ING paid $619 million for falsifying records of the movement of billions of dollars through the U.S. financial system on behalf of Iranian and Cuban clients; (5) in August 2012, Standard Chartered paid $340 million to New York State regulators for processing transactions with Iran;[22] (6) in January 2014, Luxembourg-based Clearstream Banking paid $152 million for permitting Iran to evade restrictions on dealing with U.S. banks; (7) in January 2014, the Bank of Moscow paid $9.5 million for illicitly moving money through the U.S. financial system on behalf of Bank Melli;[23] and (8) in June 2014, BNP Paribas paid $9 billion in fines for helping Iran (and Sudan and Cuba) violate U.S. sanctions.

CISADA: Sanctioning Foreign Banks That Conduct Transactions with Sanctioned Iranian Banks

The Treasury Department efforts were enhanced substantially by Section 104 of CISADA (P.L. 111-195, signed July 1, 2010) and U.N. and EU sanctions. The intent of Section 104 was, in large part, to weaken Iran's economy by preventing Iranian traders from obtaining "letters of credit" (trade financing) to buy or sell goods. The binding provisions of Section 104 of CISADA require the Secretary of the Treasury to prescribe several sets of regulations to forbid U.S. banks from opening new "correspondent accounts" or "payable-through accounts" (or force the cancellation of existing such accounts) for foreign banks that process "significant transactions" with

- Any foreign entity that is sanctioned by Executive Order 13224 or 13382 (terrorism and proliferation activities, respectively). These orders are discussed elsewhere in this report. To date, several hundred entities (including individuals), many of them Iran-based or of Iranian origin, have been sanctioned under these two Orders; a full list is at the end of this report.
- Any entity designated under by U.N. Security Council resolutions that impose sanctions on Iran.
- Iran's energy, shipping, and shipbuilding sectors, including with NIOC, NITC, and IRISL. (This provision was added by Section 1244(d) of the FY2013 National Defense Authorization Act (P.L. 112-239) *but it does not specifically amend CISADA*).

Foreign banks that do not have operations in the United States typically establish correspondent accounts or payable-through accounts with U.S. banks as a means of accessing the U.S. financial system. The Treasury Department has authority to determine what constitutes a "significant" financial transaction.

Implementation of Section 104: Sanctions Imposed

On July 31, 2012, the Administration announced the first sanctions under Section 104 of CISADA. Sanctioned were the Bank of Kunlun in China and the Elaf Islamic Bank in Iraq. However, on May 17, 2013, the Treasury Department lifted sanctions on Elaf Islamic Bank in Iraq, asserting that the bank had reduced its exposure to the Iranian financial sector and stopped providing services to an Iranian bank sanctioned by the EU (Export Development Bank of Iran).

Waiver and Termination

Under Section 401(a) of CISADA, the Section 104 sanctions provisions would terminate 30 days after the President certifies to Congress that Iran (1) has met the requirements for removal from the terrorism list, AND (2) has ceased pursuit, acquisition or development of, and verifiably dismantled its nuclear weapons and other WMD programs.

The Secretary of the Treasury may waive sanctions under Section 104, with the waiver taking effect 30 days after the Secretary determines that a waiver is necessary to the national interest and submits a report to Congress describing the reason for that determination.

Waivers of CISADA were not required to implement the JPA. Iran is likely to demand that this sanction no longer apply after any comprehensive nuclear deal.

Iran Designated a Money-Laundering Jurisdiction

On November 21, 2011, the Administration took further steps to isolate Iran's banking system by identifying Iran as a "jurisdiction of primary money laundering concern"[24] under Section 311 of the USA Patriot Act (31 U.S.C. 5318A). The Treasury Department determined that Iran's financial system, including the Central Bank, constitutes a threat to governments or financial institutions that do business with these banks. The designation carried no immediate penalty, but it imposed additional requirements on U.S. banks to ensure against improper Iranian access to the U.S. financial system.

LAWS THAT PROMOTE DIVESTMENT

Some U.S. laws require or call for divestment of shares of firms that conduct certain transactions with Iran. A divestment-promotion provision was contained in CISADA, providing a "safe harbor" for investment managers who sell shares of firms that invest in Iran's energy sector at levels that would trigger U.S. sanctions under the Iran Sanctions Act.

Another provision, Section 219 of the Iran Threat Reduction and Syria Human Rights Act of 2012, requires company reports to the Securities and Exchange Commission to disclose whether it or any corporate affiliate has engaged in any transactions with Iran that could trigger sanctions under ISA, CISADA, and other applicable laws.

SANCTIONS AND SANCTIONS EXEMPTIONS TO SUPPORT DEMOCRATIC CHANGE/CIVIL SOCIETY IN IRAN

A trend in U.S. policy and legislation since the June 12, 2009, election-related uprising in Iran has been to support the ability of the domestic opposition in Iran to communicate, to reduce the regime's ability to monitor or censor Internet communications, and to sanction Iranian officials that commit human rights abuses. Sanctions on the IRGC (see box above) represent one facet of that trend because the IRGC is not only involved in Iran's WMD programs but it is also the key instrument through which the regime has suppressed oppositionists. Earlier, the Iran Freedom Support Act (IFSA; P.L. 109-293) authorized "sums as may be necessary" to assist Iranians who are "dedicated" to "democratic values ... and the adoption of a democratic form of government in Iran"; and "advocates the adherence by Iran to nonproliferation regimes."

General Implementation: Individuals and entities designated under the Executive Orders and provisions discussed below are listed in the tables at the end of this report. For those provisions that ban visas to enter the United States, the State Department interprets the provisions to apply to all members of the designated entity.[25] Similar sanctions against many of these same officials—as well as several others—have been imposed by the European Union.

No suspension of U.S. sanctions on Iran for its human rights practices was required by the JPA. U.S. statements indicate that sanctions related specifically to human rights issues will not be eased as part of a comprehensive nuclear settlement, if reached.

Expanding Internet and Communications Freedoms

Some laws and Administration action focus on expanding Internet freedom in Iran or preventing the Iranian government from using the Internet to identify opponents. Subtitle D of the FY2010 Defense Authorization Act (P.L. 111-84), called the "VOICE" (Victims of Iranian Censorship) Act, contained several provisions to increase U.S. broadcasting to Iran and to identify (in a report to be submitted 180 days after enactment) companies that are selling Iran technology equipment that it can use to suppress or monitor the Internet usage of Iranians. The act authorized funds to document Iranian human rights abuses since the June 2009 Iranian presidential election. Section 1241 of the act also required an Administration report by January 31, 2010, on U.S. enforcement of sanctions against Iran, and the effect of those sanctions on Iran.

Sanctions and Actions to Counter Iranian Censorship of the Internet

- Section 106 of CISADA incorporated the "Reduce Iranian Cyber-Suppression Act" (111th Congress, S. 1475 and H.R. 3284), prohibiting U.S. government contracts with foreign companies that sell technology that Iran could use to monitor or control Iranian usage of the Internet. The provisions were directed, in part, against a joint venture between Nokia (Finland) and Siemens (Germany) that reportedly sold Internet monitoring and censorship technology to Iran in 2008.[26]

- On April 23, 2012, President Obama issued an executive order (13606) directly addressing the issue by sanctioning persons who commit "Grave Human Rights Abuses by the Governments of Iran and Syria Via Information Technology (GHRAVITY)." The order blocks the U.S.-based property and essentially bars U.S. entry and bans any U.S. trade with persons and entities listed in an Annex and persons or entities subsequently determined to be (1) operating any technology that allows the Iranian (or Syrian) government to disrupt, monitor, or track computer usage by citizens of those countries or assisting the two governments in such disruptions or monitoring; or (2) selling to Iran (or Syria) any technology that enables those governments to carry out such disruptions or monitoring.
- Section 403 of the Iran Threat Reduction and Syria Human Rights Act (P.L. 112- 158, August 10, 2012) sanctions (visa ban, U.S.-based property blocked) persons/firms determined to have engaged in censorship in Iran, limited access to media, or—for example, a foreign satellite service provider—supported Iranian government jamming or frequency manipulation. On October 9, 2012, the President issued Executive Order 13628 reinforcing Section 403 by blocking the property of persons/firms determined to have committed the censorship, limited free expression, or assisted in jamming communications. The Order also specifies the sanctions authorities of the Department of State and of the Treasury.

Laws and Administration Actions to Promote Internet Communications by Iranians

- On March 8, 2010, OFAC amended the Iran Transactions Regulations to allow for a general license for providing free mass market software to Iranians. The ruling incorporated major features of the Iran Digital Empowerment Act (H.R. 4301 in the 111th Congress). The OFAC determination required a waiver of the provision of the Iran-Iraq Arms Nonproliferation Act (Section 1606 waiver provision) discussed above.

- Section 103(b)(2) of CISADA exempts equipment to help Iranians communicate and use the Internet from the U.S. export ban on Iran.
- On March 20, 2012, the Treasury Department amended U.S.-Iran trade regulations to permit several additional types of software and information technology products to be exported to Iran under general license, provided the products were available at no cost to the user.[27]The items included personal communications, personal data storage, browsers, plug-ins, document readers, and free mobile applications related to personal communications.
- On May 30, 2013, the Treasury Department further amended the trade regulations to allow for the sale, *on a cash basis* (no U.S. financing), to Iran of equipment (e.g., cellphones, laptops, satellite Internet, website hosting, and related products and services) that Iranians can use to communicate.

Measures to Sanction Human Rights Abuses and Promote the Opposition

Another part of the effort to help Iran's opposition has been legislation to sanction regime officials involved in suppressing the domestic opposition in Iran.

- Sanctions Against Iranian Human Rights Abusers. Section 105 of CISADA was modeled on a Senate bill, S. 3022, the Iran Human Rights Sanctions Act, in the 111th Congress. The section bans travel and freezing assets of those Iranians determined to be human rights abusers. On September 29, 2010, pursuant to Section 105, President Obama signed an Executive Order (13553) providing for the CISADA sanctions against Iranians determined to be responsible for or complicit in post-2009 Iran election human rights abuses. Those sanctioned under the provisions are listed in the tables at the end of this report. Section 105 contains its own specific authority to terminate the section through Administration action. Section 105 can be terminated if the President certifies to Congress that Iran has (1) unconditionally released all political prisoners detained in the aftermath of the June 2009 uprising; (2) ceased its practices of violence, unlawful detention, torture, and abuse of citizens who were engaged in peaceful protest; (3) fully investigated abuses of political activists that occurred after the uprising; and (4) committed to and is making progress toward establishing an independent judiciary and respecting human rights recognized in the Universal Declaration of Human Rights.

- *Sanctions on Sales of Anti-Riot Equipment.* Section 402 of the Iran Threat Reduction and Syria Human Rights Act of 2012 (P.L. 112-158) amended Section 105 by adding provisions that sanctions (visa ban, U.S. property blocked) for any person or company that sells the Iranian government goods or technologies that it can use to commit human rights abuses against its people. Such goods include firearms, rubber bullets, police batons, chemical or pepper sprays, stun grenades, tear gas, water cannons, and like goods. Under that section, ISA sanctions are additionally to be imposed on any person determined to be selling such equipment to the IRGC.
- *Sanctions Against Iranian Government Broadcasters.* Section 1248 of IFCA (Subtitle D of P.L. 112-239) mandates inclusion of the Islamic Republic of Iran Broadcasting (IRIB), the state broadcasting umbrella group, as a human rights abuser, thereby imposing CISADA Section 105 sanctions (travel ban, asset freeze) on that entity.
- *Sanctions Against Iranian Profiteers.* Section 1249 of IFCA amends CISADA by making sanctionable under Section 105 any person determined to have engaged in corruption or to have diverted or misappropriated humanitarian goods or funds for such goods for the Iranian people. The measure is intended to sanction Iranian profiteers who are, for example, using official connections to corner the market for vital medicines. This essentially codifies a similar provision of Executive Order 13645.
- *Separate Visa Bans.* On July 8, 2011, the State Department imposed visa restrictions on more than 50 Iranian officials for participating in political repression in Iran. The State Department announcement stated that the names of those subject to the ban would not be released because visa records are confidential. The action was taken under the authorities of Section 212(a)(3)(C) of the Immigration and Nationality Act, which renders inadmissible to the United States a foreign person whose activities could have serious consequences for the United States. On May 30, 2013, the State Department announced it had imposed visa restrictions on an additional 60 Iranian officials and

other individuals who participated in human rights abuses related to political repression in Iran.[28]

- There are certain exemptions in the case of high level Iranian visits to attend the United Nations. Under the U.N. Participation Act (P.L. 79-264) that provides for U.S. participation in the United Nations and as host nation of U.N. headquarters in New York, visas are routinely issued to heads of state and members of their entourage attending these meetings. In September 2012, however, the State Department refused visas for 20 members of Iranian President Ahmadinejad's traveling party on the grounds of past involvement in terrorism or human rights abuses. Still, in line with U.S. obligations under the act, then President Ahmadinejad was allowed to fly to the United States on Iran Air, even though Iran Air is a U.S.-sanctioned entity, and his plane reportedly was allowed to stay at Andrews Air Force base for the duration of his visit.

U.N. Sanctions

U.N. sanctions apply to all U.N. member states. As part of a multilateral process of attempting to convince Iran to choose the path of negotiations or face further penalty, during 2006-2008, three U.N. Security Council resolutions—1737, 1747, and 1803—imposed sanctions primarily on Iran's weapons of mass destruction (WMD) infrastructure.

Resolution 1929 was adopted on June 9, 2010, by a vote of 12-2 (Turkey and Brazil), with one abstention (Lebanon). (Iranian entities and persons under U.N. sanctions are in Table 5.) A summary of the major provisions of all four of these resolutions is contained in the table below.

U.N. Security Council action was not needed to implement the JPA. The JPA makes reference to a comprehensive settlement satisfying all provisions of U.N. resolutions on Iran, indicating that Security Council action might be taken to implement any comprehensive agreement.

Table 3. Summary of Provisions of U.N. Resolutions on Iran Nuclear Program (1737, 1747, 1803, and 1929)

Requires Iran to suspend uranium enrichment, to suspend construction of the heavy-water reactor at Arak, ratify the "Additional Protocol" to Iran's IAEA Safeguards Agreement. (1737)
Freezes the assets of Iranian persons and entities named in annexes to the resolutions, and requires that countries ban the travel of named Iranians. (1737, 1747, 1803, and 1929)
Prohibits transfer to Iran of nuclear, missile, and dual use items to Iran, except for use in light-water reactors. (1737, and 1747)
Prohibits Iran from exporting arms or WMD-useful technology (1747)
Prohibits Iran from investing abroad in uranium mining, related nuclear technologies or nuclear capable ballistic missile technology, and prohibits Iran from launching ballistic missiles (including on its territory). (1929)
Requires Iran to refrain from any development of ballistic missiles that are nuclear capable. (1929)
Mandates that countries not export major combat systems to Iran, but does not bar sales of missiles that are not on the U.N. Registry of Conventional Arms. (1929)
Calls for voluntary restraint on transactions with Iranian banks, particularly Bank Melli and Bank Saderat. (1929)
Calls for vigilance on international lending to Iran and providing trade credits and other financing. (1929)
Calls on countries to inspect cargoes carried by Iran Air Cargo and Islamic Republic of Iran Shipping Lines—or by any ships in national or international waters—if there are indications they carry cargo banned for carriage to Iran. Searches in international waters would require concurrence of the country where the ship is registered. (1929)
A Sanctions Committee, composed of the 15 members of the Security Council, monitors implementation of all Iran sanctions and collects and disseminates information on Iranian violations and other entities involved in banned activities. A "panel of experts" is empowered by 1929 to assist the U.N. sanctions committee in implementing the resolution and previous Iran resolutions, and to suggest ways of more effective implementation.

Source: Text of U.N. Security Council resolutions 1737, 1747, 1803, and 1929. http://www.un.org. More information on specific provisions of each of these resolutions and the nuclear negotiations with Iran is in CRS Report RL32048, *Iran: U.S. Concerns and Policy Responses*, by Kenneth Katzman.

INTERNATIONAL IMPLEMENTATION AND COMPLIANCE[29]

During 2010-2013, converging international views on Iran produced substantial global cooperation in pressuring Iran with sanctions. Some countries apparently joined the sanctions regime primarily as a means of heading off unwanted military action against Iran by the United States or by Israel. Countries in the region cooperated largely in order to preserve their close relationships with the United States, even though many regional countries seek to avoid antagonizing Iran. A comparison between U.S., U.N., and EU sanctions against Iran is contained in **Table 4** below. On May 1, 2012, President Obama issued Executive Order 13608, giving the Treasury Department the ability to identify and sanction (cutting them off from the U.S. market) foreign persons who help Iran (or Syria) evade U.S. and multilateral sanctions.

The JPA, extended until July 6, 2015, requires Iran's oil exports to remain constant at the levels they were when it began implementation in January 2014—just over 1 million barrels per day (mbd) of crude oil. Iran's oil customers are not required to cut average purchases further but are not permitted to increase those purchases either. Because U.S. sanctions laws do not penalize increases in purchases of condensates (which are produced in association with crude oil or natural gas), Iran's oil buyers appear to have increased condensate purchases during the JPA period by about 200,000 barrels per day (crude oil equivalent),[30] making Iran's exports of crude and condensates combined about 1.3 mbd.

The following countries have active exemptions under Section 1245 of the FY2012 NDAA (on dealings with the Central Bank for oil purchases or other transactions): (1) 10 EU countries,[31] for complying with an EU embargo on Iran oil purchases; (2) China, India, Turkey, South Korea, Japan, and Taiwan, for significantly reducing oil purchases from Iran; and (3) Singapore, Malaysia, South Africa, and Sri Lanka for ending oil purchases from Iran.

The United States and its partners have also sought to stop Iran from using traditional trading patterns common to its neighborhood to evade sanctions. On January 10, 2013, the Treasury Department's Office of Foreign Assets Control issued an Advisory to highlight Iran's use of *hawalas* (traditional informal banking and money exchanges) in the Middle East and South Asia region to circumvent financial sanctions. Because the involvement of an Iranian client is often opaque, banks have sometimes inadvertently processed *hawala* transactions involving Iranians.

Europe

U.S. and European approaches on Iran have converged since 2002, when it was revealed that Iran was developing a uranium enrichment capability. Previously, European and other countries appeared less concerned than the United States about Iranian policies and were reluctant to sanction Iran. Since the passage of Resolution 1929 in June 2010, European Union (EU) sanctions on Iran have become nearly as extensive as those of the United States. The EU is a party to the JPA. The following outlines European sanctions policy on Iran

- A ban on EU oil imports from Iran went into effect on July 1, 2012, pursuant to a January 23, 2012, EU decision. Collectively, the EU bought about 600,000 barrels per day of Iranian oil in 2011, about a quarter of Iran's total oil exports. The embargo was imposed despite the fact that the most vulnerable EU economies—Spain, Italy, and Greece—were each buying more than 10% of their oil from Iran. Because of the embargo, 10 EU countries have maintained exemptions from sanctions under (P.L. 112-81). A ban on EU imports of natural gas from Iran went into effect in October 2012 and intended to stall Iran's efforts to expand gas exports to Europe. *The JPA did not alter the EU ban on imports of oil or gas from Iran.*
- An EU ban on insurance for shipping oil or petrochemicals from Iran took full effect on July 1, 2012. Earlier, most EU-based insurers closed their offices in Iran. *The EU has eased this sanction to implement the JPA.*
- The EU has banned all trade with Iran in gold, precious metals, diamonds, and petrochemical products. *The EU has eased this sanction to implement the JPA.*
- The EU has frozen the assets of Iran's Central Bank, although transactions are permitted for approved legitimate trade, and it froze the assets of several Iranian firms involved in shipping. *The JPA does not alter this sanction.*
- As of October 15, 2012, there has been a ban on transactions between European and all Iranian banks, unless specifically authorized, and the EU has banned short-term export credits, guarantees, and insurance. *The EU has eased this sanction in accordance with the JPA.*
- The EU banned exports to Iran of graphite, semi-finished metals such as aluminum and steel, industrial software, shipbuilding technology, oil storage capabilities, and flagging or classification services for

Iranian tankers and cargo vessels. *With the exception of exports to Iran's automotive sector, the JPA did not alter EU implementation of these sanctions.*

SWIFT Cutoff. Section 220 of the Iran Threat Reduction and Syria Human Rights Act (P.L. 112- 158, signed in August 2012), required reports on electronic payments systems such as the Brussels-based SWIFT (Society of Worldwide Interbank Financial Telecommunications) that might be doing business with Iran, but does not mandate sanctions against such systems. Subsequently, the EU requested that SWIFT cut off sanctioned Iranian banks from the network. SWIFT acceded to that request on March 17, 2012, denying access to 14 Iranian banks blacklisted by the EU. Iranian banks not sanctioned by the EU can still access the SWIFT system.[32] (The United States has sanctioned about 50 Iranian banks, but only those sanctioned by the EU have been cut off from SWIFT.) And, some experts report that Iranian banks are still able to conduct electronic transactions with the European Central Bank via an electronic payments system called "Target II." The SWIFT cutoff was not suspended to implement the JPA, but most experts assess that this ban would be lifted as part of a comprehensive nuclear deal with Iran.

The harmonization of U.S. and European sanctions on Iran differs from early periods. During the 1990s, EU countries maintained a policy of "critical dialogue" with Iran, and the EU and Japan refused to join the 1995 U.S. trade and investment ban on Iran. The European dialogue with Iran was suspended in April 1997 in response to the German terrorism trial ("Mykonos trial") that found high-level Iranian involvement in killing Iranian dissidents in Germany, but resumed in May 1998 during Mohammad Khatemi's presidency of Iran. In the 1990s, European and Japanese creditors bucked U.S. objections and rescheduled about $16 billion in Iranian debt bilaterally, in spite of Paris Club rules that call for multilateral rescheduling. In July 2002, Iran tapped international capital markets for the first time since the Islamic revolution, selling $500 million in bonds to European banks. During 2002-2005, there were active negotiations between the European Union and Iran on a "Trade and Cooperation Agreement" (TCA) that would have lowered the tariffs or increased quotas for Iranian exports to the EU countries.[33] Negotiations were discontinued in late 2005 after Iran abrogated an agreement with several EU countries to suspend uranium enrichment. Similarly, there has, to date, been insufficient international support to grant Iran membership in the World Trade Organization (WTO), even though U.S. Administrations ceased blocking Iran from applying in May 2005.

China and Russia

The position of Russia and China, two permanent members of the U.N. Security Council, is that they will impose only those sanctions required by U.N. Security Council resolutions. Russia earns significant revenues from large projects in Iran, such as the Bushehr nuclear reactor, and it also seeks not to provoke Iran into supporting Islamist movements in the Muslim regions of Russia and the Central Asian states. In August 2014, the two countries reportedly agreed to a broad trade and energy deal which might include an exchange of Iranian oil (500,000 barrels per day) for Russian goods. That deal could potentially violate the JPA, if implemented.[34] Russia is an oil exporter, but Iranian oil that Russia might buy under this arrangement would presumably free up additional Russian oil for export.

China remains Iran's largest oil customer and its cooperation has been pivotal to U.S. efforts to reduce Iran's revenue from oil sales. According to U.S. officials in May 2013, China had cut its buys of oil from Iran by 21% since the end of 2011—to about 435,000 barrels per day from its 2011 average of about 550,000 barrels per day. Iran's oil exports to China fell further thereafter, as shown in the table above. Because China is the largest buyer of Iranian oil, percentage cuts by China have a large impact in reducing Iran's oil sales by volume—explaining State Department's maintenance of China's sanctions exemption. As is the case with other Iranian oil customers, some months might show spikes to higher levels as oil shipments get scheduled. Several Chinese energy firms invested in Iran's energy sector, but some of these projects have been given to Iranian or other country firms or show little evidence of actual development work.

A February 6, 2013, U.S. sanction requiring that Iran be paid in local currency accounts caused Iran to increase importation of clothing and household appliances from China. Even before that sanction was imposed, China had begun to settle much of its trade balance with Iran with goods rather than hard currency. Doing so was highly favorable to China financially. In August 2013, it was reported that China might settle some of its Iran oil bill by providing 315 subway cars for the Tehran metro.[35] Press reports indicated that Iran's automotive sector obtains a significant proportion of its parts from China, and two Chinese companies, Geelran and Chery, produce cars in Iran. These exports were reduced substantially during 2013 because of U.S. sanctions, but recovered somewhat during the JPA period, which eased sanctions on Iran's automotive sector.

Japan/Korean Peninsula/Other East Asia

Since 2010, in part in deference to their alliances with the United States, Japan and South Korea have imposed trade, banking, and energy sanctions on Iran—similar to those of the EU. Both countries have cut imports of Iranian oil sharply since 2011. Some South Korean firms have been active in energy infrastructure construction in Iran but, on December 16, 2011, South Korea banned sales to Iran of energy sector equipment. The main South Korean refiners that import Iranian crude are SK Energy and Hyundai Oilbank.

The U.S. sanctions that require on oil buyers pay Iran in local accounts to avoid U.S. sanctions— a requirement that took effect on February 6, 2013—did not affect Japan and South Korea's trading patterns with Iran significantly. South Korea generally paid Iran's Central Bank through local currency accounts at its Industrial Bank of Korea and Woori Bank, and it exported to Iran mainly iron, steel, consumer electronics, and appliances. Japan exports to Iran significant amounts of chemical and rubber products, as well as consumer electronics. These exports continued after 2010, and since the JPA went into effect, using local currency accounts. The two countries also have comprised a large portion of the $700 million per month in direct hard currency payments to Iran for oil, as provided for by the JPA.

Iran reportedly has ordered from Singapore (Yangzijiang Shipbuilding Holdings Ltd.) 10 ships that Iran (IRISL) is expected to use to transport iron ore and copper to foreign buyers.[36] The purchased could potentially violate IFCA, as discussed above.

North Korea

North Korea is an ally of Iran and, like Iran, is a subject of international sanctions. North Korea generally does not comply with international sanctions against Iran, and reportedly cooperates with Iran on a wide range of WMD-related ventures. Press reports in April 2013 said that Iran might supply oil directly to North Korea, but it has not been reported that any such arrangement was finalized. Currently, according to experts, a portion of China's purchases of oil from Iran and other suppliers is re-exported to North Korea.

South Asia: Afghanistan, India, and Pakistan

India has implemented U.N.-mandated sanctions against Iran but its cultural, economic, and historic ties to Iran—and their common interests in

Afghanistan—have made the Indian government hesitant to impose sanctions on Iran to the extent the United States and EU have. Yet, India's private sector has come to view Iran as a "controversial market"—a term used by many international firms to describe markets that entail reputational and financial risks.

India began reducing economic relations with Iran in 2010, when India's central bank ceased using a Tehran-based regional body, the Asian Clearing Union, to handle transactions with Iran. In January 2012, Iran agreed to accept India's local currency, the rupee, to settle 45% of its sales to India. That local account funds the sale to Iran of Indian wheat, pharmaceuticals, rice, sugar, soybeans, auto parts, and other products. Still, there is a large trade imbalance, because the oil Iran exports to India are worth far more than the value of the products that India sells to an.

Even though purchases of Iranian oil are financially advantageous because of the barter nature of their trade, India has reduced its imports of Iranian oil substantially since 2011 in an effort to conform to U.S. and EU policy. By the time of the JPA, Iran was only supplying about 6% of India's oil imports (down from over 16% in 2008). India has incurred significant costs to retrofit refineries that were handling Iranian crude. In advance of President Obama's visit to India in late January 2015, the Indian government reportedly requested refiners to further cut purchases from Iran. As shown in the table later in this report, some Indian firms have ended or slowed actual work on investments in Iranian oil and gas fields since 2012.

India hopes to develop Iran's Chahbahar port that would enable India to trade with Afghanistan unimpeded by Pakistan, but Indian investment in the project appears to be contingent on an international nuclear deal with Iran that would result in an easing of sanctions. Iranian and Indian officials reportedly have periodically discussed the issue of constructing an underwater natural gas pipeline, which would avoid going through Pakistani territory. However, such a route would be expensive to construct.

A test of Pakistan's compliance with sanctions is a pipeline project intended to carry Iranian gas to Pakistan. Agreement on the $7 billion project was finalized on June 12, 2010, and construction was formally inaugurated in a ceremony attended by the Presidents of both countries on March 11, 2013. In line with an agreed completion date of mid-2014, Iran reportedly completed the pipeline on its side of the border. However, Pakistan has not completed its portion of the project. In March 2013, the State Department reiterated earlier comments that the project might be sanctioned under ISA, and Pakistani officials said U.S. sanctions precluded construction on the Pakistan side of the border.[37] Still, Pakistan is obligated to begin buying gas from Iran as of January 1, 2015, lest it incur a $200 million per month penalty due Iran. (In 2009, India dissociated itself from the project, which was initially conceived as bringing Iranian gas to India. India had concerns about the security of the pipeline, the location at which the gas would be transferred to India, pricing of the gas, and tariffs.)

Afghanistan

Iran has extensive security interests in Afghanistan. However, Afghanistan's economy is small, and very few Iran-Afghanistan economic interactions are subject to international sanctions. Iranian firms have been involved in road and building construction in Afghanistan, mostly near the Iranian border and in Kabul. Some reports say that Iranian currency traders acquire dollars that are plentiful in Afghanistan but in short supply in Iran. Iranian traders—acting on behalf of wealthy Iranians seeking to preserve the value of their savings—are said to be carrying local currency to Afghanistan to buy up some of the dollars available there. There have been allegations that Iran is using an Iran-owned bank in Afghanistan, Arian Bank, to move funds in and out of Afghanistan. The U.S. Treasury Department has warned Afghan traders not to process dollar transactions for Iran. The Special Inspector General for Afghanistan Reconstruction reported in late January 2013 that Afghan security forces might have used some of U.S. aid funds to purchase fuel from Iran. In September 2013, it was reported that Anham FZCO, a U.S. contractor building food storage shelters for U.S. troops in Afghanistan, might have violated U.S. sanctions by transshipping building materials through Iran.[38]

Turkey/South Caucasus

Even though Turkey and Iran differ sharply on the Syria civil conflict, Turkey remains a significant buyer of Iranian oil. In 2011, it purchased about 200,000 bpd, but it subsequently reduced those buys and Turkey has maintained a Section 1245 NDAA sanctions exemption. Overall Iran-Turkey trade fell to $15 billion in 2013 from $22 billion in 2012. However, on June 9, 2014, Iran's President Hassan Rouhani visited Ankara, accompanied by more than 100 Iranian businessmen, and vowed to double bilateral trade to $30 billion by 2015.

Turkey is Iran's main gas customer via a pipeline built in 1997. During the pipeline's construction, the State Department testified that Turkey would be importing gas originating in Turkmenistan, not Iran, under a swap arrangement, and the State Department did not determine that the project was a violation of ISA. Even though direct Iranian gas exports to Turkey through the line began in 2001, no ISA sanctions were imposed, possibly because the State Department views the line as crucial to the energy security of Turkey. Prior to the EU decision on October 15, 2012, to bar sales of Iranian gas to Europe, Turkey was also the main conduit for Iranian gas exports to Europe (primarily Bulgaria and Greece). Turkey said in December 2012 that it is constructing a second Iran-Turkey gas pipeline (the work is being performed by Som Petrol). No determination of ISA sanctions violation has been announced.[39] Earlier, press reports accused Turkey's Halkbank of settling much of Turkey's payments to Iran for oil or natural gas with shipments to Iran of gold. U.S. officials testified on May 15, 2013, that Turkey is not paying for its gas imports from Iran with gold, but that the gold going from Turkey to Iran consists mainly of Iranian private citizens' purchases of Turkish gold to hedge against the value of the *rial.*

On January 6, 2014, the Commerce Department issued an emergency order blocking a Turkey-based firm (3K Aviation Consulting and Logistics) from re-exporting two U.S.-made jet engines to Iran. That and other firms reportedly involved in the deal denied that the engines were bound for an Iranian airline (Pouya Airline).[40]

Caucasus: Azerbaijan, Armenia, and Georgia

The Clinton and George W. Bush Administrations used the threat of ISA sanctions to deter oil pipeline routes involving Iran and thereby successfully promoted an alternate route from Azerbaijan (Baku) to Turkey (Ceyhan). The route became operational in 2005. Section 6 of Executive Order 13622 exempts from sanctions any pipelines that bring gas from Azerbaijan to Europe and Turkey. In part because Iran and Azerbaijan are often at odds, Iran and Armenia—Azerbaijan's adversary—enjoy extensive economic relations. Armenia is Iran's largest direct gas customer, after Turkey. In May 2009, Iran and Armenia inaugurated a natural gas pipeline between the two, built by Gazprom of Russia. No determination of ISA sanctions has been issued. Armenia has said its banking controls are strong and that Iran is unable to process transactions illicitly through Armenia's banks.[41] However, Azerbaijani officials assert that Iran is using Armenian banks operating in the Armenia-occupied Nagorno-Karabakh territory to circumvent international financial sanctions. These institutions could include Artsakhbank and Ameriabank.[42] In May 2014, Iran and Armenia increased weekly flights between the two from 3 to 50, suggesting that commerce between the two is growing.

Some press reports say that Iran might have used another Caucasian state, Georgia, to circumvent sanctions. IRGC companies reportedly have established 150 front companies in Georgia for the purpose of importing dual-use items and to boost Iran's non-oil exports with sales of products such as roofing materials and jams. On the other hand, observers assert that since extensive Iran-Georgia economic ties were highly publicized in mid-2013, Georgia has obtained cooperation from its businessmen in reducing transactions with Iran.

Persian Gulf and Iraq[43]

The Persian Gulf countries are oil exporters and close allies of the United States. As Iranian oil exports decreased 2012 and 2013, the Gulf states supplied the global oil market with additional oil. The Gulf states have generally sought to prevent the re-exportation to Iran of U.S. technology, and have curtailed banking relationships with Iran. On the other hand, in order not to antagonize Iran, the Gulf countries still conduct relatively normal trade with Iran and several of them allow some sanctioned Iranian banks to operate in their countries. Gulf-based shipping companies such as United Arab Shipping Company have continued to pay port loading fees to such sanctioned IRGC-controlled port operators as Tidewater.[44]

The UAE is particularly closely watched by U.S. officials because of the large presence of Iranian firms there. Several UAE-based firms have been sanctioned for efforts to evade sanctions, as noted in the tables at the end of the report. U.S. officials praised the UAE's March 1, 2012, ban on transactions with Iran by Dubai-based Noor Islamic Bank. Iran reportedly used the bank to process a substantial portion of its oil payments. Some Iranian gas condensates (120,000 barrels per day) reportedly are imported by Emirates National Oil Company (ENOC) and refined into jet fuel, gasoline, and other products.

Iran and Kuwait have held talks on the construction of a 350-mile pipeline that would bring Iranian gas to Kuwait. No construction has been reported. The two have apparently reached agreement on volumes (8.5 million cubic meters of gas would go to Kuwait each day) but not on price.[45] Kuwait's Amir visited Iran in early June 2014. Iran has sought to use its close relations with Iraq's Shiite-dominated government to evade some sanctions. As noted above, the United States sanctioned an Iraqi bank that has cooperated with Iran's efforts, but lifted those sanctions when the bank reduced that business. Iraq presented the United States with a more significant Iran sanctions-related dilemma on July 23, 2013, when it signed an agreement with Iran to buy 850 million cubic feet per day of natural gas through a joint pipeline that enters Iraq at Diyala province and will supply several power plants. The two countries signed a contract for the pipeline construction, estimated at $365 million, in July 2011, and it reportedly has been completed on both sides of the border.[46] It is not clear whether the offensive against the Iraqi government by the Islamic State organization has affected the project.

Iran has intervened with advisers and weapons supplies to help Iraq fend off Islamic State forces. U.S. officials assert that the Iranian intervention complements U.S. policy and the Iranian activity has not been sanctioned, even though Iranian arms exports are prohibited by U.N. Security Council Resolution 1747. The United States has, however, cited that Resolution in pressing Iraq to halt military resupply flights from Iran to Syria. Iran supports the Assad government of Syria, whereas the United States has called for Assad to step down in the face of the armed uprising that began as peaceful protests in 2011.[47]

Latin America

Iran, during the term of President Ahmadinejad, looked to several Latin American countries, particularly Venezuela, to try to avoid or reduce the effects of international sanctions. For the most part, however, Iran's trade and other business dealings with Latin America remain modest and likely to reduce the effect of sanctions on Iran only marginally. And, Iran lost a key Latin American ally with the March 2013 death of Venezuelan President Hugo Chavez. As noted elsewhere in this report, several Venezuelan firms have been sanctioned for dealings with Iran.

Africa

During the term of Ahmadinejad, Iran sought to cultivate relations with some African countries to try to circumvent sanctions. However, African countries have tended to avoid dealings with Iran in order to avoid pressure from the United States. South Africa has ended its buys of Iranian oil. In June

2012, Kenya contracted to buy about 30 million barrels of Iranian oil, but cancelled the contract the following month after the United States warned that going ahead with the purchase could hurt U.S.-Kenya relations. Tanzania has re-flagged about 6-10 Iranian tankers. Perhaps fearing similar criticism, in September 2012 Sierra Leone removed nine vessels from its shipping register after determining they belonged to IRISL.

World Bank Loans

The July 27, 2010, EU measures narrowed substantially the prior differences between the EU and the United States over international lending to Iran. As noted above, the United States representative to international financial institutions is required to vote against international lending, but that vote, although weighted, is not sufficient to block international lending. No new loans have been approved to Iran since 2005, including several environmental projects under the Bank's "Global Environmental Facility" (GEF). The initiative has slated more than $7.5 million in loans for Iran to dispose of harmful chemicals.[48] Earlier, in 1993, the United States voted its 16.5% share of the World Bank against loans to Iran of $460 million for electricity, health, and irrigation projects, but the loans were approved. To block that lending, the FY1994-FY1996 foreign aid appropriations (P.L. 103-87, P.L. 103-306, and P.L. 104-107) cut the amount appropriated for the U.S. contribution to the bank by the amount of those loans. The legislation contributed to a temporary halt in new bank lending to Iran. In the 111th Congress, a provision of H.R. 6296—Title VII—cut off U.S. contributions to the World Bank, International Finance Corp., and the Multilateral Investment Guarantee Corp. if the World Bank approves a new Country Assistance Strategy for Iran or makes a loan to Iran. During 1999-2005, Iran's moderating image had led the World Bank to consider new loans over U.S. opposition. In May 2000, the United States' allies outvoted the United States to approve $232 million in loans for health and sewage projects. During April 2003-May 2005, a total of $725 million in loans were approved for environmental management, housing reform, water and sanitation projects, and land management projects, in addition to $400 million in loans for earthquake relief.

Table 4. Comparison Between U.S., U.N., and EU and Allied Country Sanctions

U.S. Sanctions	U.N. Sanctions	Implementation by EU and Some Allied Countries
General Observation: Most sweeping sanctions on Iran of virtually any country in the world	Increasingly sweeping, but still intended to primarily target Iran's nuclear and other WMD programs. No mandatory sanctions on Iran's energy sector.	EU closely aligns its sanctions tightening—as well as sanctions relief in the context of the nuclear deal—with those of the U.S. Japan and South Korean sanctions also increasingly extensive.
Ban on U.S. Trade with and Investment in Iran: Executive Order 12959 bans (with limited exceptions) U.S. firms from exporting to Iran, importing from Iran, or investing in Iran. There is an exemption for sales to Iran of food and medical products.	U.N. sanctions do not ban civilian trade with Iran or general civilian sector investment in Iran. Nor do U.N. sanctions mandate restrictions on provision of trade financing or financing guarantees by national export credit guarantee agencies.	No general EU ban on trade in civilian goods with Iran, but bans on certain types of trade as discussed. Japan and South Korea have banned medium- and long-term trade financing and financing guarantees. Short-term credit still allowed.
Sanctions on Foreign Firms that Do Business with Iran's Energy Sector: The Iran Sanctions Act, P.L. 104-172, and subsequent laws and executive orders, discussed throughout the report, mandate sanctions on virtually any type of transaction with/in Iran's energy sector.	No U.N. equivalent exists. However, preambular language in Resolution 1929 "not[es] the potential connection between Iran's revenues derived from its energy sector and the funding of Iran's proliferation-sensitive nuclear activities." This wording is interpreted by most observers as providing U.N. support for countries who want to ban their companies from investing in Iran's energy sector.	With certain exceptions likely to fulfill the nuclear deal, the EU bans almost all dealings with Iran's energy sector. Japanese and South Korean measures ban new energy projects in Iran and call for restraint on ongoing projects. South Korea in December 2011 cautioned its firms not to sell energy or petrochemical equipment to Iran. Both have cut oil purchases from Iran sharply.

Table 4. (Continued)

U.S. Sanctions	U.N. Sanctions	Implementation by EU and Some Allied Countries
Some exemptions are permitted for firms of countries that have “significantly reduced” purchases of Iranian oil each 180 days.		
Ban on Foreign Assistance: U.S. foreign assistance to Iran— other than purely humanitarian aid— is banned under §620A of the Foreign Assistance Act, which bans U.S. assistance to countries on the U.S. list of “state sponsors of terrorism.” Iran is also routinely denied direct U.S. foreign aid under the annual foreign operations appropriations acts (most recently in §7007 of division H of P.L. 111-8).	No U.N. equivalent	EU measures of July 27, 2010, ban grants, aid, and concessional loans to Iran. Also prohibit financing of enterprises involved in Iran’s energy sector. Japan and South Korea measures do not specifically ban aid or lending to Iran, but no such lending by these countries is under way.
Ban on Arms Exports to Iran: Iran is ineligible for U.S. arms exports under several laws, as discussed in the report.	Resolution 1929 (operative paragraph 8) bans all U.N. member states from selling or supplying to Iran major weapons systems, including tanks, armored vehicles, combat aircraft, warships, and most missile systems, or related spare parts or advisory services for such weapons systems.	EU sanctions include a comprehensive ban on sale to Iran of all types of military equipment, not just major combat systems. No similar Japan and South Korean measures announced, but neither has exported arms to Iran.

U.S. Sanctions	U.N. Sanctions	Implementation by EU and Some Allied Countries
Restriction on Exports to Iran of "Dual Use Items": Primarily under §6(j) of the Export Administration Act (P.L. 96-72) and §38 of the Arms Export Control Act, there is a denial of license applications to sell Iran goods that could have military applications.	The U.N. resolutions on Iran, cumulatively, ban the export of almost all dual-use items to Iran.	EU bans the sales of dual use items to Iran, in line with U.N. resolutions. Japan and S. Korea have announced full adherence to strict export control regimes when evaluating sales to Iran.
Sanctions Against International Lending to Iran: Under §1621 of the International Financial Institutions Act (P.L. 95-118), U.S. representatives to international financial institutions, such as the World Bank, are required to vote against loans to Iran by those institutions.	Resolution 1747 (oper. paragraph 7) requests, but does not mandate, that countries and international financial institutions refrain from making grants or loans to Iran, except for development and humanitarian purposes.	The July 27, 2010, measures prohibit EU members from providing grants, aid, and concessional loans to Iran, including through international financial institutions. No specific similar Japan or South Korea measures announced.
Sanctions Against Foreign Firms that Sell Weapons of Mass Destruction-Related Technology to Iran: As discussed in this report, several laws and regulations provide for sanctions against entities, Iranian or otherwise, that are determined to be involved in or supplying Iran's	Resolution 1737 (oper. paragraph 12) imposes a worldwide freeze on the assets and property of Iranian entities named in an Annex to the Resolution. Each subsequent resolution has expanded the list of Iranian entities subject to these sanctions.	The EU measures imposed July 27, 2010, commit the EU to freezing the assets of entities named in the U.N. resolutions, as well as numerous other named Iranian entities. Japan and South Korea froze assets of U.N.-sanctioned entities.

Table 4. (Continued)

U.S. Sanctions	U.N. Sanctions	Implementation by EU and Some Allied Countries
WMD programs (asset freezing, ban on transaction with the entity).		
Ban on Transactions with Terrorism Supporting Entities: Executive Order 13224 bans transactions with entities determined by the Administration to be supporting international terrorism. Numerous entities, including some of Iranian origin, have been so designated.	No direct equivalent, but Resolution 1747 (oper. paragraph 5) bans Iran from exporting any arms—a provision widely interpreted as trying to reduce Iran's material support to groups such as Lebanese Hezbollah, Hamas, Shiite militias in Iraq, and insurgents in Afghanistan.	No direct equivalent, but many of the Iranian entities named as blocked by the EU, Japan, and South Korea overlap or complement Iranian entities named as terrorism supporting by the United States.
Travel Ban on Named Iranians: CISADA and H.R. 1905 provide for a prohibition on travel to the U.S., blocking of U.S.-based property, and ban on transactions with Iranians determined to be involved in serious human rights abuses against Iranians since the June 12, 2009, presidential election there, or with persons selling Iran equipment to commit such abuses.	Resolution 1803 imposed a binding ban on international travel by several Iranians named in an Annex to the Resolution. Resolution 1929 extended that ban to additional Iranians, and forty Iranians are now subject to the ban. However, the Iranians subject to the travel ban are so subjected because of their involvement in Iran's WMD programs, not because of involvement in human rights abuses.	The EU sanctions announced July 27, 2010, contains an Annex of named Iranians subject to a ban on travel to the EU countries. An additional 60+ Iranians involved in human rights abuses were subjected to EU sanctions since. Japan and South Korea have announced bans on named Iranians.

U.S. Sanctions	U.N. Sanctions	Implementation by EU and Some Allied Countries
Restrictions on Iranian Shipping: Under Executive Order 13382, the U.S. Treasury Department has named Islamic Republic of Iran Shipping Lines and several affiliated entities as entities whose U.S.-based property is to be frozen.	Resolution 1803 and 1929 authorize countries to inspect cargoes carried by Iran Air and Islamic Republic of Iran Shipping Lines (IRISL)—or any ships in national or international waters—if there is an indication that the shipments include goods whose export to Iran is banned.	The EU measures announced July 27, 2010, bans Iran Air Cargo from access to EU airports. The measures also freeze the EU-based assets of IRISL and its affiliates. Insurance and re-insurance for Iranian firms is banned. Japan and South Korean measures took similar actions against IRISL and Iran Air.
Banking Sanctions: During 2006-2011, several Iranian banks have been named as proliferation or terrorism supporting entities under Executive Orders 13382 and 13224, respectively (see Table 5 at end of report). CISADA prohibits banking relationships with U.S. banks for any foreign bank that conducts transactions with Iran's Revolutionary Guard or with Iranian entities sanctioned under the various U.N. resolutions.	No direct equivalent However, two Iranian banks are named as sanctioned entities under the U.N. Security Council resolutions.	The EU froze Iran Central Bank assets January 23, 2012, and banned all transactions with Iranian banks unless authorized on October 15, 2012. Brussels-based SWIFT expelled sanctioned Iranian banks from the electronic payment transfer system. Japan and South Korea measures similar to the 2010 EU sanctions, with South Korea adhering to the same 40,000 Euro authorization requirement. Japan and S. Korea froze the assets of 15 Iranian banks; South Korea targeted Bank Mellat for freeze. Some measures by these allies likely to be eased to implement nuclear deal.

Table 4. (Continued)

U.S. Sanctions	U.N. Sanctions	Implementation by EU and Some Allied Countries
FY2012 Defense Authorization (P.L. 112-81) prevents U.S. accounts with foreign banks that process transactions with Iran's Central Bank (with specified exemptions). No direct equivalent, although, as discussed above, U.S. proliferations laws provide for sanctions against foreign entities that help Iran with its nuclear and ballistic missile programs.	Resolution 1929 (oper. paragraph 7) prohibits Iran from acquiring an interest in any country involving uranium mining, production, or use of nuclear materials, or technology related to nuclear-capable ballistic missiles. Paragraph 9 prohibits Iran from undertaking "any activity" related to ballistic missiles capable of delivering a nuclear weapon.	EU measures on July 27, 2010, require adherence to this provision of Resolution 1929.

Private-Sector Cooperation and Compliance

The imposition of sanctions on Iran by many governments has caused Iran to be viewed by many worldwide corporations as a "controversial market"—a market that carries political and reputational risks. On the other hand, travelers to Iran say many foreign products, including U.S. products, are readily available in Iran, suggesting that such products are being re-exported to Iran from neighboring countries. Examples of major non-U.S. companies that, prior to the JPA, had discontinued business with Iran include the following:

- ABB of Switzerland said in January 2010 it would cease doing business with Iran. Siemens of Germany followed suit in February 2010. Finemeccanica, a defense and transportation conglomerate of Italy, and Thyssen-Krupp, a German steelmaker, subsequently left the Iran market as well. Indian conglomerate Tata is ending its Iran business.
- Selling cars to Iran has not been sanctionable at any time, yet, in 2010, the following firms suspended such sales: Germany's Daimler (Mercedes-Benz) and Porsche; Toyota (Japan); Fiat (Italy); and South Korea's Hyundai and Kia Motors.
- As of 2007, BNP Paribas of France ceased pursuing new business in Iran, according to attorneys for the company.
- The State Department reported on September 30, 2010, that Hong Kong company NYK Line Ltd. had ended shipping business with Iran on any goods. On June 30, 2011, the Danish shipping giant Maersk said that it would no longer operate out of Iran's three largest ports. The firm's decision reportedly was based on the U.S. announcement on June 23, 2011, of sanctions on the operator of those ports, Tidewater Middle East Co., under Executive Order 13382.
- Well before Executive Order 13590 was issued (see above), one large oil services firm, Schlumberger, incorporated in the Netherlands Antilles, said it would wind down its business with Iran.[49]

Foreign Subsidiaries of U.S. Firms That Have Exited the Iran Market

Many foreign subsidiaries of U.S. firms had exited the Iran market voluntarily, before any of their business activities with Iran became sanctionable (for example sales to Iran of equipment that can be used in Iran's oil, gas, and petrochemicals sectors).

- Chemical manufacturer Huntsman announced in January 2010 its subsidiaries would halt sales to Iran.
- On January 11, 2005, Iran said it had contracted with U.S. company Halliburton and an Iranian company, Oriental Kish, to drill for gas in Phases 9 and 10 of South Pars. Halliburton reportedly provided $30 million to $35 million worth of services per year through Oriental Kish, leaving unclear whether Halliburton would be considered in violation of the U.S. trade and investment ban or the Iran Sanctions Act (ISA),[50] because the deals involved a subsidiary of Halliburton (Cayman Islands-registered Halliburton Products and Service, Ltd., based in Dubai). On April 10, 2007, Halliburton announced that its subsidiaries were no longer operating in Iran, as promised in January 2005.
- General Electric (GE) announced in February 2005 that it would seek no new business in Iran, and it reportedly wound down preexisting contracts by July 2008. GE was selling Iran equipment and services for hydroelectric, oil, and gas services. However, GE subsidiary sales of medical diagnostic products such as MRI machines, sold through Italian, Canadian, and French subsidiaries, are not generally sanctionable and are believed to be continuing.
- On March 1, 2010, Caterpillar Corp. said it had altered its policies to prevent foreign subsidiaries from selling equipment to independent dealers that have been reselling the equipment to Iran.[51] Ingersoll Rand, maker of air compressors and cooling systems, followed suit.[52]
- In April 2010, it was reported that foreign partners of several U.S. or other multinational accounting firms had cut their ties with Iran, including KPMG of the Netherlands, and local affiliates of U.S. firms PricewaterhouseCoopers and Ernst and Young.[53]
- Oilfield services firm Smith International said on March 1, 2010, it would stop sales to Iran by its subsidiaries. Another oil services firm, Flowserve, said its subsidiaries have voluntarily ceased new business with Iran as of 2006.[54] FMC Technologies took similar action in 2009, as did Weatherford[55] in 2008. However, in November 2013, Weatherford was fined by the Treasury Department for violating sanctions against Iran and other countries.

Foreign Firms Reportedly Remaining in the Iran Market

Still, many major firms continue to do business with Iran, including major consumer products companies of Europe and Asia. Some of the foreign firms that trade with Iran, such as Mitsui and Co. of Japan, Alstom of France, and Schneider Electric of France, are discussed in a March 7, 2010, *New York Times* article on foreign firms that do business with Iran and also receive U.S. contracts or financing. The *Times* article does not claim that these firms have violated any U.S. sanctions laws. Internet and communications-related foreign firms remaining in or having departed the Iranian market are discussed in the section below on human rights effects of sanctions.

Some foreign firms still active in Iran are subsidiaries of U.S. firms and some of them also received U.S. government contracts, grants, loans, or loan guarantees. They include:

- An Irish subsidiary of the Coca Cola Company, which provides syrup for the U.S.-brand soft drink to an Iranian distributor, Khoshgovar. Local versions of both Coke and of Pepsi (with Iranian-made syrups) are also marketed in Iran by distributors who licensed the recipes for those soft drinks before the Islamic revolution and before the trade ban was imposed on Iran.
- Via a Swiss-based subsidiary, Transammonia Corp. has helped Iran develop its exports of ammonia.
- Kansas-based Koch Industries may have sold equipment to Iran to be used in petrochemical plants (making methanol) and possibly oil refineries, until 2007— before such sales became subject to sanctions under ISA.[56]
- Some subsidiaries of U.S. energy equipment and energy-related shipping firms were in the Iranian market as late as 2010, including Natco Group,[57] Overseas Shipholding Group,[58] UOP (United Oil Products, a Honeywell subsidiary based in Britain),[59] Itron,[60] Fluor,[61] Parker Drilling, Vantage Energy Services,[62] PMFG, Ceradyne, Colfax, Fuel Systems Solutions, General Maritime Company, Ameron International Corporation, and World Fuel Services Corp. As of mid-2010 almost all energy sector-related sales to Iran are subject to sanctions and these companies have likely exited Iran's markets.

EFFECTIVENESS OF SANCTIONS ON IRAN

The following sections examine the effectiveness of sanctions on a variety of criteria and goals.

Effect on Iran's Nuclear Program Decisions and Intentions

Iran's acceptance of the JPA and progress in the talks on a comprehensive nuclear accord are widely considered evidence that sanctions helped produce a possible shift in Iran's nuclear policies. The JPA agreement came after the June 14, 2013, presidential election in Iran in which Iranians elected as president the relatively moderate mid-ranking cleric Hassan Rouhani, who ran on a platform of achieving an easing of sanctions and ending Iran's international isolation. The talks on a comprehensive solution on Iran's nuclear program between Iran and the "P5+1" countries (United States, Britain, France, Russia, China, and Germany) began in February 2014. the talks have not reached final agreement, but, based on reported progress in the negotiations, Iran and the P5+1 have extended the JPA twice—until November 24, 2014, and then until July 6, 2015. However, a comprehensive agreement, if reached, will likely have a duration of no more than 20 years. Director of National Intelligence James Clapper testified in his "Worldwide Threat Assessment" presentation to Congress on January 29, 2014, that Iran's ultimate nuclear intentions remain "unclear."

Effects on Iran's Defense Capabilities

A related question is whether sanctions have prevented Iran from acquiring advanced conventional weapons or technology or skills for weapons of mass destruction (WMD) or missile programs. Some U.S. officials have asserted that sanctions have complicated Iran's efforts to acquire key equipment for its enrichment program,[63] but not to the point where Iran has failed to advance its enrichment capabilities. Director of National Intelligence James Clapper has testified that Iran continues to expand the scale, reach, and sophistication of its ballistic missile arsenal. On March 16, 2014, Principal Deputy Assistant Secretary of State for International Security and Nonproliferation Vann Van Diepen said that Iran was still "very actively" creating front companies and engaging in other activity to conceal procurement.[64]

With respect to Iran's conventional military capabilities, sanctions might have eroded those aspects of Iran's conventional capabilities that are most dependent on foreign supplies. Resolution 1929 of June 2010 prohibited the sale to Iran of major combat systems, and there have been no reports of sales to Iran of tanks or combat aircraft since then. Iran's arsenal of these systems are aging and a failure to modernize likely reduces Iran's ability to project power. As an example, in early December 2014, Iran used 40 year-old aircraft (U.S.-supplied F-4 jets) to strike Islamic State targets in Iraq, near the Iranian border.

On the other hand, Iran's indigenous arms industry has grown over the past two decades, partly mitigating the limited foreign supplies of weaponry. Iran is able to produce some advanced conventional weaponry indigenously, including short range ballistic and cruise missiles. In addition, Iran might be acquiring some systems, such as smaller ships and small submarines, from foreign suppliers such as North Korea that are willing to disobey U.N. restrictions.[65]

Effects on Iran's Regional Influence

Another question is whether sanctions have weakened Iran's ability to accomplish its foreign policy objectives. To date, neither sanctions nor oil prices that have fallen nearly 50% since June 2014 appear to have materially reduced Iran's ability to arm militant movements in the Middle East and to provide military equipment and advisers to the embattled governments of Syria and Iraqi. In December 2014, one of Iran's Vice Presidents stated that Iran's economic support for Syria would continue uninterrupted despite the fall in oil prices since June 2014.[66] Iran reportedly also has continued to export arms to the Shiite rebel Houthi faction in Yemen, and to militant Palestinian Islamist factions, and has sought to supply arms to radical Shiite factions in Bahrain. Iran's assistance might have helped the Houthis expand their control of Yemen's capital, Sanaa, in January 2015 and force the resignation of President Abd Rabbu Mansur Al Hadi. Iran's arms exports contravene Resolution 1747, which bans Iran's exportation of arms.[67]

General Political Effects

Sanctions might have produced some political change in Iran. The support of Iranians seeking reintegration with the international community helped power the most moderate candidate, Rouhani, to a first round victory in the June 2013 presidential election. The Supreme Leader welcomed Rouhani's election and has publicly backed the JPA and subsequent negotiations on a comprehensive solution, while at the same time expressing skepticism about the prospects for an agreement.

No U.S. Administration has stated that sanctions on Iran are intended to bring about the change of Iran's regime. However, some Iran sanctions advocates have stated that outcome should be the goal of the sanctions. The major unrest in Iran in 2009 was, by all accounts, a response to repression and alleged fraud in the June 2009 re-election of Mahmoud Ahmadinejad as president—and not to international sanctions. Since 2012 there has been labor and other public unrest over escalating food prices and the fall of the value of Iran's currency, but the unrest has not been large or sustained.

Press reports indicate that Iranians were highly disappointed when no comprehensive nuclear deal was reached by the November 24, 2014, deadline (subsequently extended). Some experts assess that popular unrest could re-emerge if no comprehensive nuclear deal is reached by the new deadline of July 6, 2015, and sanctions are not eased more substantially.

Human Rights-Related Effects

Recent State Department human rights reports and reports of the U.N. Special Rapporteur on Iran's human rights practices assess that there has not been significant net improvement in Iran's human rights practices in recent years. President Rouhani has achieved the release of a few political prisoners and press reports say media freedoms have increased slightly since he took office, but executions have become more frequent.

Sanctions have apparently not reduced the regime's ability to monitor and censor use of the Internet, according to observers in and outside Iran. However, that capability might decrease because, as assessed by the Government Accountability Office (GAO) in a January 13, 2015, report (GAO-15-258R), no foreign firms were reported to have exported technologies to the Iranian government for blocking telecommunications by monitoring, filtering, or disrupting information and communication flows during November 8, 2013, and December 1, 2014. This GAO analysis suggests that firms that pledged to stop selling the Iranian government such equipment, including German telecommunications firm Siemens, Chinese Internet infrastructure firm Huawei, and South African firm, MTN Group, have done so. In October 2012, Eutelsat, a significant provider of satellite service to Iran's state broadcasting establishment, ended that relationship following EU sanctioning in March 2012 of the head of the Islamic Republic of Iran Broadcasting (IRIB), Ezzatollah Zarghami.

Economic Effects

Sanctions have taken a toll on Iran's economy, by all accounts, as indicated below.

- *GDP Decline*. Sanctions caused Iran to suffer its first gross domestic product (GDP) contraction in two decades—about 5% contraction in 2013. Under Secretary of the Treasury for Terrorism and Financial Intelligence David Cohen testified before the Senate Foreign Relations Committee on January 21, 2015, that Iran's economy is 15%-20% smaller than it would have been had post-2010 sanctions not been imposed. Many Iranian businesses have failed, the number of nonperforming loans held by Iranian banks increased to about 15%-30%,[68] and many employees in the private sector have gone unpaid or are subject to long delays in payments. The unemployment rate is about 20%, although the Iranian government reports the rate at 13%. The sanctions relief of the JPA has stabilized the economy modestly—Iran's economy achieved slight growth of about 1%- 1.5% for 2014, according to the International Monetary Fund.
- *Oil Exports*. As noted in **Table 2**, sanctions drove Iran's crude oil sales down about 60% from the 2.5 mbd of sales in 2011, reducing Iran's crude oil sales revenue from $100 billion in 2011 to about $35 billion in 2013 and even less in 2014—in part because oil prices fell sharply in the second half of 2014. The JPA, still in effect, caps Iran's crude oil exports at *about* 1 mbd.[69] When it was submitted to the *Majles* in December 2014, Iran's 2015 budget was initially based on an oil price of $72 per barrel and anticipated $34 billion in oil revenues for 2015, but a budget revision in January 2015 lowered that estimate to assume $40 per barrel average price and oil revenues in 2015 of only about $20 billion.
- *Falling Oil Production*. When the JPA began implementation in early 2014, Iran's oil production stood at about 2.6-2.8 mbd down from nearly 4.0 mbd at the end of 2011.[70] Iran has tried to avoid further production cuts by storing millions of barrels of unsold crude oil on tankers in the Persian Gulf and by building additional storage tanks on

shore. U.S. officials say that production has held steady at the early 2014 level and that Iran has largely succeeded in preventing damage to shut or inactive wells.

- *Hard Currency Inaccessible.* Not only have Iran's oil exports fallen by volume, but Iran is not paid in hard currency for its oil (other than the $700 million per month agreed under the JPA) and cannot access most of its hard currency held in accounts abroad. Iran's hard currency reserves were estimated in late 2013 to be about $100 billion. Of that, about $80 billion cannot be repatriated due to compliance by banks with U.S. sanctions.
- *Currency Decline.* Sanctions caused the value of the rial on unofficial markets to decline about 56% from January 2012 until January 2014. The unofficial rate is about 37,000 to the dollar, and the government has repeatedly adjusted the official rate (currently about 27,000 to the dollar) to reduce the spread between it and the unofficial rate.
- *Inflation.* The drop in value of the currency caused inflation to accelerate during 2011-2013. The Iranian Central Bank acknowledged an inflation rate of 45% in July 2013, but many economists asserted that the actual inflation rate was between 50% and 70%. The sanctions relief of the JPA has helped reduce that to about 35%, and it is projected to fall further to about 25% by March 2015.[71] Some assert that inflation was fed by the policies of Ahmadinejad, particularly the substitution of subsidies with cash payments, rather than the effect of sanctions.
- *Industrial Production.* Iran's economy is widely assessed as industrializing, but the manufacturing sector remains dependent on imported parts. The currency decline and financial sanctions have created difficulties for that sector. Many Iranian manufacturers are unable to obtain credit and must pre-pay, often through time-consuming and circuitous mechanisms, to obtain parts from abroad. This difficulty is particularly acute in the automotive sector; Iran's production of automobiles fell by about 40% from 2011 to 2013. The JPA has benefitted the auto sector because of the sanctions easing on that sector, but press reports say that manufacturing overall has rebounded only modestly since the JPA implementation began. The JPA's easing of sanctions on Iran's sales of petrochemicals and on its automotive manufacturing sector enable Iran to earn only $378 million from these sectors in the first half of 2014. That is far below

the $2.5 billion that diplomats predicted would be earned by these sectors.[72]

Iran's Economic Coping Strategies

Iran has had moderate success mitigating the economic effect of sanctions, primarily by implementing austerity measures and promoting non-oil exports. Iran has key inherent economic strengths, including an educated workforce—including the highest percentage of engineering graduates in the world—that is familiar with the use of the Internet and other modern technologies.

Promoting Non-Oil Exports. Iran's primary strategy has been to substitute for crude oil sales by increasing sales of non-oil products. Some of the non-oil exports that have grown in recent years include minerals, cement, urea fertilizer, and other agricultural and basic industrial goods. The main customers for Iran's non-oil exports reportedly are countries in the immediate neighborhood. As of 2014, non-oil exports generate about two-thirds of the revenue required to fund Iran's imports of goods and services, greatly reducing the centrality of oil exports to Iran's budget.[73]

Oil Products/Condensate Sales. Iran has sought to increase sales of oil products such as petrochemicals and condensates, which are allowed under the JPA, to compensate for some lost crude oil export revenue. In 2014, Iran exported to its main oil customers the equivalent of about 200,000 barrels per day of crude oil in condensates,[74] producing about $4.7 billion in additional revenue (but not in the form of retrievable hard currency) in the first half of 2014 as compared to the latter half of 2013.[75]

Reallocation of Investment Funds and Import Substitution. Iranian manufacturers have increased production of some goods as Iranians cut back on purchases of imported goods. This trend is considered positive by Iranian economists—and some Iranian political leaders including Supreme Leader Khamene'i—that have long maintained that Iran should expand domestic manufacturing capabilities and reduce dependence on oil revenues and imported goods. In addition, some private funds are going into the Tehran stock exchange and hard assets, such as property. However, many of these trends generally benefit the urban elite.

Subsidy Reductions. In 2007, Ahmadinejad's government instituted a program to wean the population off of generous subsidies by compensating families with cash payments of about $40 per month. Gasoline prices began to run on a tiered system that brought them closer to regional prices—and far above the subsidized price of 40 cents per gallon. However, as sanctions began to crimp government revenues, in late 2012 Ahmadinejad postponed "phase two" of the subsidy phase-out effort. In April 2014, Rouhani instituted phase two by raising gasoline prices further and limiting the cash payments to only those families who could claim financial hardship. On December 1, 2014, subsidies on bread were reduced and bread prices rose 30%. Rouhani also has improved collections of taxes and of price increases charged for electricity and natural gas utilities.[76]

Import Restrictions. To conserve hard currency, Iran has reduced the supply of hard currency to importers of luxury goods, such as cars or cellphones, in order to maintain hard currency supplies to importers of essential goods. As noted above, the government has sought to align the official "reference" rate with the free market (or "black market") exchange rate.

Effect on Energy Sector Long-Term Development

Sanctions have been intended, in part, to reduce Iran's oil and gas production capacity over the longer term by denying Iran the outside technology and investment to maintain, let alone boost, production. U.S. officials estimated in 2011 that Iran had lost $60 billion in investment in the sector as numerous major firms have announced pullouts from some of their Iran projects, declined to make further investments, or resold their investments to other companies. Iran says it needs $130 billion-$145 billion in new investment by 2020 to keep oil production capacity from falling.[77] Of that amount, further development of the large South Pars gas field alone requires $100 billion.[78]

Even though some international firms remain invested in Iran's energy sector, observers at key energy fields in Iran say there is little evidence of foreign company development activity sighted at Iran's various oil and gas development sites, as discussed in **Table 5**. The declining foreign activity appears to be a product of international firms' decisions not to risk triggering U.S. sanctions. Some of the ongoing investments have avoided sanctions either through Administration waivers or invocation of the "special rule" (see above). Other ongoing foreign investment projects have not been determined as ISA violations and may be under State Department investigation.

Table 5. Post-1999 Major Investments/Major Development Projects in Iran's Energy Sector

Date	Field/Project	Company(ies)/Status (If Known)	Value	Output/Goal
Feb. 1999	Doroud (oil) (Energy Information Agency, Department of Energy, August 2006.) Total and ENI exempted from sanctions on September 30 because of pledge to exit Iran market	Total (France)/ENI (Italy)	$1 billion	205,000 bpd
April 1999	Balal (oil) ("Balal Field Development in Iran Completed," World Market Research Centre, May 17, 2004.)	Total/ Bow Valley (Canada)/ENI	$300 million	40,000 bpd
Nov. 1999	Soroush and Nowruz (oil) ("News in Brief: Iran." Middle East Economic Digest, (MEED) January 24, 2003.) Royal Dutch exempted from sanctions on 9/30 because of pledge to exit Iran market	Royal Dutch Shell (Netherlands)/Japex (Japan)	$800 million	190,000 bpd
April 2000	Anaran bloc (oil) (MEED Special Report, December 16, 2005, pp. 48-50.)	Norsk Hydro and Statoil (Norway) and Gazprom and Lukoil (Russia) No production to date; Statoil and Norsk exited.	$105 million	65,000

Table 5. (Continued)

Date	Field/Project	Company(ies)/Status (If Known)	Value	Output/Goal
July 2000	Phase 4 and 5, South Pars (gas) ENI exempted 9/30 based on pledge to exit Iran market	ENI Gas onstream as of Dec. 2004	$1.9 billion	2 billion cu. ft./day (cfd)
March 2001	Caspian Sea oil exploration—construction of submersible drilling rig for Iranian partner (IPR Strategic Business Information Database, March 11, 2001.)	GVA Consultants (Sweden)	$225 million	NA
June 2001	Darkhovin (oil) ("Darkhovin Production Doubles." Gulf Daily News, May 1, 2008.) ENI told CRS in April 2010 it would close out all Iran operations by 2013. ENI exempted from sanctions on 9/30, as discussed above	ENI Field in production	$1 billion	100,000 bpd
May 2002	Masjid-e-Soleyman (oil) ("CNPC Gains Upstream Foothold." MEED, September 3, 2004.)	Sheer Energy (Canada)/China National Petroleum Company (CNPC). Local partner is Naftgaran Engineering	$80 million	25,000 bpd

Date	Field/Project	Company(ies)/Status (If Known)	Value	Output/Goal
Sept. 2002	Phase 9 + 10, South Pars (gas) ("OIEC Surpasses South Korean Company in South Pars." IPR Strategic Business Information Database, November 15, 2004.)	LG Engineering and Construction Corp. (now known as GS Engineering and Construction Corp., South Korea) On stream as of early 2009	$1.6 billion	2 billion cfd
October 2002	Phase 6, 7, 8, South Pars (gas) (Source: Statoil, May 2011) Field began producing late 2008; operational control handed to NIOC in 2009. Statoil exempted from sanctions on 9/30/2010 after pledge to exit Iran market.	Statoil (Norway)	$750 million	3 billion cfd
January 2004	Azadegan (oil)—South and North October 15, 2010: Inpex announced it would exit the Azadegan project entirely by selling its 10% stake; "special rule" exempting it from ISA investigation invoked November 17, 2010. China National Petroleum Corp. took a majority stake in South and North Azadegan fields in January 2009.	Inpex (Japan) and CNPC (China)	$200 million (Inpex stake); China $2.5 billion	260,000 bpd

Table 5. (Continued)

Date	Field/Project	Company(ies)/Status (If Known)	Value	Output/Goal
	However, on April 29, 2014, Iran cancelled the South Azadegan contract citing CNPC for performing “no effective work” since taking the stake in 2009. Industry sources say CNPC likely to also lose North Azadegan project also. (Iran-CNPC Breakup: Tehran Eyes the West, Christian Science Monitor, May 5, 2014.			
August 2004	Tusan Block Oil found in block in Feb. 2009, but not in commercial quantity, according to the firm. (“Iran-Petrobras Operations.” APS Review Gas Market Trends, April 6, 2009; “Brazil’s Petrobras Sees Few Prospects for Iran Oil,” (http://www.reuters.com/ article/idUSN0317110720090703.)	Petrobras (Brazil)	$178 million	No production
October 2004	Yadavaran (oil) Christian Science Monitor reports May 5, 2014, (op.cit.) that Iran says Sinopec has “experienced problems with regards to progress” on the field, which also extends into Iraq. But International Oil Daily quotes company on May 7, 2014, as saying project is on course to produce an initial 85,000 bpd by the end of 2014.	Sinopec (China), deal finalized Dec. 9, 2007	$2 billion	300,000 bpd

Date	Field/Project	Company(ies)/Status (If Known)	Value	Output/Goal
2005	Saveh bloc (oil) GAO report, cited below	PTT (Thailand)	?	?
June 2006	Garmsar bloc (oil) Deal finalized in June 2009 ("China's Sinopec signs a deal to develop oil block in Iran—report," Forbes, 20 June 2009, http://www.forbes.com/feeds/afx/2006/06/20/afx2829188.html.)	Sinopec (China)	$20 million	?
July 2006	Arak Refinery expansion (GAO reports; Fimco FZE Machinery website; http://www.fimco.org/index.php?option=com_content&task=view&id=70&Itemid=78.)	Sinopec (China); JGC (Japan). Work may have been taken over or continued by Hyundai Heavy Industries (S. Korea)	$959 million (major initial expansion; extent of Hyundai work unknown)	Expansion to produce 250,000 bpd
Sept. 2006	Khorramabad block (oil) Seismic data gathered, but no production is planned. (Statoil factsheet, May 2011)	Norsk Hydro and Statoil (Norway).	$49 million	?
Dec. 2006	North Pars Gas Field (offshore gas). Includes gas purchases Work crews reportedly pulled from the project in early-mid 2011. ("China Curbs Iran Energy Work" Reuters, September 2, 2011)	China National Offshore Oil Co.	$16 billion	3.6 billion cfd
Feb. 2007	LNG Tanks at Tombak Port Contract to build three LNG tanks at Tombak, 30 miles north of Assaluyeh Port.	Daelim (S. Korea)	$320 million	200,000 ton capacity

Table 5. (Continued)

Date	Field/Project	Company(ies)/Status (If Known)	Value	Output/Goal
	(May not constitute "investment" as defined in pre-2010 version of ISA, because that definition did not specify LNG as "petroleum resource" of Iran.) "Central Bank Approves $900 Million for Iran LNG Project." Tehran Times, June 13, 2009.			
Feb. 2007	Phase 13, 14—South Pars (gas) Deadline to finalize as May 20, 2009, apparently not met; firms submitted revised proposals to Iran in June 2009. (http://www.rigzone.com/news/ article.asp?a_id=77040&hmpn=1.) State Department said on September 30, 2010, that Royal Dutch Shell and Repsol will not pursue this project any further	Royal Dutch Shell, Repsol (Spain)	$4.3 billion	?
March 2007	Esfahan refinery upgrade ("Daelim, Others to Upgrade Iran's Esfahan Refinery." Chemical News and Intelligence, March 19, 2007.)	Daelim (S. Korea)		NA
July 2007	Phase 22, 23, 24—South Pars (gas) Pipeline to transport Iranian gas to Turkey, and on to Europe and building three power plants in Iran. Contract not finalized to date.	Turkish Petroleum Company (TPAO)	$12. billion	2 billion cfd

Date	Field/Project	Company(ies)/Status (If Known)	Value	Output/Goal
Dec. 2007	Golshan and Ferdowsi onshore and offshore gas and oil fields and LNG plant contract modified but reaffirmed December 2008 (GAO reports; Oil Daily, January 14, 2008.)	Petrofield Subsidiary of SKS Ventures (Malaysia)	$15 billion	3.4 billion cfd of gas/250,000 bpd of oil
2007 (unspec.)	Jofeir Field (oil) GAO report cited below. Belarusneft, a subsidiary of Belneftekhim, sanctioned under ISA on March 29, 2011. Naftiran sanctioned on September 29, 2010, for this and other activities.	Belarusneft (Belarus) under contract to Naftiran. No production to date	$500 million	40,000 bpd
2008	Dayyer Bloc (Persian Gulf, offshore, oil) GAO reports	Edison (Italy)	$44 million	?
Feb. 2008	Lavan field (offshore natural gas) GAO report cited below invested. PGNiG invested, but delays caused Iran to void PGNiG contract in December 2011. Project to be implemented by Iranian firms. (Fars News, December 20, 2011)	PGNiG (Polish Oil and Gas Company, Poland)	$2 billion	
March 2008	Danan Field (on-shore oil) "PVEP Wins Bid to Develop Danan Field." Iran Press TV, March 11, 2008	Petro Vietnam Exploration and Production Co. (Vietnam)	?	?
April 2008	Iran's Kish gas field Includes pipeline from Iran to Oman	Oman (co-financing of project)	$7 billion	1 billion cfd

Table 5. (Continued)

Date	Field/Project	Company(ies)/Status (If Known)	Value	Output/Goal
April 2008	Moghan 2 (onshore oil and gas, Ardebil province) Jan. 7, 2014, GAO report says INA has withdrawn from Iran.	INA (Croatia)	$40-$140 million (dispute over size)	?
2008	Kermanshah petrochemical plant (new construction) GAO reports	Uhde (Germany)		300,000 metric tons/yr
June 2008	Resalat Oilfield Status of work unclear	Amona (Malaysia). Joined in June 2009 by CNOOC and another China firm, COSL.	$1.5 billion	47,000 bpd
January 2009	Bushehr Polymer Plants Production of polyethelene at two polymer plants in Bushehr Province. GAO Jan. 7, 2014, report says Sasol has withdrawn from Iran.	Sasol (South Africa)	?	Capacity is 1 million tons per year. Products are exported from Iran.
March 2009	Phase 12 South Pars (gas)—Incl. LNG terminal construction and Farsi Block gas field/Farzad-B bloc.	Taken over by Indian firms (Oil and Natural Gas Corp. of India, Oil India Ltd., India Oil Corp. Ltd. in 2007); may also include minor stakes by Sonanagol (Angola) and PDVSA (Venezuela)..	$8 billion from Indian firms/$1.5 billion Sonangol/$780 million PDVSA	20 million tonnes of LNG annually by 2012

Date	Field/Project	Company(ies)/Status (If Known)	Value	Output/Goal
August 2009	Abadan refinery Upgrade and expansion; building a new refinery at Hormuz on the Persian Gulf coast	Sinopec	up to $6 billion if new refinery is built	
Oct. 2009	South Pars Gas Field—Phases 6-8, Gas Sweetening Plant CRS conversation with Embassy of S. Korea in Washington, D.C, July 2010 Contract signed but then abrogated by S. Korean firm	G and S Engineering and Construction (South Korea)	$1.4 billion	
Nov. 2009	South Pars: Phase 12—Part 2 and Part 3 ("Italy, South Korea To Develop South Pars Phase 12." Press TV (Iran), November 3, 2009, http://www.presstv.com/pop/Print/?id=110308.)	Daelim (S. Korea)—Part 2; Tecnimont (Italy)—Part 3	$4 billion ($2 bn each part)	
Feb. 2010	South Pars: Phase 11 Drilling was to begin in March 2010, but CNPC pulled out in October 2012. (Economist Intelligence Unit "Oil Sanctions on Iran: Cracking Under Pressure." 2012)	CNPC (China)	$4.7 billion	

Table 5. (Continued)

Date	Field/Project	Company(ies)/Status (If Known)	Value	Output/Goal
2011 Dec. 2011	Azar Gas Field Gazprom contract voided in late 2011 by Iran due to Gazprom's unspecified failure to fulfill its commitments. Zagheh Oil Field Preliminary deal signed December 18, 2011(Associated Press, December 18, 2011)	Gazprom (Russia) Tatneft (Russia)	$1 billion	55,000 barrels per day within five years

Sources: As noted in table, as well as CRS conversations with officials of the State Department Bureau of Economics, and officials of embassies of the parent government of some of the listed companies. Some information comes from various GAO reports, the latest of which was January 13, 2015 (GAO-15-258R).

Note: CRS has neither the mandate,the authority, nor the means to determine which of these projects, if any, might constitute a violation of the Iran Sanctions Act. CRS has no way to confirm the precise status of any of the announced investments; some investments may have been resold to other firms or terms altered since agreement. In virtually all cases, such investments and contracts represent private agreements between Iran and its instruments and the investing firms, and firms are not necessarily required to confirm or publicly release the terms of their arrangements with Iran. Reported $20 million+ investments in oil and gas fields, refinery upgrades, and major project leadership are included in this table. Responsibility for a project to develop Iran's energy sector is part of ISA investment definition.

Some foreign investors have left the Iran market entirely, and their work has been picked up by domestic companies, particularly those controlled or linked to the Revolutionary Guard (IRGC). Foreign firms are reluctant to partner with IRGC firms as international sanctions have increasingly targeted the IRGC. The energy companies still active in Iran, particularly the Iranian firms, are reportedly not as technically capable as the international firms that have withdrawn.

The JPA does not ease sanctions against investing in Iran's energy sector. However, there are numerous reports of international firms' discussing with Iranian energy officials future investment subsequent to a comprehensive nuclear deal. Iran is reportedly working actively to lure foreign investors back into the sector, including by hiring back many of the former officials that successfully negotiated past investments.

Others maintain that Iran's gas sector can compensate for declining oil exports, although Iran has used its gas development primarily to reinject into its oil fields rather than to export. Iran exports about 3.6 trillion cubic feet of gas, primarily to Turkey and Armenia. On the other hand, sanctions have rendered Iran unable to develop a liquefied natural gas (LNG) export business. EU sanctions have also derailed several gas ventures, including BP-NIOC joint venture in the Rhum gas field, 200 miles off the Scotland coast, and inclusion of Iran in planned gas pipeline projects to Europe.

Effect on Gasoline Availability and Importation

In March 2010, well before the enactment of CISADA, several suppliers announced that they had stopped or would stop selling gasoline to Iran.[79] Others have ceased since the enactment of CISADA. Some observers say that gasoline deliveries to Iran fell from about 120,000 barrels per day before CISADA to about 30,000 barrels per day immediately thereafter, although importation later increased to about 50,000 barrels per day. The GAO report of January 7, 2014, identified no foreign firms selling Iran gasoline between October 1, 2012, and November 7, 2013, suggesting that a phaseout of gasoline subsidies had reduced demand for gasoline.

Table 6. Firms That Sold Gasoline to Iran

Vitol of Switzerland (notified GAO it stopped selling to Iran in early 2010)
Trafigura of Switzerland (notified GAO it stopped selling to Iran in November 2009)
Glencore of Switzerland (notified GAO it stopped selling in September 2009)

Table 6. (Continued)

Total of France (notified GAO it stopped sales to Iran in May 2010)
Reliance Industries of India (notified GAO it stopped sales to Iran in May 2009)
Petronas of Malaysia (said on April 15, 2010, it had stopped sales to Iran)80
Lukoil of Russia was reported to have ended sales to Iran in April 2010,81 although some reports continue that Lukoil affiliates are supplying Iran.
Royal Dutch Shell of the Netherlands (notified GAO it stopped sales in October 2009)
Kuwait's Independent Petroleum Group (told U.S. officials it stopped selling gasoline to Iran as of September 2010)82
Tupras of Turkey (stopped selling to Iran as of May 2011, according to the State Department)
British Petroleum of United Kingdom, Shell, Q8, Total, and OMV are no longer selling aviation fuel to Iran Air, according to U.S. State Department officials on May 24, 2011
A UAE firm, Golden Crown Petroleum FZE, told the author in April 2011 that, as of June 29, 2010, it no longer lease vessels for the purpose of shipping petroleum products from or through Iran
Munich Re, Allianz, Hannover Re (Germany) were providing insurance and re-insurance for gasoline shipments to Iran. However, they reportedly have exited the market for insuring gasoline shipments for Iran83
Lloyd's (Britain). The major insurer had been the main company insuring Iranian gas (and other) shipping, but reportedly ended that business in July 2010.
According to the State Department on May 24, 2011, Linde of Germany said it had stopped supplying gas liquefaction technology to Iran, contributing to Iran's decision to suspend its LNG program.
Some of the firms sanctioned by the Administration on May 24, 2011, (discussed above), may still be providing service to Iran, including PCCI (Jersey/Iran); Associated Shipbroking (Monaco); and Petroleos de Venezuela (Venezuela). Tanker Pacific representatives told the author in January 2013 that the firm had stopped dealing with Iran in April 2010 but may have been deceived by IRISL into a transaction with Iran after that time.
Zhuhai Zhenrong, Unipec, ZhenHua Oil, and China Oil of China. Zhuhai Zhenrong is no longer selling Iran gasoline, according to the January 7, 2014, GAO report (GAO-14-281R). ZhenHua, a subsidiary of arms manufacturer Norinco, supplied one third of Iran's gasoline in March 2010, but there is little information on supplies since.

Emirates National Oil Company of UAE has been reported by GAO to still be selling to Iran, as have three other UAE energy traders, FAL, Royal Oyster Group, and Speedy Ship (UAE/Iran).
Hin Leong Trading of Singapore may still be selling gasoline to Iran, as might Kuo Oil of Singapore.

Source: CRS conversations with various firms, GAO reports, various press reports.

Humanitarian Effects/Air Safety

Humanitarian-related effects of sanctions have been noted in several sectors, and some of the sanctions easing in the interim nuclear deal are intended to mitigate these effects. Press reports have mounted since mid-2012 that sanctions are hurting the population's ability to obtain Western-made medicines, such as expensive chemo-therapy medicines. Some of the scarcity is caused by banks' refusal to finance such sales, even though doing so is technically allowed under all applicable sanctions. Some observers say the Iranian government is exaggerating reports of medicine shortages to generate opposition to the sanctions. Other accounts say that Iranians, particularly those with connections to the government, are taking advantage of medicine shortages by cornering the market for importing key medicines.

Some human rights and other groups have suggested potential solutions. The JPA provides for the international community to provide enhanced financial channels for Iran to import medicines, although the exact mechanism has generally been limited to a U.S.-led information campaign for international banks. In July 2014, the U.S. Administration asked European medical firms to expedite sales of medical goods to Iran, and the Administration reportedly cleared banks in Switzerland and Japan to process financing for the shipments.[84]

In the aviation sector, some Iranian pilots have complained publicly and stridently that U.S. sanctions are causing Iran's passenger airline fleet to deteriorate to the point of jeopardizing safety. Since the U.S. trade ban was imposed in 1995, 1,700 passengers and crew of Iranian aircraft have been killed in air accidents, although it is not clear how many of the crashes, if any, were due to difficultly in acquiring U.S. spare parts.[85] The JPA provides for new sales of civilian aircraft parts to address this issue and Boeing and GE have applied for and obtained licenses to sell spare part and operating manuals to Iranian airlines.

Other reports say that pollution in Tehran and other big cities has worsened because Iran is making gasoline itself with methods that cause more impurities than imported gasoline. As noted above, Iran's efforts to deal with environment hazards and problems might be hindered by denial of World Bank lending for that purpose.

JPA Sanctions Easing and Additional Sanctions Debate

The further easing of sanctions, or imposition of additional sanctions, might depend at least in part on the outcome of the ongoing P5+1-Iran talks on a comprehensive nuclear settlement.

Sanctions Easing under the JPA

U.S. officials have said that the JPA requires "limited, temporary, targeted, and reversible" easing of international sanctions. And, despite such developments as the visits to Iran of business delegations, U.S. officials say there has not been any significant decline in international compliance with the sanctions regime since JPA implementation began in January 2014.

Under the JPA:[86]

- Iran's oil exports are to remain at the level of about 1 million barrels per day. This implies that Iran's current oil customers will not reduce their oil purchases from Iran "significantly" while the JPA is in effect. Such reduction is a requirement to avoid sanctions on the banks of those countries under Section 1245 of P.L. 112-81. To avoid penalizing these oil buyers, the Administration has exercised waiver authority under Section 1245(d)(1) of the National Defense Authorization Act for FY2012 (P.L. 112-81) and Section 1244c(1) of the Iran Freedom and Counter-Proliferation Act of 2012 ("IFCA," Title XII, subtitle D, of the FY2013 National Defense Authorization Act, P.L. 112-239); the Administration has said it will not impose sanctions on foreign banks under Executive Orders 13622, 13645, and 13382 and related regulations. Waivers of Section 302(a) of the Iran Threat Reduction and Syria Human Rights Act of 2012 (P.L. 112-

158) and of Section 5(A)(7) of the Iran Sanctions Act (P.L. 104-172, as amended) have been issued to permit transactions with Iran's national oil company (NIOC). The European Union has based its own regulations to allow shipping insurers to provide insurance for ships carrying oil from Iran.[87] *The waivers and sanctions suspensions under the JPA do not permit U.S. companies to trade in such goods with Iran.*

- Iran is able to repatriate $700 million per month in oil sales proceeds while the JPA is in effect. As of December 2014, Iran has been able to access a total of about $8.4 billion from this JPA provision. Iran is also able to access about $65 million per month to make tuition payments for Iranian students abroad (paid directly to the educational institutions). The waiver authority under Section 1245(d)(1), discussed above, enables Iran to receive these proceeds directly.
- The JPA permits Iran to resume sales of petrochemicals and trading in gold and other precious metals, and to resume transactions with foreign firms involved in Iran's automotive manufacturing sector. The Administration estimated the value of the revenue Iran will accrue from these changes would be about $2.5 billion in a six month period. However, Iran apparently earned far less from these activities than expected in the first half of 2014 (less than $400 million earned compared to $2 billion estimated for that period). To enable these transactions, the Administration suspended application of Executive Orders 13622 and 13645, several provisions of U.S. trade regulations with Iran, and several sections of IFCA.
- The parties to the JPA pledged to facilitate humanitarian transactions that are already allowed by U.S. and partner country laws, such as sales of medicine to Iran, but which many banks refuse to finance. Steps to facilitate humanitarian shipments to Iran are discussed above. The United States also committed to license safety-related repairs and inspections inside Iran for certain Iranian airlines. Such licensing is specifically permitted under U.S. trade regulations written pursuant to Executive Order 12959 (May 6, 1995) and Executive Order 13059 (August 19, 1997), discussed above. To implement this commitment, the Administration issued a new "Statement of Licensing Policy" to enable U.S. aircraft manufacturers to sell the appropriate equipment to Iranian airlines. Several Iranian airlines, including Iran Air, have been designated for sanctions under Executive Order 13382, which blocks U.S.-based property of entities designated as "proliferation

supporters." The Administration has suspended application of Executive Order 13382 and certain provisions of U.S. trade regulations with Iran to allow the supply of equipment to Iran Air.

- The P5+1 and Iran agreed to set up a Joint Commission whose tasks will include evaluating P5+1 compliance with its commitments for sanctions relief. The commission is empowered to consider Iranian complaints about foreign firms that Tehran believes have been sanctioned inappropriately for commercial interactions with Iran.
- The JPA requires that the P5+1 "not impose new nuclear-related sanctions," if Iran abides by its commitments under this deal, to the extent permissible within their political systems.[88]

Sanctions in the Context of Ongoing Nuclear Talks

A comprehensive nuclear deal between Iran and the P5+1 will presumably require a broad easing of international sanctions against Iran. The JPA indicates that "nuclear-related" sanctions would be eased in a comprehensive deal, but in practice many sanctions are related to Iran's nuclear program even if they are not specifically proliferation-related. Iran apparently is demanding that a comprehensive agreement ease those sanctions imposed in recent years (since Resolution 1929 was adopted in June 2010) for the specific purpose of compelling Iran to negotiate limits to its nuclear program. Those post-Resolution 1929 sanctions include those that limit its oil and oil products exports, those that restrict its use of the international financial system, and those that prevent it from repatriating hard currency. Iran reportedly has accepted that a nuclear deal will not ease sanctions addressing purely human rights and Iranian foreign policy issues. However, there are several outstanding questions:

- The P5+1 continue to insist that sanctions be eased stepwise as Iran complies with the terms of a comprehensive nuclear deal, whereas Iran reportedly seeks immediate implementation of all agreed sanctions relief.
- There are questions whether Iran will be satisfied with an initial suspension of sanctions rather than outright lifting. The Administration has said that, at least initially, it would use its waiver and other authorities to implement the agreed sanctions relief[89] and, after testing Iran's compliance over a period of perhaps one year, ask

Congress to repeal or terminate sanctions imposed by statue.[90] However, some Iranian leaders, particularly Supreme Leader Khamene'i, continue to express distrust that the United States will implement permanent sanctions relief. (The requirements for lifting sanctions are discussed in this report and in CRS Report R43311, *Iran: U.S. Economic Sanctions and the Authority to Lift Restrictions*, by Dianne E. Rennack.)[91]

- There is a question whether a comprehensive nuclear accord will provide for a lifting of U.S. sanctions (Iran Sanctions Act) on longer-term investment in Iran's energy sector.
- There is question of whether there will be a congressional vote on any comprehensive agreement reached. The Administration argues that an Iran nuclear deal will constitute an executive agreement—U.S. participation in a multilateral agreement with Iran—and not represent a U.S.-Iran or other "treaty" requiring Senate advice and consent. The Administration has opposed legislation that would require formal submission to Congress of the comprehensive agreement for approval or disapproval. Such a provision was contained in S. 2650 in the 113th Congress, and incorporated into draft legislation in the 114th Congress (Nuclear Weapon Free Iran Act).[92]

Possible Additional Sanctions While P5+1-Iran Talks Continue

A major issue is whether the 114th Congress might seek to enact additional sanctions while P5+1 Iran talks on a comprehensive accord are continuing. The potential for congressional passage of such legislation has increased in the 114th Congress because Senate Majority Leader Mitch McConnell has expressed support for such legislation. Supporters of additional sanctions express doubts that the negotiating process will produce a result that ensures that Iran's nuclear program can only be used for peaceful purposes and argue that the threat of additional sanctions—even if such sanctions would not take effect while new talks are going on—could prod Iran into agreeing to a deal that Congress considers acceptable.

In his January 21, 2015, State of the Union message, President Obama has stated that he will veto any new Iran sanctions legislation while talks continue. The Administration argues that imposing new sanctions during the talks—even if actual penalties would not go into effect while negotiations are going on—will cause Iran to walk away from talks and fracture the international coalition that imposed Iran sanctions.[93] The potential for fracturing the coalition was underscored in January 2015 in comments by visiting British

Prime Minister David Cameron and an editorial in the *Washington Post* by three top European diplomats.[94] Iran's Foreign Minister Mohammad Javad Zarif has repeatedly said that any U.S. imposition of new sanctions during the JPA period would void the deal, even if such sanctions do not take effect while talks are going on.

113th Congress: H.R. 850 and S. 1881

It is possible that any new Iran sanctions legislation would be modeled on two bills that received varying degrees of consideration in the 113th Congress. One is S. 1881, the "Nuclear Weapon Free Iran Act of 2013," which was introduced on December 19, 2013. Its operative provisions were similar to those of H.R. 850, a House bill that was passed 400-20 in July 2013.

- Both bills contain virtually identical provisions to require those countries that have exemptions allowing them to pay Iran's Central Bank for oil to accelerate their Iran oil import reductions to an aggregate cut of an additional 1 million barrels per day within one year of enactment. Countries that do not "dramatically reduce" their Iran oil buys would lose their exemptions.
- Both bills would add sectors of the Iranian economy with which transactions would be subject to sanctions (under IFCA; P.L. 112-239). H.R. 850 references the automotive and mining sectors; S. 1881 references the shipbuilding, construction, engineering, and mining sectors—defining them, along with the energy and shipping sectors, as "strategic sectors."
- H.R. 850 authorizes, but does not mandate, sanctions for conducting financial transaction with Iran's Central Bank or other sanctioned Iranian banks for trade with Iran in any goods.
- Both bills would sanction foreign banks that help Iran exchange its foreign currency abroad.
- H.R. 850 would require the Administration to determine whether the Revolutionary Guard should be named a Foreign Terrorist Organization.
- S. 1881 contains provisions to delay the effective date of the sanctions beyond the duration of the JPA, provided the President certifies Iran is implementing the JPA, is negotiating in good faith on a final deal, has not (directly or through proxies) supported an act of terrorism against the United States, and has not conducted any tests of ballistic missiles of over 500 kilometer range. The suspension can be continued for an

additional 60 days (two 30-day extensions) if the President certifies that a comprehensive nuclear deal that would "terminate" Iran's "illicit" nuclear program is imminent. A waiver provision enables the President to forestall reinstatement of the act's sanctions.

- S. 1881 also provides for sanctions to be suspended if there is a comprehensive nuclear agreement. The sanctions in the bill can be suspended for one year, with additional one-year periods, if the President certifies there is a final deal under which Iran agrees to dismantle its "illicit" nuclear infrastructure, is brought into compliance with U.N. Security Council resolutions, resolves all issues of possible military dimensions of its nuclear program, and permits constant monitoring of all "suspect" facilities in Iran. Under S. 1881, this sanctions suspension could be terminated if Congress enacts a joint resolution of disapproval. None of these delay provisions are contained in H.R. 850.

Critics of S. 1881 asserted that the bill adds requirements to avoid new sanctions that are not in the JPA—particularly that Iran not test new longer-range missiles. Others say S. 1881 imposes unattainable conditions on a final nuclear deal—that Iran's nuclear infrastructure be eliminated. Supporters of the bill say that the term "illicit" allows flexibility to allow Iran to continue some enrichment as part of a final deal.

114th Congress: Nuclear Weapon Free Iran Act and S.Res. 40

At the start of the 114th Congress, some Members sought to build support for legislation that would require a congressional vote on any comprehensive nuclear deal, and to stipulate additional sanctions that would go into effect if stated deadlines for the comprehensive nuclear deal with Iran are not met. A major initiative was draft legislation entitled the "Nuclear Weapon Free Iran Act of 2015." The bill was reportedly to be marked up by the Senate Banking Committee, which has jurisdiction over sanctions legislation affecting the U.S. financial system. However, President Obama's threat to veto the legislation appears to have contributed to a statement by its main sponsors to delay further consideration of the bill until the end of March—the deadline for a political framework accord that will stipulate the outlines of a comprehensive nuclear deal with Iran. The bill was modeled, in significant respects, on S. 1881, but with significant changes:

- The bill did not set out the parameters of a final accord that Congress would find acceptable as binding. The bill describes Congress's views of an acceptable deal in nonbinding preambular language.
- The bill sets out sets of sanctions that would take effect in successive months in late 2015. The core provision adopts the elements of S. 1881 that would compel Iran's remaining oil customers to make "dramatic" (30%) cuts in purchases of Iranian oil, every successive eight months, in order to retain an exemption of their banks from U.S. sanctions.
- The draft legislation would expand the authorities of IFCA (see above) to sanction transactions not only with Iran's shipping, shipbuilding, and energy sector but also with Iran's automotive, construction, engineering, and mining sectors.
- The draft legislation incorporates elements of S. 2650 from the 113th Congress requiring congressional consideration of a comprehensive nuclear deal with Iran.

President Obama's stated intent to veto the Nuclear Free Iran Act apparently also contributed to the introduction of alternative legislation that would not likely jeopardize the nuclear talks. S.Res. 40 was introduced on January 26, 2015, expressing the non-binding sense of Congress that new sanctions should be enacted if the talks fail to produce an accord.

Other Possible U.S. and International Sanctions

There are a number of other possible sanctions that might receive consideration—either in a global or multilateral framework—presumably if no comprehensive nuclear deal is reached and Iran returns to expanding its nuclear program.

- *Sanctioning All Trade with Iran.* Some organizations, such as United Against Nuclear Iran, advocate sanctions against virtually all trade with Iran, with exceptions for food and medical products. The concept of a global trade ban on Iran has virtually no support in the United Nations Security Council, and U.S. allies strongly oppose U.S. measures that would compel allied firms to end commerce with Iran in purely civilian, non-strategic goods.

- *Comprehensive Ban on Energy Transactions with Iran.* Many experts believe that a U.N.-mandated, worldwide embargo on the purchase of any Iranian crude oil would put significant pressure on Iran. This concept would likely require support from the U.N. Security Council. Some advocate a U.N. Security Council ban on all investment in and equipment sales to Iran's energy sector. During the 1990s, U.N. sanctions against Libya for the Pan Am 103 bombing banned the sale of energy equipment to Libya.
- *Iran Oil Free Zone.* Prior to the EU oil embargo on Iran, there was discussion of forcing a similar result by closing the loophole in the U.S. trade ban under which Iranian crude oil, when mixed with other countries' oils at foreign refineries in Europe and elsewhere, can be imported as refined product. Some argue this concept has been mooted by the EU oil embargo, while others say the step still has value in making sure the EU oil embargo on Iran is not lifted or modified.
- *Mandating Reductions in Diplomatic Exchanges with Iran or Prohibiting Travel by Iranian Officials.* Some have suggested that the United States organize a worldwide ban on travel by senior Iranian civilian officials, a pullout of all diplomatic missions in Tehran, and expulsion of Iranian diplomats worldwide. The EU came close to adopting this option after the November 29, 2011, attack on the British Embassy in Tehran.
- *Barring Iran from International Sporting Events.* An option is to limit sports or cultural exchanges with Iran, such as Iran's participation in the World Cup soccer tournament. However, many experts oppose using sporting events to accomplish political goals.
- *Sanctioning Iranian Profiteers and Other Abusers.* Some experts believe that, despite the provision of P.L. 112-239 discussed earlier, the United States and international community should more aggressively target for sanctions Iranians who are exploiting special rights, monopolies, or political contacts for economic gain at the expense of average Iranians. Others believe that human rights sanctions should be extended to Iranian officials who are responsible for depriving Iranian women and other groups of internationally accepted rights.
- *Banning Passenger Flights to and from Iran.* Bans on flights to and from Libya were imposed on that country in response to the finding that its agents were responsible for the December 21, 1988, bombing

of Pan Am 103 (now lifted). A variation of this idea could be the imposition of sanctions against airlines that are in joint ventures or codeshare arrangements with Iranian airlines.

- *Limiting Lending to Iran by International Financial Institutions.* Resolution 1747 calls for restraint on but does not outright ban international lending to Iran. An option is to make a ban on such lending mandatory. Some U.S. groups have called for the International Monetary Fund (IMF) to withdraw all its holdings in Iran's Central Bank and suspend Iran's membership in the body.
- *Banning Trade Financing or Official Insurance for Trade Financing.* Another option is to mandate a worldwide ban on official trade credit guarantees. This was not mandated by Resolution 1929, but several countries imposed this sanction subsequently. A ban on investment in Iranian bonds reportedly was considered but deleted to attract China and Russia's support.
- *Restricting Operations of and Insurance for Iranian Shipping.* One option, reportedly long under consideration, has been a worldwide ban on provision of insurance or reinsurance for any shipping to or from Iran. A call for restraint is in Resolution 1929, but is not mandatory. As of July 1, 2012, the EU has banned such insurance, and many of the world's major insurers are in Europe.

Table 7. Entities Sanctioned Under U.N. Resolutions and U.S. Laws and Executive Orders

(Persons listed are identified by the positions they held when designated; some have since changed. Sanctions imposed, revoked, or exempted under the Iran Sanctions Act, CISADA, and IFCA are discussed above and not included in this table)

Entities Sanctioned Under Resolution 1737
Atomic Energy Organization of Iran (AEIO) Mesbah Energy Company (Arak supplier); Kalaye Electric (Natanz supplier); Pars Trash Company (centrifuge program); Farayand Technique (centrifuge program); Defense Industries Organization (DIO); 7th of Tir (DIO subordinate); Shahid Hemmat Industrial Group (SHIG)—missile program; Shahid Bagheri Industrial Group (SBIG)—missile program; Fajr Industrial Group (missile program); Mohammad Qanadi, AEIO Vice President; Behman Asgarpour (Arak manager); Ehsan Monajemi (Natanz construction manager); Jafar Mohammadi (Adviser to AEIO); Gen. Hosein Salimi (Commander, IRGC Air Force); Dawood Agha

Jani (Natanz official); Ali Hajinia Leilabadi (director of Mesbah Energy); Lt. Gen. Mohammad Mehdi Nejad Nouri (Malak Ashtar University of Defence Technology rector); Bahmanyar Morteza Bahmanyar (AIO official); Reza Gholi Esmaeli (AIO official); Ahmad Vahid Dastjerdi (head of Aerospace Industries Org., AIO); Maj. Gen. Yahya Rahim Safavi (Commander in Chief, IRGC)
Entities/Persons Added by Resolution 1747
Ammunition and Metallurgy Industries Group (controls 7th of Tir); Parchin Chemical Industries (branch of DIO); Karaj Nuclear Research Center; Novin Energy Company; Cruise Missile Industry Group; Sanam Industrial Group (subordinate to AIO); Ya Mahdi Industries Group; Kavoshyar Company (subsidiary of AEIO); Sho'a Aviation (produces IRGC light aircraft for asymmetric warfare); Bank Sepah (funds AIO and subordinate entities); Esfahan Nuclear Fuel Research and Production Center and Esfahan Nuclear Technology Center; Qods Aeronautics Industries (produces UAV's, para-gliders for IRGC asymmetric warfare); Pars Aviation Services Company (maintains IRGC Air Force equipment); Gen. Mohammad Baqr Zolqadr (IRGC officer serving as deputy Interior Minister; Brig. Gen. Qasem Soleimani (Qods Force commander); Fereidoun Abbasi-Davani (senior defense scientist); Mohasen Fakrizadeh-Mahabai (defense scientist); Seyed Jaber Safdari (Natanz manager); Mohsen Hojati (head of Fajr Industrial Group); Ahmad Derakshandeh (head of Bank Sepah); Brig. Gen. Mohammad Reza Zahedi (IRGC ground forces commander); Amir Rahimi (head of Esfahan nuclear facilities); Mehrdada Akhlaghi Ketabachi (head of SBIG); Naser Maleki (head of SHIG); Brig. Gen. Morteza Reza'i (Deputy commander-in-chief, IRGC); Vice Admiral Ali Akbar Ahmadiyan (chief of IRGC Joint Staff); Brig. Gen. Mohammad Hejazi (Basij commander)
Entities Added by Resolution 1803
Thirteen Iranians named in Annex 1 to Resolution 1803; all reputedly involved in various aspects of nuclear program. Bans travel for five named Iranians. Electro Sanam Co.; Abzar Boresh Kaveh Co. (centrifuge production); Barzaganin Tejaral Tavanmad Saccal; Jabber Ibn Hayan; Khorasan Metallurgy Industries; Niru Battery Manufacturing Co. (Makes batteries for Iranian military and missile systems); Ettehad Technical Group (AIO front co.); Industrial Factories of Precision; Joza Industrial Co.; Pshgam (Pioneer) Energy Industries; Tamas Co. (involved in uranium enrichment); Safety Equipment Procurement (AIO front, involved in missiles)

Table 7. (Continued)

Entities Added by Resolution 1929	
Over 40 entities added; makes mandatory a previously nonbinding travel ban on most named Iranians of previous resolutions. Adds one individual banned for travel—AEIO head Javad Rahiqi Amin Industrial Complex; Armament Industries Group; Defense Technology and Science Research Center (owned or controlled by Ministry of Defense); Doostan International Company; Farasakht Industries; First East Export Bank, PLC (only bank added by Resolution 1929); Kaveh Cutting Tools Company; M. Babaie Industries; Malek Ashtar University (subordinate of Defense Technology and Science Research Center, above); Ministry of Defense Logistics Export (sells Iranian made arms to customers worldwide); Mizan Machinery Manufacturing; Modern Industries Technique Company; Nuclear Research Center for Agriculture and Medicine (research component of the AEIO); Pejman Industrial Services Corp.; Sabalan Company; Sahand Aluminum Parts Industrial Company; Shahid Karrazi Industries; Shahid Sattari Industries; Shahid Sayyade Shirazi Industries (acts on behalf of the DIO); Special Industries Group (another subordinate of DIO); Tiz Pars (cover name for SHIG); Yazd Metallurgy Industries The following Revolutionary Guard affiliated firms (several are subsidiaries of Khatam ol-Anbiya, the main Guard construction affiliate): Fater Institute; Garaghe Sazendegi Ghaem; Gorb Karbala; Gorb Nooh; Hara Company; Imensazan Consultant Engineers Institute; Khatam ol-Anbiya; Makin; Omran Sahel; Oriental Oil Kish; Rah Sahel; Rahab Engineering Institute; Sahel Consultant Engineers; Sepanir; Sepasad Engineering Company The following entities owned or controlled by Islamic Republic of Iran Shipping Lines (IRISL): Irano Hind Shipping Company; IRISL Benelux; and South Shipping Line Iran	
Entities Designated Under U.S. Executive Order 13382 (many designations coincident with designations under U.N. resolutions)	
Entity	**Date Named**
Shahid Hemmat Industrial Group (Iran)	June 2005, September 2007
Shahid Bakeri Industrial Group (Iran)	June 2005, February 2009
Atomic Energy Organization of Iran	June 2005
Novin Energy Company (Iran) and Mesbah Energy Company (Iran)	January 2006

Entity	Date Named
Four Chinese entities: Beijing Alite Technologies, LIMMT Economic and Trading Company, China Great Wall Industry Corp, and China National Precision Machinery Import/Export Corp.	June 2006
Sanam Industrial Group (Iran) and Ya Mahdi Industries Group (Iran)	July 2006
Bank Sepah (Iran)	January 2007
Defense Industries Organization (Iran)	March 2007
June 2007	
Pars Trash (Iran, nuclear program); Farayand Technique (Iran, nuclear program); Fajr Industries Group (Iran, missile program); Mizan Machine Manufacturing Group (Iran, missile prog.)	
Aerospace Industries Organization (AIO) (Iran)	September 2007
Korea Mining and Development Corp. (N. Korea)	September 2007
October 21, 2007	
Islamic Revolutionary Guard Corps (IRGC); Ministry of Defense and Armed Forces Logistics; Bank Melli (Iran's largest bank, widely used by Guard); Bank Melli Iran Zao (Moscow); Melli Bank PC (U.K.); Bank Kargoshaee; Arian Bank (joint venture between Melli and Bank Saderat). Based in Afghanistan; Bank Mellat (provides banking services to Iran's nuclear sector); Mellat Bank SB CJSC (Armenia). Reportedly has $1.4 billion in assets in UAE; Persia International Bank PLC (U.K.); Khatam ol Anbiya Ghorargah Sazendegi Nooh (main IRGC construction and contracting arm, with $7 billion in oil, gas deals); Oriental Oil Kish (Iranian oil exploration firm); Ghorb Karbala; Ghorb Nooh (synonymous with Khatam ol Anbiya); Sepasad Engineering Company (Guard construction affiliate); Omran Sahel (Guard construction affiliate); Sahel Consultant Engineering (Guard construction affiliate); Hara Company; Ghorargahe Sazandegi Ghaem Individuals: Bahmanyar Morteza Bahmanyar (AIO, Iran missile official, see above under Resolution 1737); Ahmad Vahid Dastjerdi (AIO head, Iran missile program); Reza Gholi Esmaeli (AIO, see under Resolution 1737); Morteza Reza'i (deputy commander, IRGC) See also Resolution 1747; Mohammad Hejazi (Basij commander). Also, Resolution 1747; Ali Akbar Ahmadian (Chief of IRGC Joint Staff). Resolution 1747; Hosein Salimi (IRGC Air Force commander). Resolution 1737; Qasem Soleimani (Qods Force commander). Resolution 1747.	

Table 7. (Continued)

March 12, 2008
Future Bank (Bahrain-based but allegedly controlled by Bank Melli)
July 8, 2008
Yahya Rahim Safavi (former IRGC Commander in Chief); Mohsen Fakrizadeh-Mahabadi (senior Defense Ministry scientist); Dawood Agha-Jani (head of Natanz enrichment site); Mohsen Hojati (head of Fajr Industries, involved in missile program); Mehrdada Akhlaghi Ketabachi (heads Shahid Bakeri Industrial Group); Naser Maliki (heads Shahid Hemmat Industrial Group); Tamas Company (involved in uranium enrichment); Shahid Sattari Industries (makes equipment for Shahid Bakeri); 7th of Tir (involved in developing centrifuge technology); Ammunition and Metallurgy Industries Group (partner of 7th of Tir); Parchin Chemical Industries (deals in chemicals used in ballistic missile programs)
August 12, 2008
Karaj Nuclear Research Center; Esfahan Nuclear Fuel Research and Production Center (NFRPC); Jabber Ibn Hayyan (reports to Atomic Energy Org. of Iran, AEIO); Safety Equipment Procurement Company; Joza Industrial Company (front company for Shahid Hemmat Industrial Group, SHIG)
September 10, 2008
Islamic Republic of Iran Shipping Lines (IRISL) and 18 affiliates, including Val Fajr 8; Kazar; Irinvestship; Shipping Computer Services; Iran o Misr Shipping; Iran o Hind; IRISL Marine Services; Iriatal Shipping; South Shipping; IRISL Multimodal; Oasis; IRISL Europe; IRISL Benelux; IRISL China; Asia Marine Network; CISCO Shipping; and IRISL Malta
September 17, 2008
Firms affiliated to the Ministry of Defense, including Armament Industries Group; Farasakht Industries; Iran Aircraft Manufacturing Industrial Co.; Iran Communications Industries; Iran Electronics Industries; and Shiraz Electronics Industries
October 22, 2008
Export Development Bank of Iran (EDBI). Provides financial services to Iran's Ministry of Defense and Armed Forces Logistics
Banco Internacional de Desarollo, C.A., Venezuelan-based Iranian bank, sanctioned as an affiliate of the Export Development Bank
Assa Corporation (alleged front for Bank Melli involved in managing property in New York City on behalf of Iran) December 17, 2008

March 3, 2009
11 Entities Tied to Bank Melli: Bank Melli Iran Investment (BMIIC); Bank Melli Printing and Publishing; Melli Investment Holding; Mehr Cayman Ltd.; Cement Investment and Development; Mazandaran Cement Co.; Shomal Cement; Mazandaran Textile; Melli Agrochemical; First Persian Equity Fund; BMIIC Intel. General Trading
February 10, 2010
IRGC General Rostam Qasemi, head of Khatem ol-Anbiya Construction Headquarters (main IRGC corporate arm) and several entities linked to Khatem ol-Anbiya, including: Fater Engineering Institute, Imensazen Consultant Engineers Institute, Makin Institute, and Rahab Institute
June 16, 2010
- Post Bank of Iran
- IRGC Air Force
- IRGC Missile Command
- Rah Sahel and Sepanir Oil and Gas Engineering (for ties to Khatem ol-Anibya IRGC construction affiliate)
- Mohammad Ali Jafari—IRGC Commander-in-Chief since September 2007
- Mohammad Reza Naqdi—Head of the IRGC's Basij militia force that suppresses dissent (since October 2009)
- Ahmad Vahedi—Defense Minister
- Javedan Mehr Toos, Javad Karimi Sabet (procurement brokers or atomic energy managers)
- Naval Defense Missile Industry Group (controlled by the Aircraft Industries Org that manages Iran's missile programs)
- Five front companies for IRISL: Hafiz Darya Shipping Co.; Soroush Sarzamin Asatir Ship Management Co.; Safiran Payam Darya; and Hong Kong-based Seibow Limited and Seibow Logistics.
Also identified on June 16 were 27 vessels linked to IRISKL and 71 new names of already designated IRISL ships.
Several Iranian entities were also designated as owned or controlled by Iran for purposes of the ban on U.S. trade with Iran.
November 30, 2010
- Pearl Energy Company (formed by First East Export Bank, a subsidiary of Bank Mellat
- Pearl Energy Services, SA
- Ali Afzali (high official of First East Export Bank)

Table 7. (Continued)

- IRISL front companies: Ashtead Shipping, Byfleet Shipping, Cobham Shipping, Dorking Shipping, Effingham Shipping, Farnham Shipping, Gomshall Shipping, and Horsham Shipping (all located in the Isle of Man).- IRISL and affiliate officials: Mohammad Hosein Dajmar, Gholamhossein Golpavar, Hassan Jalil Zadeh, and Mohammad Haji Pajand.
December 21, 2010
- Bonyad (foundation) Taavon Sepah, for providing services to the IRGC; Ansar Bank (for providing financial services to the IRGC); Mehr Bank (same justification as above); Moallem Insurance Company (for providing marine insurance to IRISL, Islamic Republic of Iran Shipping Lines)
May 17, 2011
Bank of Industry and Mine (BIM)
June 23, 2011
- Tidewater Middle East Company; Iran Air; Mehr-e Eqtesad Iranian Investment Co.
March 28, 2012
Iran Maritime Industrial Company SADRA (owned by IRGC engineering firm Khatem-ol-Anbiya, has offices in Venezuela); Deep Offshore Technology PJS (subsidiary of the above); Malship Shipping Agency and Modality Ltd (both Malta-based affiliates of IRISL); Seyed Alaeddin Sadat Rasool (IRISL legal adviser); Ali Ezati (IRISL strategic planning and public affairs manager)
July 12, 2012
- Electronic Components Industries Co. (ECI) and Information Systems Iran (ISIRAN); Advanced Information and Communication Technology Center (AICTC) and Hamid Reza Rabiee (software engineer for AICTC); Digital Medial Lab (DML) and Value Laboratory (owned or controlled by Rabiee or AICTC); Ministry of Defense Logistics Export (MODLEX); Daniel Frosh (Austria) and International General Resourcing FZE)—person and his UAE-based firm allegedly supply Iran's missile industry.
November 8, 2012
- National Iranian Oil Company; Tehran Gostaresh, company owned by Bonyad Taavon Sepah; Imam Hossein University, owned by IRGC; Baghyatollah Medical Sciences University, owned by IRGC or providing services to it.
December 13, 2012
Atomic Energy Organization of Iran (AEOI) chief Fereidoun Abbasi Davain; Seyed Jaber Safdari of Novin Energy, a designated affiliate of AEOI; Morteza

Ahmadi Behazad, provider of services to AEOI (centrifuges); Pouya Control— provides goods and services for uranium enrichment; Iran Pooya—provides materials for manufacture of IR-1 and IR-2 centrifuges; Aria Nikan Marine Industry—source of goods for Iranian nuclear program; Amir Hossein Rahimyar— procurer for Iran nuclear program; Mohammad Reza Rezvanianzadeh—involved in various aspects of nuclear program; Faratech—involved in Iran heavy water reactor project; Neda Industrial Group—manufacturer of equipment for Natanz enrichment facility; Tarh O Palayesh—designer of elements of heavy water research reactor; Towlid Abzar Boreshi Iran—manufacturer for entities affiliated with the nuclear program.
December 21, 2012
SAD Import Export Company (also designated by U.N. Sanctions Committee a few days earlier for violating Resolution 1747 ban on Iran arms exports, along with Yas Air) for shipping arms and other goods to Syria's armed forces; Marine Industries Organization—designated for affiliation with Iran Ministry of Defense and Armed Forces Logistics; Mustafa Esbati, for acting on behalf of Marine Industries; Chemical Industries and Development of Materials Group—designated as affiliate of Defense Industries Org.; Doostan International Company—designated for providing services to Iran Aerospace Industries Org, which oversees Iran missile industries.
April 11, 2013
Babak Morteza Zanjani—chairmen of Sorinet Group that Iran uses to finance oil sales abroad; International Safe Oil— provides support to NIOC and NICO; Sorinet Commercial Trust Bankers (Dubai) and First Islamic Investment Bank (Malaysia)—finance NIOC and NICO; Kont Kosmetik and Kont Investment Bank—controlled by Babak Zanjani; Naftiran Intertrade Company Ltd.—owned by NIOC
May 9, 2013
Iranian-Venezuelan Bi-National Bank (IVBB), for activities on behalf of the Export Development Bank of Iran that was sanctioned on October 22, 2008, (see above). EDBI was sanctioned for providing financial services to Iran's Ministry of Defense.
May 31, 2013
Bukovnya AE (Ukraine) for leasing aircraft to Iran Air.
December 12, 2013

Table 7. (Continued)

Several Iranian firms and persons: Eyvaz Technic Manufacturing Company; The Exploration and Nuclear Raw Materials Company; Maro Sanat Company; Navid Composite Material Company; Negin Parto Khavar; Neka Novin Officials Iradj Mohammadi Kahvarin and Mahmoud Mohammadi Dayeni; Neka Novin alisaes including Kia Nirou; Qods Aviation Industries (operated by IRGC, produces UAVs, paragliders, etc); iran Aviation Industries Organization; Reza Amidi; Fan Pardazan; Ertebat Gostar Novin
February 6, 2014
Ali Canko (Turkey) and Tiva Sanat Group, for procuring IRGC-Navy fast boats; Advance Electrical and Industrial Technologies (Spain), for procurement for Neka Novin; Ulrich Wipperman and Deutsche Forfait (Germany), and Deutsche Forfait Americas (U.S.) for facilitating oil deals for NIOC.
April 29, 2014
Karl Lee (aka Li Fangwei) and 8 China-based front companies: Sinotech Industry Co. Ltd.; MTTO Industry and Trade Limited; Success Move Ltd.; Sinotech Dalian Carbon and Graphite Manufacturing Corporation; Dalian Zhongchuang Char-White Co., Ltd.; Karat Industry Co., Ltd.; Dalian Zhenghua Maoyi Youxian Gongsi; and Tereal Industry and Trade Ltd.
August 29, 2014 (by both State and Treasury)
By State: Organization of Defensie Innovation and Research (nuclear weapons research); Nuclear Science and Technology Research Institute (implements nuclear projects including heavy water reactor at Arak); Jahan Tech Rooyan Pars: and Mandegar Baspar Kimiya Company (latter two are involved in procuring carbon fiber for proscribed aspects of Iran's nuclear program).
By Treasury: Mohammad Javad and Arman Imanirad (for acting on behalf of Aluminat, which procures aluminum products for Iran's nuclear program); Nefertiti Shipping (IRISL's agent in Egypt); Sazeh Morakab (provides services to Shahid Hemat Industrial Group, SHIG, and Iran's Aircraft Manufacturing Industrial Co., HESA); Ali Gholami and Marzieh Bozorg (officials of Sazeh Morakab). SHIG aliases identified: Sahand Aluminum Parts Co and Ardalan Machineries Co.
Iran-Related Entities Sanctioned under Executive Order 13224 (Terrorism Entities)
July 25, 2007
Martyr's Foundation (Bonyad Shahid), a major Iranian foundation (bonyad)—for providing financial support to Hezbollah and PIJ; Goodwill Charitable

Organization, a Martyr's Foundation office in Dearborn, Michigan; Al Qard Al Hassan—part of Hezbollah's financial infrastructure (and associated with previously designated Hezbollah entities Husayn al-Shami, Bayt al-Mal, and Yousser Company for Finance and Investment); Qasem Aliq—Hezbollah official, director of Martyr's Foundation Lebanon branch, and head of Jihad al-Bina, a previously designated Lebanese construction company run by Hezbollah; Ahmad al-Shami—financial liaison between Hezbollah in Lebanon and Martyf's Foundation chapter in Michigan
October 21, 2007
Qods Force and Bank Saderat (allegedly used to funnel Iranian money to Hezbollah, Hamas, PIJ, and other Iranian supported terrorist groups)
January 16, 2009
Al Qaeda Operatives in Iran: Saad bin Laden; Mustafa Hamid; Muhammad Rab'a al-Bahtiyti; Alis Saleh Husain
August 3, 2010
Qods Force senior officers: Hushang Allahdad, Hossein Musavi,Hasan Mortezavi, and Mohammad Reza Zahedi; Iranian Committee for the Reconstruction of Lebanon, and its director Hesam Khoshnevis, for supporting Lebanese Hezbollah; Imam Khomeini Relief Committee Lebanon branch, and its director Ali Zuraik, for providing support to Hezbollah; Razi Musavi, a Syrian based Iranian official allegedly providing support to Hezbollah
December 21, 2010
Liner Transport Kish (for providing shipping services to transport weapons to Lebanese Hezbollah)
October 11, 2011 (For alleged plot against Saudi Ambassador to the U.S.):
Qasem Soleimani (Qods Force commander); Hamid Abdollahi (Qods force); Abdul Reza Shahlai (Qods Force); Ali Gholam Shakuri (Qods Force); Manssor Arbabsiar (alleged plotter)
October 12, 2011
Mahan Air (for transportation services to Qods Force)
February 16, 2012
Ministry of Intelligence and Security of Iran (MOIS)
March 27, 2012
Yas Air (successor to Pars Air); Behineh Air (Iranian trading company); Ali Abbas Usman Jega (Nigerian shipping agent); Qods Force officers: Esmail Ghani, Sayyid Ali Tabatabaei, and Hosein Aghajani
These entities and persons were sanctioned for weapons shipments to Syria and an October 2011 shipment bound for Gambia, intercepted in Nigeria.

Table 7. (Continued)

May 31, 2013	
Ukraine-Mediterranean Airlines (Um Air, Ukraine) for helping Mahan Air and Iran Air conduct illicit activities; Rodrigue Elias Merhej (owner of Um Air); Kyrgyz Trans Avia (KTA, Kyrgyzstan) for leasing aircraft to Mahan Air Lidia Kim, director of KTA; Sirjanco (UAE) for serving as a front for Mahan Air acquisition of aircraft; Hamid Arabnejad, managing director of Mahan Air.	
February 6, 2014	
Several persons/entities in UAE aiding Mahan Air (see above): Blue Sky Aviation FZE; Avia Trust FZE; Hamidreza Malekouti Pour; Pejman Mahmood Kosrayanifard; and Gholamreza Mahmoudi.	
Several IRGC-Qods Force offices or facilitators involved in Iran's efforts in Afghanistan: Sayyed Kamal Musavi; Alireza Hemmati; Akbar Seyed Alhosseini; and Mahmud Afkhami Rashidi.	
One Iran-based Al Qaeda facilitator (supporting movement of Al Qaeda affiliated fightes to Syria): Olimzhon Adkhamovich Sadikov (aka Jafar al-Uzbeki or Jafar Muidinov).	
August 29, 2014	
Meraj Air (for delivering weapons to Syria from Iran); Caspian Air (supports IRGC by transporting personnel and weapons to Syria); Sayyed Jabar Hosseini (manager of Liner Transport Kish which IRGC uses to support terrorist activities outside Iran); Pioneer Logistics (Turkey, helps Mahan Air evade sanctions); Asian Aviation Logistics (Thailand, helps Mahan Air evade sanctions). Pouya Air designated as alias of Yas Air.	
Entities Sanctioned Under the Iran North Korea Syria Nonproliferation Act or Executive Order 12938	
The designations are under the Iran, North Korea, Syria Nonproliferation Act (INKSNA) unless specified. These designations expire after two years, unless re-designated	
Baltic State Technical University and Glavkosmos, both of Russia	July 30, 1998
(Both removed —Baltic on January 29, 2010, and Glavkosmos on March 4, 2010)	
D. Mendeleyev University of Chemical Technology of Russia and Moscow Aviation Institute (Both removed on May 21, 2010)	January 8, 1999
Norinco (China). For alleged missile technology sale to Iran.	May 2003

Taiwan Foreign Trade General Corporation (Taiwan)	July 4, 2003
Tula Instrument Design Bureau (Russia). For alleged sales of laser-guided artillery	September 17, 2003, removed
shells to Iran. (Also designated under Executive Order 12938)	May 21, 2010
13 entities sanctioned including companies from Russia, China, Belarus, Macedonia, North Korea, UAE, and Taiwan.	April 7, 2004
14 entities from China, North Korea, Belarus, India (two nuclear scientists, Dr. Surendar and Dr. Y.S.R. Prasad), Russia, Spain, and Ukraine.	September 29, 2004
14 entities, mostly from China, for alleged supplying of Iran's missile program. Many, such as North Korea's Changgwang Sinyong and China's Norinco and Great Wall Industry Corp, have been sanctioned several times previously. Newly sanctioned entities included North Korea's Paeksan Associated Corporation, and Taiwan's Ecoma Enterprise Co.	December 2004 and January 2005
9 entities, including those from China (Norinco yet again), India (two chemical companies), and Austria. Sanctions against Dr. Surendar of India (see September 29, 2004) were ended, presumably because of information exonerating him.	December 26, 2005
7 entities. Two Indian chemical companies (Balaji Amines and Prachi Poly Products); two Russian firms (Rosobornexport and aircraft manufacturer Sukhoi); two North Korean entities (Korean Mining and Industrial Development, and Korea Pugang Trading); and one Cuban entity (Center for Genetic Engineering and Biotechnology).	August 4, 2006 (see below for Rosobornexport removal)
9 entities. Rosobornexport, Tula Design, and Komna Design Office of Machine Building, and Alexei Safonov (Russia); Zibo Chemical, China National Aerotechnology, and China National Electrical (China). Korean Mining and Industrial Development (North Korea) for WMD or advanced weapons sales to Iran (and Syria).	January 2007 (see below for Tula and Rosoboronexport removal)

Table 7. (Continued)

14 entities, including Lebanese Hezbollah. Some were penalized for transactions with Syria. Among the new entities sanctioned for assisting Iran were Shanghai Non-Ferrous Metals Pudong Development Trade Company (China); Iran's Defense Industries Organization; Sokkia Company (Singapore); Challenger Corporation (Malaysia); Target Airfreight (Malaysia); Aerospace Logistics Services (Mexico); and Arif Durrani (Pakistani national).	April 23, 2007
13 entities: China Xinshidai Co.; China Shipbuilding and Offshore International Corp.; Huazhong CNC (China); IRGC; Korea Mining Development Corp. (North Korea); Korea Taesong Trading Co. (NK); Yolin/Yullin Tech, Inc. (South Korea); Rosoboronexport (Russia sate arms export agency); Sudan Master Technology; Sudan Technical Center Co; Army Supply Bureau (Syria); R and M International FZCO (UAE); Venezuelan Military Industries Co. (CAVIM). (Rosoboronexport removed May 21, 2010.)	October 23, 2008.
16 entities: Belarus: Belarusian Optical Mechanical Association; Beltech Export; China: Karl Lee; Dalian Sunny Industries; Dalian Zhongbang Chemical Industries Co.; Xian Junyun Electronic; Iran: Milad Jafari; DIO; IRISL; Qods Force; SAD Import-Export; SBIG; North Korea: Tangun Trading; Syria: Industrial Establishment of Defense; Scientific Studies and Research Center; Venezuela: CAVIM.	May 23, 2011
Mohammad Minai, senior Qods Force member involved in Iraq; Karim Muhsin al-Ghanimi, leader of Kata'ib Hezbollah (KH) militia in Iraq; Sayiid Salah Hantush al-Maksusi, senior KH member; and Riyad Jasim al-Hamidawi, Iran based KH member	November 8, 2012
Entities Designated as Threats to Iraqi Stability under Executive Order 13438	
January 8, 2008	
Ahmad Forouzandeh. Commander of the Qods Force Ramazan Headquarters, accused of fomenting sectarian violence in Iraq and of organizing training in Iran for Iraqi Shiite militia fighters; Abu Mustafa al-Sheibani. Iran based	

leader of network that funnels Iranian arms to Shiite militias in Iraq; Isma'il al-Lami (Abu Dura). Shiite militia leader, breakaway from Sadr Mahdi Army, alleged to have committed mass kidnapings and planned assassination attempts against Iraqi Sunni politicians; Mishan al-Jabburi. Financier of Sunni insurgents, owner of pro-insurgent Al-Zawra television, now banned; Al Zawra Television Station
July 2, 2009
Khata'ib Hezbollah (pro-Iranian Mahdi splinter group); Abu Mahdi al-Muhandis
Iranians Sanctioned Under September 29, 2010, Executive Order 13553 on Human Rights Abusers
September 29, 2010
1. IRGC Commander Mohammad Ali Jafari
2. Minister of Interior at time of June 2009 elections Sadeq Mahsouli
3. Minister of Intelligence at time of elections Qolam Hossein Mohseni-Ejei
4. Tehran Prosecutor General at time of elections Saeed Mortazavi
5. Minister of Intelligence Heydar Moslehi
6. Former Defense Minister Mostafa Mohammad Najjar
7. Deputy National Police Chief Ahmad Reza Radan
8. Basij (security militia) Commander at time of elections Hossein Taeb
February 23, 2011
9. Tehran Prosecutor General Abbas Dowlatabadi (appointed August 2009). Has indicted large numbers of Green movement protesters.
10. Basij forces commander (since October 2009) Mohammad Reza Naqdi (was head of Basij intelligence during post 2009 election crackdown)
June 9, 2011
11. Islamic Revolutionary Guard Corps (IRGC)
12. Basij Resistance Force
13. Law Enforcement Forces (LEF)
14. LEF Commander Ismail Ahmad Moghadam
February 16, 2012
15. Ministry of Intelligence and Security of Iran (MOIS)
May 30, 2013
16. Ashgar Mir-Hejazi for human rights abuses on/after June 12, 2009, and for
providing material support to the IRGC and MOIS.
December 30, 2014
Abyssec, for training the IRGC in cyber tradecraft and supporting its development of offensive information operations capabilities

Table 7. (Continued)

Iranians Sanctioned Under Executive Order 13572 (April 29, 2011) for Repression of the Syrian People	
Revolutionary Guard—Qods Force	April 29, 2011
Qasem Soleimani (Qods Force Commander)	May 18, 2011
Mohsen Chizari (Commander of Qods Force operations and training)	Same as above
Iranian Entities Sanctioned Under Executive Order 13606 (GHRAVITY)	
- Ministry of Intelligence and Security (MOIS); IRGC (Guard Cyber Defense Command); Law Enforcement Forces;	
Datak Telecom	
Entities Sanctioned Under Executive Order 13608 Targeting Sanctions Evaders	
- Ferland Company Ltd. for helping NITC deceptively sell Iranian crude oil	
Designations on February 6, 2014 (persons or firms that facilitated deceptive transactions for or on behalf of persons subject to U.S. sanctions on Iran)	
Three persons based in the Republic of Georgia: Pourya Nayebi, Houshang Hosseinpour, and Houshang Farsoudeh; and eight firms owned or controlled by the three: Caucasus Energy (Georgia); Orchidea Gulf Trading (UAE and/or Turkey); Georgian Business Development (Georgia and/or UAE); Great Business Deals (Georgia and/or UAE); KSN Foundation (Lichtenstein); New York General Trading (UAE); New York Money Exchange (UAE and/or Georgia); and European Oil Traders (Switzerland).	
Entities Names as Iranian Government Entities Under Executive Order 13599	
July 12, 2012:	
Petro Suisse Intertrade Company (Switzerland); Hong Kong Intertrade Company (Hong Kong); Noor Energy (Malaysia); Petro Energy Intertrade (Dubai, UAE) (all four named as front companies for NIOV, Naftiran Intertrade Company, Ltd (NICO), or NICO Sarl) 20 Iranian financial institutions (names not released but available from Treasury Dept.) 58 vessels of National Iranian Tanker Company (NITC)	
March 14, 2013:	
Dimitris Cambis and several affiliated firms named in Treasury Dept. press release.	
May 9, 2013:	
Sambouk Shipping FZC, which is tied to Dr. Dimitris Cambis and his network	

of front companies.
May 31, 2013:
Eight petrochemicals companies were designated as Iranian government entities, including Bandar Imam; Bou Ali Sina; Mobin; Nouri; Pars; Shahid Tondgooyan; Shazand; and Tabriz.
September 6, 2013:
Six individuals including Seyed Nasser Mohammad Seyyedi, director of Sima General Trading who is also associated with NIOC and NICO. The other 5 persons sanctioned manage firms associated with NIOC and NICO.
Four businesses used by Seyyedi to assist NIOC and NICO front companies. Three are based in UAE: AA Energy FZCO; Petro Royal FZE; and KASB International LLC. The other firm is Swiss Management Services Sari.
August 29, 2014
Five Iranian banks: Khavarmianeh Bank, Ghavamin Bank, Gharzolhasaneh Bank, Kish International Bank, and Kafolatbank (Tajikistan).
Entities Sanctioned Under Executive Order 13622 (For Oil and Petrochemical Purchases from Iran and Precious Metal Transactions with Iran)
May 31, 2013:
Jam Petrochemical Company (for purchasing petrochemical products from Iran); Niksima Food and Beverage JLT (for receiving payments on behalf of Jam Petrochemical)
August 29, 2014:
Asia Bank (for delivering from Moscow to Tehran of $13 million in U.S. bank notes paid to representatives of the Iranian government).
December 30, 2014
Five individuals and one company for helping Iran acquire U.S. banknotes: Hossein Zeidi, Seyed Kamal Yasini, Azizullah Qulandary, Asadollah Seifi, Teymour Ameri, and Belfast General Trading.
Anahita Nasirbeik – Asia Bank official (see above)
Entities Designated as Human Rights Abusers or Limiting Free Expression Under Executive Order 13628 (Exec. order pursuant to Iran Threat Reduction and Syria Human Rights Act)
November 8, 2012:
Ali Fazli, deputy commander of the Basij; Reza Taghipour, Minister of Communications and Information Technology; LEF Commander Moghaddam (see above); Center to Investigate Organized Crime (established by the IRGC to protect the government from cyber attacks; Press Supervisory Board, established in 1986 to issue licenses to publications and oversee news agencies; Ministry of Culture and Islamic Guidance;

Table 7. (Continued)

Rasool Jalili, active in assisting the government's Internet censorship activities; Anm Afzar Goster-e-Sharif, company owned by Jalili, above, to provide web monitoring and censorship gear; PekyAsa, another company owned by Jalili, to develop telecom software.
February 6, 2013:
- Islamic Republic of Iran Broadcasting (IRIB) and Ezzatollah Zarghami (director and head of IRIB); Iranian Cyber Police (filters websites and hacks email accounts of political activists); Communications Regulatory Authority (filters Internet content); Iran Electronics Industries (producer of electronic systems and products including those for jamming, eavesdropping
May 30, 2013:
Committee to Determine Instances of Criminal Content for engaging in censorship activities on/after June 12, 2009; Ofogh Saberin Engineering Development Company for providing services to the IRGC and Ministry of Communications to override Western satellite communications.
May 23, 2014:
Morteza Tamaddon for cutting mobile phone communications and harassing opposition leaders Mir Hosein Musavi and Mehdi Karrubi when Tamaddon was governor-general of Tehran Province in 2009.
December 30, 2014
Douran Software Technologies, for acting on behalf of the Committee to Determine Instances of Criminal Content (see above).
Entities Designated Pursuant to Executive Order I3645
December 12, 2012 (all for providing material support to NITC)
Mid Oil Asia (Singapore); Singa Tankers (Singapore); Siqiriya Maritime (Philippines); Ferland Company Limited (previously designated under other E.O.); Vitaly Sokolenko (general manager of Ferland)
April 29, 2014, (for connections to deceptive oil dealings for Iran)
Saeed Al Aqili (co-owner of Al Aqili Group LLC) ; Al Aqili Group LLC; Anwar Kamal Nizami (Dubai-based Pakistani facilitator, manages bank relations for affilates of Al Aqili and Al Aqili Group. Also works for Sima General Trading, sanctioned under E.O. 13599)
August 29, 2014
Faylaca Petroleum (for obscuring the origin of Iranian sales of gas condensates); Lissome Marine Services LLC and six of its vessels (for supporting NITC with ship-to-ship transfers); Abdelhak Kaddouri (manages Iranian front comp;anies on behalf of NICO); Mussafer Polat (for obscuring origin of Iran's gas condensate sales); Seyedeh Hanje Seyed Nasser Seyyedi (managing director of Faylaca).

End Notes

[1] http://www.regulations.gov/#!documentDetail;D=DOS_FRDOC_0001-2175.

[2] http://www.treasury.gov/resource-center/sanctions/Documents/tar2010.pdf.

[3] http://global.factiva.com/hp/printsavews.aspx?pp=Print&hc=Publication.

[4] The executive order was issued not only under the authority of IEEPA but also: the National Emergencies Act (50 U.S.C. 1601 et seq.; §505 of the International Security and Development Cooperation Act of 1985 (22 U.S.C. 2349aa9) and §301 of Title 3, *United States Code.*

[5] Reuters, February 21, 2014; Exclusive: Boeing Says Gets U.S. License to Sell Spare Parts to Iran. Reuters, April 4, 2014.

[6] http://www.treasury.gov/resource-center/sanctions/Programs/Documents/gl_food_exports.pdf.

[7] The information in this bullet is taken from: Jo Becker, "With U.S. Leave, Companies Skirt Iran Sanctions," *New York Times*, December 24, 2010.

[8] As amended by CISADA (P.L. 111-195), these definitions include pipelines to or through Iran, as well as contracts to lead the construction, upgrading, or expansions of energy projects. CISADA also changes the definition of investment to eliminate the exemption from sanctions for sales of energy-related equipment to Iran, if such sales are structured as investments or ongoing profit-earning ventures.

[9] Under §4(d) of the original act, for Iran, the threshold dropped to $20 million, from $40 million, one year after enactment, when U.S. allies did not join a multilateral sanctions regime against Iran. However, P.L. 111-195 explicitly sets the threshold investment level at $20 million. For Libya, the threshold was $40 million, and sanctionable activity included export to Libya of technology banned by Pan Am 103-related Security Council Resolutions 748 (March 31, 1992) and 883 (November 11, 1993).

[10] The original ISA definition of energy sector included oil and natural gas, and CISADA added to that definition: liquefied natural gas (LNG), oil or LNG tankers, and products to make or transport pipelines that transport oil or LNG.

[11] A definition of chemicals and products considered "petrochemical products" is found in a Policy Guidance statement. See, *Federal Register*, November 13, 2012, http://www.regulations.gov/#!documentDetail;D= DOS_FRDOC_0001-2175.

[12] A definition of what chemicals and products are considered "petroleum products" for the purposes of the order are in the policy guidance issued November 13, 2012, http://www.regulations.gov/#!documentDetail;D= DOS_FRDOC_0001-2175.

[13] Other ISA amendments under that law included recommending against U.S. nuclear agreements with countries that supply nuclear technology to Iran and expanding provisions of the USA Patriot Act (P.L. 107-56) to curb money-laundering for use to further WMD programs.

[14] This termination requirement added by P.L. 109-293, which formally removed Libya from the Act. Application of the Act to Libya terminated on April 23, 2004, with a determination that Libya had fulfilled U.N. requirements.

[15] http://dawn.com/2012/03/01/tough-us-warning-on-iran-gas-pipeline/.

[16] Dollar figures for investments in Iran represent public estimates of the amounts investing firms are expected to spend over the life of a project, which might in some cases be several decades.

[17] Text of announcement of waiver decision by then-Secretary of State Madeleine Albright, containing expectation of similar waivers in the future, at http://www.parstimes.com /law/albright_southpars.html.

[18] Text of letter from Senators Mark Kirk and Robert Menendez to Secretary Geithner, January 19, 2012.

[19] Announcements by the Department of State, March 20, 2012, June 11, 2012, and June 28, 2012.

[20] The provision contains certain exceptions to ensure the safety of astronauts, but it nonetheless threatened to limit U.S. access to the international space station after April 2006, when Russia started charging the United States for transportation on its Soyuz spacecraft. Legislation in the 109th Congress (S. 1713, P.L. 109-112) amended the provision in order to facilitate continued U.S. access and extended INA sanctions provisions to Syria.

[21] Glenn Kessler, "U.S. Moves to Isolate Iranian Banks," *Washington Post*, September 9, 2006.

[22] Jessica Silver-Greenberg, "Regulator Says Bank Helped Iran Hide Deals," *New York Times*, August 7, 2012.

[23] Rick Gladstone. "U.S. Announces Actions to Enforce Iran Sanctions." *New York Times*, April 29, 2014.

[24] http://www.treasury.gov/press-center/press-releases/Pages/tg1367.aspx.

[25] U.S. Department of the Treasury, Office of Public Affairs, *Treasury Sanctions Iranian Security Forces for Human Rights Abuses*, June 9, 2011.

[26] Christopher Rhoads, "Iran's Web Spying Aided by Western Technology," *Wall Street Journal*, June 22, 2009.

[27] *Fact Sheet: Treasury Issues Interpretive Guidance and Statement of Licensing Policy on Internet Freedom in Iran*, March 20, 2012.

[28] http://www.state.gov/r/pa/prs/ps/2013/05/210102.htm.

[29] Note: CRS has no mandate or capability to "judge" compliance of any country with U.S., multilateral, or international sanctions against Iran. This section is intended to analyze some major trends in third country cooperation with U.S. policy toward Iran, noting that there are many aspects to U.S. relations with the countries discussed here.

[30] "Iran Reaps Less Cash From Eased Sanctions Than Predicted." Bloomberg, November 25, 2014.

[31] The 10 are Belgium, Czech Republic, France, Germany, Greece, Italy, the Netherlands, Poland, Spain, and Britain.

[32] Avi Jorish, "Despite Sanctions, Iran's Money Flow Continues," *Wall Street Journal*, June 25, 2013.

[33] During the active period of talks, which began in December 2002, there were working groups focused not only on the TCA terms and proliferation issues but also on Iran's human rights record, Iran's efforts to derail the Middle East peace process, Iranian-sponsored terrorism, counter-narcotics, refugees, migration issues, and the Iranian opposition PMOI.

[34] "Iran, Russia Negotiating Big Oil-for-Goods Deal." Reuters, January 10, 2014.

[35] Author conversation with journalists based in China, September 1, 2013.

[36] Iran Aims to Return to Shipping Market. *Wall Street Journal*, September 17, 2014.

[37] Asia Times, March 21, 2014. http://www.atimes.com/atimes/South_Asia/SOU-02-210314.html.

[38] "Pentagon Contractor Used Iran for Project," *Wall Street Journal*, September 26, 2013.

[39] Information provided to the author by the New York State government, July 2012.

[40] "US Acts to Block Turkish Firm from Sending GE Engines to Iran." Reuters, January 6, 2014.

[41] Louis Charbonneau, "Iran Looks to Armenia to Skirt Banking Sanctions," *Reuters*, August 21, 2012.

[42] Information provided to the author by regional observers. October 2013.

[43] The CRS Report RL32048, *Iran: U.S. Concerns and Policy Responses*, by Kenneth Katzman, discusses the relations between Iran and other Middle Eastern states.

[44] Mark Wallace, "Closing U.S. Ports to Iran-Tainted Shipping. Op-ed," *Wall Street Journal*, March 15, 2013.

[45] http://www.kuwaittimes.net/read_news.php?newsid=NDQ0OTY1NTU4; http://english.fars news.com/newstext.php?nn=8901181055.

[46] Ben Lando, "Iraq Inks Gas Supply Deal with Iran," *Iraq Oil Report*, July 23, 2013.

[47] Michael Gordon and Eric Schmitt. "Iran Secretly Sending Drones and Supplies to Iraq, U.S. Officials Say." New York Times, June 25, 2014.

[48] Barbara Slavin. "Obama Administration Holds Up Environmental Grants to Iran." Al Monitor, June 23, 2014.

[49] Farah Stockman, "Oil Firm Says It Will Withdraw From Iran," *Boston Globe*, November 12, 2010.

[50] "Iran Says Halliburton Won Drilling Contract," *Washington Times*, January 11, 2005.

[51] "Caterpillar Says Tightens 'No-Iran' Business Policy," *Reuters*, March 1, 2010.

[52] Ron Nixon, "2 Corporations Say Business With Tehran Will Be Curbed," *New York Times*, March 11, 2010.

[53] Peter Baker, "U.S. and Foreign Companies Feeling Pressure to Sever Ties With Iran," *New York Times*, April 24, 2010.

[54] In September 2011, the Commerce Department fined Flowserve $2.5 million to settle 288 charges of unlicensed exports and reexports of oil industry equipment to Iran, Syria, and other countries.

[55] Form 10-K for Fiscal year ended December 31, 2008, claims firm directed its subsidiaries to cease new business in Iran and Cuba, Syria, and Sudan as of September 2007.

[56] Asjylyn Loder and David Evans, "Koch Brothers Flout Law Getting Richer With Iran Sales," *Bloomberg News*, October 3, 2011.

[57] Form 10-K Filed for fiscal year ended December 31, 2008.

[58] Paulo Prada and Betsy McKay, "Trading Outcry Intensifies," *Wall Street Journal*, March 27, 2007; Michael Brush, "Are You Investing in Terrorism?," *MSN Money*, July 9, 2007.

[59] *New York Times*, March 7, 2010, cited previously.

[60] "Subsidiaries of the Registrant at December 31, 2009," http://www.sec.gov/Archives/edgar /data/780571/ 000078057110000007/ex_21-1.htm.

[61] "Exhibit to 10-K Filed February 25, 2009." Officials of Fluor claim that their only dealings with Iran involve property in Iran owned by a Fluor subsidiary, which the subsidiary has been unable to dispose of. CRS conversation with Fluor, December 2009.

[62] Form 10-K for Fiscal year ended December 31, 2007.

[63] Speech by National Security Adviser Tom Donilon at the Brookings Institution, November 22, 2011.

[64] William Maclean. "Iran Pursuing Banned Items for Nuclear, Missile Wor: U.S. Official." Reuters, March 16, 2014.

[65] Department of Defense, *Annual Report of Military Power of Iran*, April 2012.

[66] "Exclusive: Iran's Support for Syria Tested by Oil Price Drop." Reuters, December 20, 2014.

[67] Louis Charbonneau, "U.N. Monitors See Arms Reaching Somalia From Yemen, Iran," *Reuters*, February 10, 2013.

[68] "Iran's Pivotal Moment." http://www.euromoney.com.September, 2014.

[69] "Why Higher Iran Oil Exports Are Not Roiling Nuclear Deal." Reuters, June 13, 2014.

[70] Rick Gladstone, "Data on Iran Dims Outlook for Economy," *New York Times*, October 13, 2012.

[71] http://www.euromoney.com, op.cit.

[72] "Iran Reaps Less Cash from Eased Sanctions Than Predicted." op.cit.

[73] Testimony of Patrick Clawson before the Senate Banking Committee.January 21, 2015.

[74] Clifford Krauss. "With Gas Byproduct, Iran Sidesteps Sanctions." New York Times, August 13, 2014.

[75] "Iran Reaps Less Cash from Eased Sanctions Than Predicted." op.cit.

[76] Patrick Clawson testimony, January 21, 2015, op.cit.

[77] Khajehpour presentation at CSIS. Op. cit.

[78] Iran Faces Steep Climb to Join Gas Superpowers by 2017. International Oil Daily, April 29, 2014.

[79] Information in this section derived from Javier Blas, "Traders Cut Iran Petrol Line," *Financial Times*, March 8, 2010.

[80] http://www.ft.com/cms/s/0/009370f0-486e-11df-9a5d-00144feab49a.html.

[81] http://www.defenddemocracy.org/index.php?option=com_content&task=view&id=11788115 &Itemid=105.

[82] http://www.defenddemocracy.org/index.php?option=com_content&task=view&id=11788115& Itemid=105.

[83] http://www.defenddemocracy.org/index.php?option=com_content&task=view&id=11788115& Itemid=105.

[84] U.S. Pushes to Expedite Some Humanitarian Shipments to Iran. WSJ.com, July 28, 2014.

[85] Thomas Erdbink, "Iran's Aging Airliner Fleet Seen As Faltering Under U.S. Sanctions," July 14, 2012.

[86] The Administration sanctions suspensions and waivers are detailed at: http://www.state.gov /p/nea/rls/220049.htm.

[87] Daniel Fineren. "Iran Nuclear Deal Shipping Insurance Element May Help Oil Sales." Reuters, November 24, 2013.

[88] White House Office of the Press Secretary. "Fact Sheet: First Step Understandings Regarding the Islamic Republic of Iran's Nuclear Program." November 23, 2013.

[89] http://thehill.com/blogs/blog-briefing-room/221528-kerry-congress-consulted-on-iran-but-dont-need-initial-vote

[90] David Sanger. "Obama Sees an Iran Deal Skirting Congress, for Now." New York Times, October 20, 2014.

[91] David Sanger. "Obama Sees an Iran Deal Skirting Congress, for Now." New York Times, October 20, 2014.

[92] http://www.kirk.senate.gov/pdfs/nuclearweaponfreeiranact.pdf

[93] Ibid.

[94] Laurent Fabius, Philip Hammond, Frank-Walter Steinmeier, and Federica Mogherini. "Give Diplomacy with Iran a Chance." Washington Post op-ed, January 21, 2015.

In: The Sanctions Way
Editor: Brian Fields

ISBN: 978-1-63482-679-2

Chapter 4

NORTH KOREA: LEGISLATIVE BASIS FOR U.S. ECONOMIC SANCTIONS*

Dianne E. Rennack

SUMMARY

U.S. economic sanctions imposed on North Korea are instigated by that country's activities related to weapons proliferation; regional disruptions; terrorism; narcotics trafficking; undemocratic governance; and illicit activities in international markets, including money laundering, counterfeiting of goods and currency, and bulk cash smuggling. The sanctions have the following consequences for U.S.-North Korea relations:

- *Trade is minimal* and mostly limited to food, medicine, and other humanitarian-related goods. North Korea has no advantageous trade status and is outright denied certain goods—including luxury goods—and trade financing, primarily due to its proliferation activities. The Department of Commerce places North Korea in the two most restricted country groups for exports; imports require a license from the Treasury Department's Office of Foreign Assets Control; using a North Korea-flagged vessel for any transaction is prohibited.

---

* This is an edited, reformatted and augmented version of a Congressional Research Service publication R41438, prepared for Members and Committees of Congress, dated January 6, 2015.

- *Foreign aid is minimal* and mostly limited to refugees fleeing North Korea; broadcasting into the country; nongovernmental organization programs dedicated to democracy promotion, human rights, and governance; emergency food aid; and aid related to disabling and dismantling the country's nuclear weapons program. By law, U.S. representatives in the international financial institutions (IFI) are required to vote against any support for North Korea due to its nuclear weapons ambitions. Human rights and environmental activities would also likely result in U.S. objections to North Korea's participation in the IFI.
- *Arms sales and arms transfers* are fully denied.
- *Assets are blocked* for certain individuals and entities, should such assets come under U.S. jurisdiction.

Since the outbreak of the Korean War in 1950, the United States had imposed fairly comprehensive economic, diplomatic, and political restrictions on North Korea. In 1999, however, President Clinton announced he would lift many restrictions on U.S. exports to and imports from North Korea in areas other than those controlled for national security concerns; the Departments of Commerce, Treasury, and Transportation issued new regulations a year later that implemented the new policy. On June 26, 2008, President George W. Bush removed restrictions based on authorities in the Trading With the Enemy Act and the terrorism designation, replacing them with more circumscribed economic restrictions related to proliferation concerns.

The U.S. sanctions in place are a result both of requirements incorporated into U.S. law by Congress and decisions made in the executive branch to exercise discretionary authorities. Though the President, in accordance with the Constitution, leads the way in conducting foreign policy, Congress holds substantial power to shape foreign policy by authorizing and funding programs, advising on appointments, and specifically defining the terms of engagement in accordance with U.S. political and strategic interests. This report presents the legislative basis for U.S. sanctions policy toward North Korea. These sanctions are a critical tenet of the larger bilateral relationship, and this report highlights Congress's role and responsibility in determining the nature of U.S.-North Korea relations.

BACKGROUND

The United States imposes economic sanctions on North Korea for activities related to weapons proliferation; regional disruptions; narcotics trafficking; undemocratic governance; and illicit activities in international markets, including money laundering, counterfeiting of goods and currency, and bulk cash smuggling. In addition, although President George W. Bush removed the government of North Korea from the list of state sponsors of acts of international terrorism in June 2008, the Department of Commerce continues to identify North Korea as a terrorism-supporter for purposes of export control policy.

United States law has been applied to North Korea in the following ways in response to the North Korean government's objectionable activities:[1]

- North Korea poses a threat to U.S. national security because of "the current existence and risk of the proliferation of weapons-usable fissile material on the Korean Peninsula", as declared by President George W. Bush on June 26, 2008, under the terms of the National Emergencies Act (NEA) and the International Emergency Economic Powers Act (IEEPA);[2]
- North Korea is cited by the United Nations Security Council[3] for its nuclear weapons and ballistic missiles pursuits, withdrawal from the Treaty on the Non-Proliferation of Nuclear Weapons, and contribution to regional tensions; the United States meets the requirements as a member state of the United Nations pursuant to the United Nations Participation Act of 1945 to implement sanctions adopted by the U.N. Security Council;
- North Korea committed an unprovoked attack that resulted in the sinking of a South Korean naval vessel, *Cheonan*; announced a new nuclear test and missile launches in 2009; engaged in money laundering, counterfeiting of goods and currency, bulk cash smuggling, and narcotics trafficking, all in violation of U.N. Security Council Resolutions, leading to President Obama to expand the national emergency in 2010 and 2011;[4]
- North Korea is a Marxist-Leninist state, with a Communist government, and stated as such in the Export-Import Bank Act of 1945, as amended, and further restricted under the Foreign Assistance Act of 1961;
- North Korea has engaged in proliferation of weapons of mass destruction, the State Department finds pursuant to the Arms Export Control Act, Export Administration Act of 1979, Iran, North Korea, and Syria Nonproliferation Act of 2000, and a national emergency

declared by President George H. W. Bush relating to the proliferation of such weapons;

- North Korea is not cooperating fully with U.S. antiterrorism efforts, the State Department has determined, under terms of the Arms Export Control Act;
- North Korea has detonated a nuclear explosive device, President George W. Bush has determined, pursuant to the Arms Export Control Act, the Atomic Energy Act, and the Export-Import Bank Act of 1945; and
- North Korea engaged in "provocative, destabilizing, and repressive actions and policies," including "destructive, coercive cyber-related actions during November and December 2014," actions in violation of a multitude of U.N. Security Council resolutions, and commission of serious human rights abuses.[5]

At the President's discretion, North Korea also could be subject to economic sanctions provided in three provisions of law addressing human rights conditions: the Foreign Assistance Act of 1961, the International Religious Freedom Act of 1998, and the Trafficking Victims Protection Act of 2000.

The United States' concerns about North Korea's pursuit of nuclear weapons capability emerged in the 1980s when that country's nuclear weapons program became apparent. In the 1990s, the two countries negotiated an Agreed Framework to freeze North Korea's plutonium-based nuclear energy program and provide heavy fuel oil until light-water reactors could be brought on-line, all funded to varying degrees by the European Union, Japan, South Korea, and the United States. In October 2002, it came to light in negotiations between U.S. and North Korean government officials that North Korea was pursuing a uranium-based nuclear weapons capability. Diplomacy over North Korea's nuclear weapons program then entered a new phase; the Agreed Framework was abandoned and the United States, North Korea, South Korea, China, Japan, and Russia convened a new forum—the Six Party Talks. Despite several steps forward, including the United States ending decades-long sanctions imposed at the outset of the 1950-1953 conflict and its delisting of North Korea as a supporter of international terrorism, the Six Party Talks collapsed in late 2008.

During this period and continuing today, North Korea engaged in a number of acts that the international community has deemed provocative. Over July 5-6, 2006, in April 2009, and again in December 12, 2012, North

Korea tested short-range and long-range ballistic missiles with varying degrees of success, the first tests since 1998. On October 8, 2006, May 25, 2009 and again on February 12, 2013, North Korea reported that it had detonated a nuclear explosive device. The international community responded to the missile tests and nuclear detonations by taking the issue to the U.N. Security Council, which adopted resolutions that condemned the weapons tests and called on member states to impose economic sanctions.

On March 26, 2010, a South Korean Navy ship, the *Cheonan*, was struck by a torpedo while sailing in the West Sea. The ship sank and 46 crew members were killed. The South Korean Ministry of National Defense formed a Civilian-Military Joint Investigation Group—with participants from five other nations including the United States—which found that the *Cheonan* was torpedoed by a North Korean submarine. North Korea denied involvement. The U.N. Security Council, in a presidential statement, condemned the attack, and acknowledged both the findings of the Investigation Group and the disavowal by North Korea.[6]

President Obama assigned responsibility to North Korea for the sinking of the *Cheonan* when, on August 30, 2010, he announced he was expanding the scope of the national emergency declared in 2008, and the United States was taking additional steps to curtail economic activity with North Korea:

> the continued actions and policies of the Government of North Korea, manifested most recently by its unprovoked attack that resulted in the sinking of the Republic of Korea Navy ship *Cheonan* and the deaths of 46 sailors in March 2010; its announced test of a nuclear device and its missile launches in 2009; its actions in violation of UNSCRs 1718 and 1874, including the procurement of luxury goods; and its illicit and deceptive activities in international markets through which it obtains financial and other support, including money laundering, the counterfeiting of goods and currency, bulk cash smuggling, and narcotics trafficking, destabilize the Korean peninsula and imperil U.S. Armed Forces, allies, and trading partners in the region, and thereby constitute an unusual and extraordinary threat to the national security, foreign policy, and economy of the United States.[7]

President Obama's explicit identification of all features of North Korea's objectionable behavior constituting the threat is unusual compared to other invocations of his IEEPA authorities.[8] The statute requires only that the President find that a threat to U.S. national security, foreign policy, or economy exists, and that its source is "in whole or substantial part outside the United States." The President identified North Korea's attack of the *Cheonan* and other acts of regional destabilization, pursuit of weapons of mass destruction and the means to deliver them, noncompliance with U.N. requirements, money laundering, counterfeiting, smuggling, and narcotics trafficking as compounding the threat. To this list, the President added, in January 2015, "cyber-related actions ... and commission of serious human rights abuses," the latter a nod to ground-breaking efforts in December 2014 in the United Nations General Assembly to refer reports of human rights atrocities in North Korea's prison system to both the U.N. Security Council and the International Criminal Court. Justifying the declaration of the emergency based on these wide-ranging activities accomplishes a number of goals:

- It confirms the United States' full support of and participation in implementation of the U.N. Security Council resolutions.
- It provides a clear list of concerns members of the U.S. diplomatic corps might raise and emphasize when speaking with North Korea's trading partners and benefactors.
- It states indisputable goals for North Korea to strive toward, meet, and surpass.

It should be noted, however, that each of these forms of objectionable behavior likely would be grounds, under current law, for restricting trade, aid, arms sales, and access to assets even if the national emergency were to be revoked.

U.S. ECONOMIC SANCTIONS CURRENTLY IN PLACE

Contrary to commonly expressed views, the United States does not maintain a comprehensive embargo against North Korea. The U.S. government does not prohibit travel to North Korea, for example, nor does it deny trade in basic goods. United States economic sanctions imposed on North Korea, as a result both of requirements in U.S. law and decisions made in the executive branch to exercise discretionary authorities, have the following impact:

- *Trade is minimal* and mostly limited to food, medicine, and other humanitarian-related goods. North Korea has no advantageous trade status and is outright denied certain goods—including luxury goods—and trade financing, primarily due to its proliferation activities. The Department of Commerce places North Korea in the two most restricted country groups for exports; imports require a license from the Treasury Department's Office of Foreign Assets Control; using a North Korea-flagged vessel for any transaction is prohibited.

- *Aid is minimal* and mostly limited to refugees fleeing North Korea; broadcasting into the country; nongovernmental organization programs dedicated to democracy promotion, human rights, and governance; emergency food aid; and aid related to disabling and dismantling the country's nuclear weapons program. By law, U.S. representatives in the international financial institutions (IFI) are required to vote against any support for North Korea due to its nuclear weapons ambitions. Human rights and environmental activities would also likely result in U.S. objections to participation in the IFI.
- *Arms sales and arms transfers* are fully denied.
- *Access to assets* of certain individuals and entities, should such assets come under U.S. jurisdiction, is blocked.

Trade

The United States curtails trade with North Korea for reasons of regional stability, that country's support for acts of international terrorism (though North Korea is no longer designated as a state sponsor of terrorism), lack of cooperation with U.S. antiterrorism efforts, proliferation, and its status as a Communist country and a nonmarket economy. The United States also prohibits transactions relating to trade with certain North Korean entities identified as those who procure luxury goods, launder money, smuggle bulk cash, engage in counterfeiting goods and currency, and traffic in illicit narcotics.

National Emergency Because of Threat to U.S. National Security

Trade with North Korea is significantly restricted because of that country's demonstrated pursuit of nuclear weapons and the means to deliver them. Though President Bush, in June 2008, determined that North Korea had cleared the bar and would no longer be characterized as a state sponsor of acts of international terrorism, and Secretary of State Rice, in October 2008, removed the terrorism designation, the Department of Commerce continues to restrict exports to North Korea for anti-terrorism reasons.[9]

Commerce's primary means of controlling exports is through the administration of Export Administration Regulations (EAR), in which goods to be controlled for a variety of reasons— national security, foreign policy, short supply, compliance with international agreements, to name a few—are categorized. Recipient countries are also characterized, from allies for which little licensing is required, to rogue states for which export licensing is all but completely denied. Commerce identifies North Korea among the most restricted trade destinations—Country Group E:1, Terrorist Supporting Countries—which severely limits its access to computers, software, national security-controlled items, items on the Commerce Control List (CCL),[10] and service or repair of such items. A U.S. exporter intending to ship any goods subject to the Export Administration Regulations (EAR), except for food and medicine not on the CCL, is required to obtain an export license.

Commerce also identifies North Korea in the second most restrictive country group—Country Group D. U.S. exports to countries in Group D are restricted for reasons of national security [D:1], nuclear activities [D:2], chemical and biological weapons activities [D:3], missile technology activities [D:4], and countries subject to arms embargoes as identified by the State Department [D:5].[11] As a result, U.S. exporters are likely to be denied licenses to export any controlled item if North Korea is the destination. In June 2007, Commerce eased licensing requirements so that food, medicine, and humanitarian assistance items could be made available, but at the same time imposed new licensing prohibitions on the export and reexport of luxury goods to implement the terms of U.N. Security Council Resolution 1718.[12]

Thus, a U.S. company may apply for a license to export to North Korea, but for nearly all items other than food and medicine, there is a presumption of denial. The EAR identify license exceptions; those wishing to export to North Korea, however, are not eligible for these exceptions except in highly circumscribed instances.[13]

The Office of Foreign Assets Control, within the Department of the Treasury, must approve any U.S. importation from North Korea, and weighs all requests in the context of proliferation, money laundering, counterfeiting, bulk cash smuggling, narcotics trafficking, or other illicit economic activity, and who in North Korea might profit. Any transfer involving the government of North Korea, any senior DPRK government official, or a DPRK person or entity designated as a Specially Designated National pursuant to any of the series of executive orders relating to North Korea, to a person under U.S.

jurisdiction is prohibited.[14] The President, in Executive Order 13570 of April 18, 2011, stated:

> Except to the extent provided in statutes or in licenses, regulations, orders, or directives that may be issued pursuant to this order, and notwithstanding any contract entered into or any license or permit granted prior to the date of this order, the important into the United States, directly or indirectly, of any goods, services, or technology from North Korea is prohibited.[15]

United States persons are also prohibited from registering a vessel in North Korea; obtaining authorization to fly the North Korean flag on a vessel; or owning, leasing, operating, or insuring any vessel so flagged.[16]

Terrorism

North Korea is among those countries listed as being in violation of section 40A of the Arms Export Control Act, which prohibits the selling or licensing of defense articles or defense services to any country that the President finds "is not cooperating fully with United States antiterrorism efforts." The President is required to make such a determination annually, and the prohibition may be waived on grounds that it is in the national interest to do so.[17]

Nonmarket Economy

The Trade Agreement Extension Act of 1951 required the suspension of Most-Favored-Nation trade status (MFN, which is now known as Normal Trade Relations [NTR]) for all Communist countries except Yugoslavia. As a result, North Korea was denied MFN trade status on September 1, 1951.

North Korea remains listed in the headnotes of the Harmonized Tariff Schedule of the United States (HTSUS) as a Rate of Duty Column 2 country (along with Cuba). As a result, while trade is not prohibited with North Korea under the relevant trade laws, tariffs are set at the highest rates for imports from that country.[18] A side result of being denied MFN or NTR status is that any such country is also denied preferential trade treatment under the Generalized System of Preferences (GSP), pursuant to the Trade Act of 1974.[19] As a nonmarket economy found to deny its citizens the right or opportunity to emigrate, North Korea is not eligible to participate in any U.S. government program that makes credit, credit guarantees, or investment guarantees available, nor may the President enter into any commercial agreement with the country.[20]

Proliferator

On several occasions, North Korean entities have been found to be in violation of U.S. missile nonproliferation laws.[21] Once a finding is made, the imposition of sanctions is mandatory, though sanctions may be waived if the President finds it "essential to the national security of the United States" to do so. The severity of the sanction depends on the type of material or technology transferred. The duration of the sanction also depends on the material or technology involved; generally sanctions are imposed for two years or more.

Sanctions include, at a minimum, a denial of contracts with agencies of the U.S. government, denial of licenses for items on the U.S. Munitions List (USML),[22] and, at a maximum, a denial of all licenses for importing into the United States for the foreign person or entity.

Because North Korea is a nonmarket economy,[23] all relevant activities of the government of North Korea are also sanctioned when entities in North Korea are found to have engaged in proliferation under U.S. law.

With the nuclear weapons test of October 8, 2006, President Bush exercised the authority granted his office to cut off all foreign aid except humanitarian and food aid, deny sales or transfers of defense articles and defense services, deny export licenses for items on the USML, deny foreign military financing, deny credit underwritten or provided by government coffers, withhold U.S. support in the international financial institutions, deny export licenses for dual-use items, and withhold Export-Import Bank support.[24] At the time, the United States already maintained a fairly comprehensive sanctions regime on North Korea, thus most of these relationships were already broken or limited.

Aid

North Korea's access to U.S. foreign assistance is limited in annual foreign operations appropriations measures.[25] Under the Department of State, Foreign Operations, and Related Programs Appropriations Act,[26] North Korea is generally denied direct foreign aid, economic support funds (ESF) for energy-related programs, and direct loans, credits, insurance and guarantees of the Export-Import Bank. The prohibitions on direct foreign aid to North Korea also make that country ineligible for Millennium Challenge Account programs.[27]

At the President's discretion, North Korea is also subject to the economic sanctions provided in three provisions of law addressing human rights conditions: the Foreign Assistance Act of 1961,[28] under which North Korea is annually castigated for its human rights record; the International Religious Freedom Act of 1998,[29] under which the administration has identified North Korea as a "country of particular concern" since 2001; and the Trafficking Victims Protection Act of 2000,[30] under which the administration has, since 2003, classified North Korea as a Tier 3 (most severe) offender of standards pertaining to the trafficking of persons for slavery or sex trade. Because of North Korea's failure to comply with minimum standards relating to trafficking in persons, President Obama, in 2010, strengthened the sanctions against North Korea to deny foreign assistance and also to deny "funding for participation by officials or employees of such governments in educational and cultural exchange programs for the subsequent fiscal year."[31] Any sanctions imposed pursuant to these acts would be largely redundant, however, with penalties already prescribed to North Korea for the above-stated reasons.

Under Department of Defense Appropriations, 2015, North Korea is denied assistance under that act "unless specifically appropriated for that purpose."[32]

Nonmarket Economy

The Export-Import Bank Act of 1945 singles out Marxist-Leninist countries for denial of guarantees, insurance, credit, or other Bank funding programs. North Korea is specifically cited as a Marxist-Leninist country for purposes of the Export-Import Bank.[33]

The Foreign Assistance Act of 1961 denies most non-humanitarian foreign assistance to any Communist country. North Korea is among five countries so designated, though the law is not limited to those countries named.[34]

Several laws deny benefits or assistance to Communist countries, but do not explicitly name any particular state. Because North Korea has been denied such benefits or aid in the course of the events of the early 1950s and thereafter, these other sections of law would probably be redundant if applied to or cited for North Korea.

In some instances, the President may determine that, for purposes of a particular law, North Korea is no longer a "Marxist-Leninist state." If, however, all other aspects of the U.S.-North Korea relationship were to improve, it would probably be necessary for Congress to remove North Korea from the list set out in the Export-Import Bank Act and the Foreign Assistance Act of 1961, or necessary for the President to exercise waiver authority made available to his office under those acts, to make these other laws inapplicable to North Korea.[35]

Arms Sales and Arms Transfers

The International Traffic in Arms Regulations (ITAR), administered by the Department of State, begins:

> It is the policy of the United States to deny licenses and other approvals for exports and imports of defense articles and defense services, destined for or originating in certain countries. This policy applies to Belarus, Cuba, Eritrea, Iran, North Korea, Syria, and Venezuela. This policy also applies to countries with respect to which the United States maintains an arms embargo (e.g., Burma, China, and the Republic of the Sudan) or whenever an export would not otherwise be in furtherance of world peace and the security and foreign policy of the United States.[36]

The first ITAR was issued on August 26, 1955; North Korea has been listed as a restricted country from the ITAR's inception. North Korea is also restricted under ITAR as the United States denies North Korea conventional arms to comply with U.N. Security Council requirements.[37]

Importing of defense articles and defense services is similarly restricted by the Department of Justice's Bureau of Alcohol, Tobacco, Firearms, and Explosives, the regulations of which state:

> It is the policy of the United States to deny licenses and other approvals with respect to defense articles and defense services originating in certain countries or areas. This policy applies to Afghanistan, Belarus (one of the states composing the former Soviet Union), Cuba, Iran, Iraq, Libya, Mongolia, North Korea, Sudan, Syria, and Vietnam. This policy applies to countries or areas with respect to which the United States maintains an arms embargo (e.g., Burma, China, the Democratic Republic of the Congo, Haiti, Liberia, Rwanda, Somalia, Sudan, and UNITA (Angola)). It also applies when an import would not be in furtherance of world peace and the security and foreign policy of the United States.[38]

Again, the President has the authority to change these regulations by removing North Korea from the list of restricted countries.

Access to Assets

Declaration of National Emergency

On June 26, 2008, when the Six Party Talks appeared to be making progress, President Bush determined it was no longer in the national interest to continue certain restrictions imposed on trade and transactions with North Korea, in place since 1950.[39] At the same time, however, he found that—[40]

> ...the current existence and risk of the proliferation of weapons-usable fissile material on the Korean Peninsula constitute an unusual and extraordinary threat to the national security and foreign policy of the United States, and I hereby declare a national emergency to deal with that threat. I further find that, as we deal with that threat through multilateral diplomacy, it is necessary to continue certain restrictions with respect to North Korea that would otherwise be lifted pursuant to a forthcoming proclamation that will terminate the exercise of authorities under the Trading With the Enemy Act.... Accordingly, I hereby order... the following are blocked and may not be transferred, paid, exported, withdrawn, or otherwise dealt in:
>
> - all property and interests in property of North Korea or a North Korean national that ... were blocked as of June 16, 2000,[41] and remained blocked immediately prior to the date of this order.
> - United States persons may not register a vessel in North Korea, obtain authorization for a vessel to fly the North Korean flag, or own, lease, operate, or insure any vessel flagged by North Korea.

To date, three of the four executive orders to address North Korea events issued by Presidents Bush and Obama block access to assets of designated individuals and entities:

- Executive Order 13466 of June 26, 2008 (President Bush; 73 F.R. 36787)— continuing the block of assets that were blocked as of June 16, 2000;

- Executive Order 13551 of August 30, 2010 (President Obama; 75 F.R. 53837)— blocking assets of Kim Yong Chol, and the entities Green Pine Associated Corporation, Reconnaissance General Bureau, and Office 39;[42] and
- Executive Order of January 2, 2015 (as yet, unnumbered)—blocking assets that come under U.S. jurisdiction of any agency, instrumentality, or controlled entity of the North Korean government or the Workers' Party of Korea, or any official of those entities; those found to materially support transactions with or act on behalf of those blocked entities.[43]

Generally, the President has the authority to change regulations, as long as those changes meet the requirements of any relevant law. He must also annually revisit his declaration of a state of national emergency; it expires if the President does not renew it. He could allow the declaration to expire, or he could lift it at any time. And Congress could terminate a declaration of national emergency by passing a joint resolution under terms of the National Emergencies Act.

Proliferation of Weapons of Mass Destruction

On June 28, 2005, President George W. Bush expanded the authority granted his office to address the threat posed by the proliferation of weapons of mass destruction—authority first exercised by President George H. W. Bush in 1990—to freeze assets and property of those engaged in the proliferation of weapons of mass destruction. The 41st President had declared that the United States faced a national emergency relating to weapons proliferation (in the absence, at the time, of a reauthorized Export Administration Act), and thus took steps in 1990 to control the exports of certain goods and services, and authorized a ban on foreign aid and credit, procurement contracts, imports and exports, support in international financial institutions, and landing rights.[44] Fifteen years later, the 43rd President's executive order took additional steps to block property and assets under U.S. jurisdiction of any person found, in part—

> ... to have engaged, or attempted to engage, in activities or transactions that have materially contributed to, or pose a risk of materially contributing to, the proliferation of weapons of mass destruction or their means of delivery (including missiles capable of delivering such weapons), including any efforts to manufacture, acquire,

> possess, develop, transport, transfer or use such items, by any person or foreign country of proliferation concern;
>
> ... to have provided, or attempted to provide, financial, material, technological or other support for, or goods or services in support of, any activity or transaction described [above] ... or any person whose property and interests in property are blocked pursuant to this order ...[45]

At its outset, Executive Order 13382 identified eight foreign entities as contributors to proliferation, of which three were North Korean. The Department of the Treasury's Office of Foreign Assets Control (OFAC) subsequently added another 19 North Korean entities and four individuals to this restricted list. In the same findings, OFAC identified entities operating out of Switzerland, Iran, China, South Korea, Russia, Sudan, Syria, United Arab Emirates, Venezuela, Belgium, and Belarus, as entities engaging in WMD proliferation.[46]

Counterfeiting and Money-Laundering

On September 12, 2005, the Treasury Department found that Banco Delta Asia—a Macau-based bank in which North Korea had holdings of more than $ U.S. 50 million—was a "financial institution of primary money laundering concern."[47] The Treasury Department's Financial Crimes Enforcement Center (FinCen) found that North Korea may reap as much as $500 million annually from counterfeiting, and another $100 million to $200 million annually from narcotics trafficking.

The finding authorizes the Secretary of the Treasury to require "special measures"[48] on the part of U.S. financial institutions and financial agencies that involve increased record keeping and reporting on Banco Delta Asia's transactions. Treasury issued a final rule, effective April 18, 2007, to impose the most stringent fifth special measure—to prohibit certain bank transactions— and issued regulations to implement the rule.[49] The finding and initial proposed rulemaking had a chilling effect on Banco Delta Asia's international business relations. Department of the Treasury officials testified that—

> some two dozen financial institutions across the globe have voluntarily cut back or terminated their business with North Korea, notably including institutions in China, Japan, Vietnam, Mongolia, and Singapore. The result of these voluntary actions is that it is becoming

very difficult for the Kim Jong-Il regime to benefit from its criminal conduct.[50]

North Korea's funds held in Banco Delta Asia were released in 2007; Banco Delta Asia shuttered its operations in 2010.

President Obama also addresses money laundering and counterfeiting in Executive Order 13551 as one of North Korea's many objectionable behaviors to be deterred. The order requires the access to property and interests in property be blocked for any individual or entity identified by the Secretary of the Treasury to have, directly or indirectly:[51]

- imported, exported, or reexported to, into, or from North Korea any arms or related materiel;
- provided training, advice, or other services or assistance, or engaged in financial transactions, related to the manufacture, maintenance, or use of any arms or related materiel to be imported, exported, or reexported to, into, or from North Korea, or following their importation, exportation, or reexportation to, into, or from North Korea;
- imported, exported, or reexported luxury goods to or into North Korea;
- engaged in money laundering, the counterfeiting of goods or currency, bulk cash smuggling, narcotics trafficking, or other illicit economic activity that involves or supports the Government of North Korea or any senior official thereof;
- materially assisted, sponsored, or provided financial, material, or technological support for, or goods or services to or in support of, prohibited activities or any person whose property and interests in property are blocked; or
- be owned or controlled by, or to have acted or purported to act for or on behalf of, any person whose property and interests in property are blocked.

Concluding Observations

The U.S. economic sanctions imposed on North Korea exemplify both the independent and intertwined aspects of the relationship between the legislative and executive branches. Congress defers the broadest power to the President, in the National Emergencies Act and the International Emergency Economic

Powers Act, to curtail trade and transactions between the United States and North Korea. Congress authorizes the President to fine-tune the relationship with North Korea for foreign policy and national security reasons with each waiver authority it incorporates into legislation. At the same time, Congress closely influences the President's choices by enacting issue-driven legislation—addressing human rights matters or proliferation concerns, for example—and by adopting North Korea-specific statutes—most particularly the North Korean Human Rights Act of 2004 (P.L. 108-333), the North Korean Human Rights Reauthorization Act of 2008 (P.L. 110-346), and the inclusion of North Korea into the Iran, North Korea, and Syria Nonproliferation Act of 2000 (P.L. 106-178).

As Congress and the President consider proposals to reform foreign aid, streamline export controls, fund defense and international programs, keep proliferation regimes relevant, assess and enter into treaties and international agreements, and participate in multilateral fora, the effectiveness of economic sanctions as a foreign policy and national security tool is likely to be considered. U.S. policy toward North Korea, expressed both unilaterally and in the United States' position in multilateral fora, is further complicated by other considerations—not the least of which include relations with other states in the region, security responsibilities with South Korea, trade with China, a determination to keep key stakeholders engaged in nonproliferation efforts in both North Korea and elsewhere, and finding the means to balance all U.S. foreign policy and national security interests in a meaningful way.

APPENDIX A. NORTH KOREA—ECONOMIC SANCTIONS CURRENTLY IMPOSED IN FURTHERANCE OF U.S. FOREIGN POLICY OR NATIONAL SECURITY OBJECTIVES

Rationale	Restriction	Statutory Basis [regulation]	Authority to impose	Authority to lift or waive
General foreign policy reasons	Limits the export of goods or services	Export Administration Act of 1979 (P.L. 96-72; 50 U.S.C. App. 2401 et seq.) [15 CFR Part 730-774]	President, Secretary of Commerce, generally	President, Secretary of Commerce, generally
General foreign policy reasons	Limits proportionate	Sec. 307, Foreign Assistance Act	Statutory requirement	No waiver; exemption for

Appendix A. (Continued)

Rationale	Restriction	Statutory Basis [regulation]	Authority to impose	Authority to lift or waive
	share to international organizations which, in turn, expend funds in North Korea	of 1961 (P.L. 87-195; 22 U.S.C. 2227)		certain IAEA programs
General foreign policy reasons	Prohibits assistance from defense appropriations	Sec. 8042, Department of Defense Appropriations, 2015 (Division C, P.L. 113-235; 128 Stat. 2130)	Statutory requirement	No waiver
General foreign policy reasons	Prohibits bilateral assistance	Sec. 7007, Department of State, Foreign Operations, and Related Programs Appropriations Act, 2015 (P.L. 113-235; 128 Stat. 2753)	Statutory requirement	No waiver
General foreign policy reasons	Prohibits Economic Support Funds	Sec. 7043(d), Department of State, Foreign Operations, and Related Programs Appropriations Act, 2015 (P.L. 113-235; 128 Stat. 2649)	Statutory requirement	No waiver
General foreign policy reasons	Prohibits DOD funds	Sec. 8042, Department of Defense Appropriations, 2015 (division C of P.L. 113-235).	Statutory requirement	No waiver
Diplomatic relations severed	Prohibits most foreign aid and agricultural sales under P.L. 480	Sec. 620(t), Foreign Assistance Act of 1961 (P.L. 87-195; 22 U.S.C.	Statutory requirement	No waiver

Rationale	Restriction	Statutory Basis [regulation]	Authority to impose	Authority to lift or waive
		2370(t))		
National security controls, Communism	Limits the export of goods or services	Sec. 5, Export Administration Act of 1979 (P.L. 96-72; 50 U.S.C. App. 2404) [15 CFR Part 730-774]	President	President
Communism	Prohibits foreign aid	Sec. 620(f), Foreign Assistance Act of 1961 (P.L. 87-195; 22 U.S.C. 2370(f))	Statutory requirement	President
Communism	Limits proportionate share to international organizations which, in turn, expend funds in North Korea	Sec. 307, Foreign Assistance Act of 1961 (P.L. 87-195; 22 U.S.C. 2227)	Statutory requirement	No waiver; exemption for certain IAEA programs
Communism	Prohibits Export-Import Bank funding to Marxist-Leninist states	Sec. 2(b)(2), Export-Import Bank Act of 1945 (P.L. 79-173; 12 U.S.C. 635(b)(2))	Statutory requirement	President
Communism	Prohibits support in the IFIs	Sec. 43, Bretton Woods Agreements Act (P.L. 79-171; 22 U.S.C. 286aa)	Statutory requirement	Secretary of the Treasury
Communism	Limits the export of goods or services	Sec. 5(b), Export Administration Act of 1979 (P.L. 96-72; 50 U.S.C. App. 2404(b))	Statutory requirement	President
Communism	Denies favorable trade terms	Sec. 401, Trade Act of 1974 (19 U.S.C. 2431)	Statutory requirement	President
Nonmarket economy and emigration	Denies favorable trade terms	Sec. 402, Trade Act of 1974 (19 U.S.C. 2432)	Statutory requirement	President

Appendix A. (Continued)

Rationale	Restriction	Statutory Basis [regulation]	Authority to impose	Authority to lift or waive
Nonmarket economy and emigration	Denies favorable trade terms	Sec. 409, Trade Act of 1974 (19 U.S.C. 2439)	President	President
Communism and market disruption	Denies favorable trade terms	Sec. 406, Trade Act of 1974 (19 U.S.C. 2436)	President	President
Communism	Prohibits the acquisition of property in U.S. for diplomatic mission	Sec. 205, State Department Basic Authorities Act (P.L. 84-885; 22 U.S.C. 4305)	Secretary of State	Secretary of State
Terrorism, failure to cooperate with U.S. efforts	Prohibits transactions related to defense articles and defense services	Sec. 40A, Arms Export Control Act (P.L. 90-629; 22 U.S.C. 2781)	President	President, at annual review, or waived by the President if he finds it "important to the national interests of the United States."
Excessive military expenditure, human rights violations	Prohibits the cancellation or reduction of certain debt	Sec. 501, Miscellaneous Appropriations, 2000 (H.R. 3425, enacted by reference in P.L. 106-113; 22 U.S.C. 2395a note)	Statutory requirement	President
National emergency, proliferation of weapons of mass destruction	Blocks assets of named proliferators of weapons of mass destruction	International Emergency Economic Powers Act (P.L. 95-223; esp. at 50 U.S.C. 1702); National Emergencies Act (P.L. 94-412; 50 U.S.C. 1601 et seq.)	President [Executive Order 13382, June 28, 2005; 50 U.S.C. 1701 note]	President
National	Prohibits imports,	International	President	President

Rationale	Restriction	Statutory Basis [regulation]	Authority to impose	Authority to lift or waive
emergency	exports, transactions related to transportation	Emergency Economic Powers Act (P.L. 95-223; esp. at 50 U.S.C. 1702); National Emergencies Act (P.L. 94-412; 50 U.S.C. 1601 et seq.) [31 CFR Part 510]	[Executive Order 13466, June 26, 2008; 50 U.S.C. 1701 note]	
National emergency, proliferation of weapons of mass destruction, attack of the Cheonan, nuclear detonations, missile launches, violation of UNSCR resolutions, counterfeiting of goods and currency, money laundering, smuggling, narcotics trafficking, destabilizing the region	Blocks assets of, and transactions with or on behalf of, named entities	International Emergency Economic Powers Act (P.L. 95-223; esp. at 50 U.S.C. 1702); National Emergencies Act (P.L. 94-412; 50 U.S.C. 1601 et seq.) Sec. 5, United Nations Participation Act of 1945 (P.L. 79-264; 22 U.S.C. 287c) [31 CFR Part 510]	President [Executive Order 13551, August 30, 2010; 50 U.S.C. 1701 note] [expands on the national emergency declared in E.O. 13466]	President
To ensure implementation of import restrictions agreed to in the U.N. Security Council	"Except to the extent provided in statutes or in licenses, regulations, orders, or directives that may be issued pursuant to this order…" prohibits "importation into	International Emergency Economic Powers Act (P.L. 95-223; esp. at 50 U.S.C. 1702); National Emergencies Act (P.L. 94-412; 50 U.S.C. 1601 et seq.) Sec. 5, United	President [Executive Order 13570, April 18, 2011; 50 U.S.C. 1701 note] [expands on the national emergency declared in E.O.	President

Appendix A. (Continued)

Rationale	Restriction	Statutory Basis [regulation]	Authority to impose	Authority to lift or waive
	the United States, directly or indirectly, of any goods, services, or technology from North Korea"	Nations Participation Act of 1945 (P.L. 79-264; 22 U.S.C. 287c)	13466]	
Provocative, destabilizing, and repressive actions of DPRK, including cyber-related actions; violation of UNSC resolutions; human rights abuses	Prohibits transactions with and blocks assets of any entity of the government of North Korea or the Workers' Party of Korea	International Emergency Economic Powers Act (P.L. 95-223; esp. at 50 U.S.C. 1702); National Emergencies Act (P.L. 94-412; 50 U.S.C. 1601 et seq.) Immigration and Nationality Act of 1952 (8 U.S.C. 1182(f))	President [Executive Order of January 2, 2015 (as yet unnumbered; 50 U.S.C. 1701 note]	President
Proliferation of weapons of mass destruction: missiles	Prohibits a range of transactions—U.S. Government contracts, export licenses, imports into United States	Sec. 73, Arms Export Control Act (P.L. 90-629; 22 U.S.C. 2797b)	President	President
Proliferation of weapons of mass destruction: nuclear enrichment transfers	Prohibits foreign aid, military aid	Sec. 101, Arms Export Control Act (P.L. 90-629; 22 U.S.C. 2799aa)	President	President
Proliferation of weapons of mass destruction: nuclear reprocessing transfers, nuclear detonations	Prohibits foreign aid (except humanitarian), military aid, USG defense sales and transfers, export licenses for	Sec. 102, Arms Export Control Act (P.L. 90-629; 22 U.S.C. 2799aa-1)	President	President

Rationale	Restriction	Statutory Basis [regulation]	Authority to impose	Authority to lift or waive
	USML goods and services, U.S. Government-backed credits, support in the international banks, agricultural credits or financing, U.S. commercial bank financing, licenses for export of certain goods and services			
Proliferation of weapons of mass destruction: nuclear detonations	Prohibits Export-Import Bank financing	Sec. 2(b)(4) of the Export-Import Bank Act of 1945 (P.L. 79-173; 12 U.S.C. 635(b)(4))	Statutory requirement	President
Proliferation of weapons of mass destruction: nuclear detonations	Prohibits Export-Import Bank financing	Title VI of the Department of State, Foreign Operations, and Related Programs Appropriations Act, 2015 (Division J, P.L. 113-235; 128 Stat. 2598)	Statutory requirement	No waiver
Proliferation of weapons of mass destruction: missiles	Prohibits a range of transactions—contracts, export licenses, imports into US	Sec. 11B, Export Administration Act (P.L. 96-72; 50 U.S.C. App. 2410b)	President	President
Proliferation of weapons of mass destruction	Prohibits a range of transactions—arms sales and exports, dual-use exports, procurement contracts, assistance, imports, support in the	Sec. 3, Iran, North Korea, and Syria Nonproliferation Act of 2000 (P.L. 106-178; 50 U.S.C. 1701 note)	President	President

Appendix A. (Continued)

Rationale	Restriction	Statutory Basis [regulation]	Authority to impose	Authority to lift or waive
	international banks, credit, landing rights			
Human rights (trafficking in persons)	Prohibits non-humanitarian foreign aid, cultural exchanges, support in international financial institutions	Sec. 110, Trafficking Victims Protection Act of 2000 (P.L. 106-386; 22 U.S.C. 7107)	President	President, waiver if in the national interest
Counterfeiting, money-laundering	Prohibits certain commercial bank transactions	31 U.S.C. 5318A (generally referred to by its amendatory vehicle—Sec. 311, USA PATRIOT Act)	Secretary of the Treasury	Secretary of the Treasury

End Notes

[1] Appendix A lists U.S. statutory authorities used to form the economic sanctions regime.

[2] Executive Order 13466, "Continuing Certain Restrictions With Respect to North Korea and North Korean Nationals," 73 F.R. 36787, June 26, 2008; 31 CFR Part 510, November 4, 2010. The same day, the President found that continuing the national emergency first proclaimed under authority of the Trading With the Enemy Act (Presidential Proclamation 2914; December 16, 1950; 15 F.R. 9029) was "no longer in the national interest of the United States." Presidential Proclamation 8271; June 26, 2008; 73 F.R. 36785. That day, he also certified that the Government of North Korea had met the requirements of U.S. law to be found to no longer support acts of international terrorism. Memorandum of June 26, 2008; 73 F.R. 37351. The Secretary of State, a few months later, issued a rescission of North Korea's listing as a terrorist supporter, as required by law. Department of State Public Notice 6415; October 11, 2008; 73 F.R. 63540. CRS Report RL31696, North Korea: Economic Sanctions Prior to Removal from Terrorism Designation, provides details on the statutes relating to a terrorism designation.

The President is required to continue annually any national emergency he issues under the National Emergencies Act, or it expires, along with the sanctions established under the International Emergency Economic Powers Act (IEEPA). President Obama renewed the national emergency declared in Executive Order 13466 in memoranda issued on June 24, 2009 (74 F.R. 30457), and again on June 14, 2010 (75 F.R. 34317).

[3] United Nations Security Council Resolution 1718 (2006), October 14, 2006 (U.N. document S/Res/1718 (2006); United Nations Security Council Resolution 1874 (2009), June 12, 2009 (U.N. document S/Res/1874 (2009).

[4] Executive Order 13551, "Blocking Property of Certain Persons With Respect to North Korea," 75 F.R. 53837, August 30, 2010; and Executive Order 13570, "Prohibiting Certain Transactions With Respect to North Korea," 76 F.R. 22291, April 20, 2011. President Obama cited Section 5 of the United Nations Participation Act of 1945 (P.L. 79-264; 22 U.S.C. 287c) authorities in addition to those provided in NEA and IEEPA.

[5] Executive Order (as yet unnumbered), "Imposing Additional Sanctions With Respect to North Korea, January 2, 2015 (White House Press Release). The 2015 Executive Order also draws on authorities granted the President in the Immigration and Nationality Act (8 U.S.C. 1182(f)) to deny entry into the United States of any person designated pursuant to IEEPA authorities. See Presidential Proclamation 8693 of July 24, 2011, "Suspension of Aliens Subject to United Nations Security Council Travel Bans and International Emergency Economic Powers Act Sanctions," 76 F.R. 44751.

[6] Civilian-Military Joint Investigation Group, On the Attack Against the ROK Ship Cheonan, Ministry of National Defense, Republic of Korea, September 2010; U.N. Security Council, Presidential Statement (U.N. document, S/PRST/2010/13, July 9, 2010).

[7] Executive Order 13551, "Blocking Property of Certain Persons With Respect to North Korea," 75 F.R. 53837, September 1, 2010.

[8] 50 U.S.C. 1701 notes.

[9] See, especially, 15 CFR Part 742.19, "Anti-terrorism: North Korea."

[10] The Secretary of Commerce establishes and administers the Commerce Control List (CCL), goods controlled for national security reasons, pursuant to Section 5(c) of the Export Administration Act of 1979 (P.L. 96-72; 50 U.S.C. App. 2404(c)).

[11] For arms embargoed [D:5] country designations, see 22 CFR Part 126.1. See also 15 CFR Part 740 Supp. 1 for Country Group Lists.

[12] Department of Commerce. Bureau of Industry and Security. 15 CFR Parts 732, 738, 740, 742, 746, 772, and 774. "North Korea: Imposition of New Foreign Policy Controls." January 26, 2007; 72 F.R. 3722-3730. The notice identifies luxury goods to include, in part:

> ...luxury automobiles; yachts; gems; jewelry; other fashion accessories; cosmetics; perfumes; furs; designer clothing; luxury watches; rugs and tapestries; electronic entertainment software and equipment; recreational sports equipment; tobacco; wine and other alcoholic beverages; musical instruments; art; and antiques and collectible items, including but not limited to rare coins and stamps. These and similar items have been imported by North Korea for the use and benefit of government officials and their families, rather than for the good of the North Korean people.

This language generally is stated at 15 CFR Part 746.4(b)(1). See also Supplement No. 1 to 15 CFR Part 746— Examples of Luxury Goods following 15 CFR Part 746.

[13] 15 CFR Part 746.4(b)(4) provides that licenses "are subject to a general policy of approval" if the intended export is a humanitarian item "(e.g., blankets, basic footware, heating oil, and other items meeting subsistence needs) intended for the benefit of the North Korean people; items in support of United Nations humanitarian efforts; and agricultural commodities or medical devices items that are determined by BIS [Bureau of Industry and Security]." 15 CFR Part 746.4(c) provides that some licensing is

possible for items used by news media, U.S. government, International Atomic Energy Agency (IAEA), the European Atomic Energy Community (Euratom), safe operation of civil aircraft, operation technology related to other legally exported commodities, and some gift parcels if no luxury goods are included.

[14] 31 CFR Part 510.201.

[15] Section1, Executive Order 13570, 76 F.R. 22291, April 18, 2011.

[16] Executive Order 13466, "Continuing Certain Restrictions With Respect to North Korea and North Korean Nationals," 73 F.R. 36787, June 26, 2008. See also 31 CFR Part 510, issued November 4, 2010.

[17] 22 U.S.C. 2781. The most recent certification, Department of State Public Notice 8754 of May 12, 2014 (79 F.R. 32357; June 4, 2014), includes Cuba, Eritrea, Iran, North Korea, Syria, and Venezuela. This section of law was added to the Arms Export Control Act in late 1996; North Korea has been included on the list each year since its inception.

[18] Harmonized Tariff Schedule of the United States, general note 3(b).

[19] Section 502(b)(1) of P.L. 93-618 (19 U.S.C. 2461).

[20] Section 402 of the Trade Act of 1974, popularly referred to as the Jackson-Vanik amendment (19 U.S.C. 2432), and Section 409 of that Act (19 U.S.C. 2439).

[21] Section 73 of the Arms Export Control Act (P.L. 90-629; 22 U.S.C. 2797b), Section 11B of the Export Administration Act (P.L. 96-72; 50 U.S.C. App. 2410b), and secs. 2 and 3 of the Iran, North Korea, and Syria Nonproliferation Act of 2000 (P.L. 106-178; 50 U.S.C. 1701 note), as amended. North Korea was added to the latter Act on October 13, 2006, with the signing into law of the North Korea Nonproliferation Act of 2006 (P.L. 109-353; 120 Stat. 2015). See Appendices C and D for lists of North Korean entities and individuals, respectively, cited for proliferation activities, and the country in which the trading partner was likely based (when available).

[22] "In furtherance of world peace and the security and foreign policy of the United States, the President is authorized to control the import and export of defense articles and defense services and to provide foreign policy guidance to persons of the United States involved in the export and import of such articles and services." To accomplish this, the President is authorized to designate items to be controlled—the United States Munitions List (USML). Section 38(a)(1) of the Arms Export Control Act (P.L. 90-629; 22 U.S.C. 2778(a)(1)). The USML may be found at 22 CFR Part 121.1.

[23] Section 74(a)(8)(B) of the Arms Export Control Act (P.L. 90-629; 22 U.S.C. 2797c(a)(8)(B)) applies restrictions to a government of a country deemed to be a nonmarket economy when an entity under the jurisdiction of that government engages in missile proliferation activities, because the separation between government and commerce is not distinct. Section 74 provides, in part: "...in the case of countries with non-market economies ... the term 'person' means ... all activities of that government relating to the development or production of any missile equipment or technology; and ... all activities of that government affecting the development or production of electronics, space systems or equipment, and military aircraft...."

[24] Section 102 of the Arms Export Control Act (P.L. 90-629; 22 U.S.C. 2799aa-1), popularly referred to as the Glenn amendment; Section 2(b)(4) of the Export-Import Bank Act of 1945 (P.L. 79-173; 12 U.S.C. 635(b)(4)); and the Department of State, Foreign Operations, and Related Programs Appropriations Act, 2010 (division F of the Consolidated Appropriations Act, 2010; P.L. 111-117; 123 Stat. 3034 at 3312), relating to Export-Import Bank funding. On December 7, 2006, President Bush determined that North Korea, a non-nuclear-weapon state, had detonated a nuclear explosive device,

citing Section 102(b) of the Arms Export Control Act and Section 129 of the Atomic Energy Act. Presidential Determination No. 2007-07. Public Papers of the President. December 18, 2006.

[25] When appropriations law prohibits the availability of foreign aid, however, numerous exceptions to the law allow aid to be made available for targeted programs. Thus, programs in nonproliferation, demining, child survival, conservation and biodiversity, food aid, debt buybacks, health and disease prevention, unanticipated contingencies, international disaster assistance, and antiterrorism, may be funded or supported in spite of country-specific restrictions. The President also is authorized, under Section 614 of the Foreign Assistance Act of 1961 (22 U.S.C. 2364) to furnish foreign aid "without regard to any provision of this Act, the Arms Export Control Act, any law relating to receipts and credits accruing to the United States, and any Act authorizing or appropriating funds for use under this Act...."

[26] Division J of the Consolidated and Further Continuing Appropriations Act, 2015 (P.L. 113-2325; 128 Stat. 2130 at 2573), See particularly Section 7007—Prohibition Against Direct Funding for Certain Countries (128 Stat. 2603); and Section 7043(d)— East Asia and the Pacific (128 Stat. 2649). Sec, 7032(h)—Democracy Programs (128 Stat. 2621) also continues funding the State Department's database of North Korea's gulags and prisons, begun the previous appropriations cycle by Section 7032(i) of P.L. 113-76 (128 Stat. 513). Previously, Section 2120(d)(6) of P.L. 112-10 removed a discretionary restriction on food aid for FY2011 stated in the FY2010 Act, which read, in part: "(6) ... the Secretary of State shall report to the Committees on Appropriations the amount the Secretary determines the Government of North Korea owes the Government of the United States for the unsupervised distribution of food assistance provided by the United States: Provided, that the Secretary of State should reduce any assistance made available to the Government of North Korea by such amount, unless the Secretary reports ... that the Government of North Korea provided such food assistance to eligible recipients as intended ...."

Subsequent to its nuclear tests, North Korea would also be denied U.S. Export-Import Bank support under this Act— see title VI (128 Stat. 2598). In the Korean Human Rights Act of 2004 (P.L. 108-333; 22 U.S.C. 7801 et seq.), as amended, Congress authorizes funding for FY2013 through 2017 for various aid and diplomacy programs for refugees from North Korea (migration and refugee assistance); up to $2 million per year for broadcasting into the country; $5 million per year in economic support funds for programs promoting democracy, human rights, and governance; and Economic Support Funds to promote human rights, address needs of North Korean refugees, improve accountability of humanitarian assistance inside the country, improve the flow of information into and out of the country, and promote a peaceful reunification of the peninsula under a democratic government.

[27] Millennium Challenge Act of 2003 (division D of title VI of P.L. 108-199; 22 U.S.C. 7701 et seq.); Millennium Challenge Corporation, "Report on Countries That Are Candidates for Millennium Challenge Account Eligibility in Fiscal Year 2015 and Countries that Would Be Candidates But for Legal Prohibitions," Notice of August 25, 2014 (79 F.R. 50704).

[28] Sections 116 and 502B of P.L. 87-195 (22 U.S.C. 2151n and 2304, respectively), as amended.

[29] P.L. 105-292 (22 U.S.C. 6401 et seq.). Department of State. "Secretary of State's Determination Under the International Religious Freedom Act of 1998," Public Notice 8875 of September 16, 2014 (79 F.R. 57171; September 24, 2014).

[30] P.L. 106-386 (22 U.S.C. 7101 et seq.). Department of State. Trafficking in Persons Report 2014. http://www.state.gov/documents/organization/226844.pdf

[31] Section 110(d)(1)(A)(ii) of P.L. 106-386; Presidential Determination No. 2011-15 of September 10, 2010 (75 F.R. 67017).

[32] Section 8042 of the Department of Defense Appropriations, 2015 (division C of P.L. 113-235).

[33] Section 2(b)(2) of P.L. 79-173 (12 U.S.C. 635(b)(2)); amended in 1986 to include this ban on funding to Marxist-Leninist states.

[34] Section 620(f) of P.L. 87-195 (22 U.S.C. 2370(f)). Consider also subsec. (h) of that section, which requires the President to "adopt regulations and establish procedures to insure that United States foreign aid is not used in a manner which, contrary to the best interests of the United States, promotes or assists the foreign aid projects or activities of any country that is a Communist country for purposes of subsection (f)." Consider also Section 5(b) of the Export Administration Act of 1979 (P.L. 96-72; 50 U.S.C. App. 2404(b)), which requires the President to "establish as a list of controlled countries those countries set forth in section 620(f) of the Foreign Assistance Act of 1961...."

[35] For example: Section 620(h) of the Foreign Assistance Act of 1961 (P.L. 87-195; 22 U.S.C. 2370(h)), secs. 502(b)(1) and (b)(2)(A) of the Trade Act of 1974 (P.L. 93-618; 19 U.S.C. 2462(b)(2)(A)), Section 5(b) of the Export Administration Act of 1979 (P.L. 96-72; 50 U.S.C. App. 2404(b)), and Section 43 of the Bretton Woods Agreements Act (P.L. 79-171; 22 U.S.C. 286aa), the latter of which requires the U.S. Executive Directors to the International Monetary Fund "to actively oppose any facility involving use of Fund credit by any Communist dictatorship...."

[36] 22 CFR Part 126.1(a), authorized pursuant to Section 38 of the Arms Export Control Act (P.L. 90-629; 22 U.S.C. 2778).

[37] U.N. Security Council Resolution 1718 (2006), October 14, 2006 (U.N. document S/Res/1718 (2006)); U.N. Security Council Resolution 1874 (2009), June 12, 2009 (U.N. document S/Res/1874 (2009)).

[38] 27 CFR Part 447.52, also authorized under Section 38 of the Arms Export Control Act.

[39] The President. "Termination of the Exercise of Authorities Under the Trading With the Enemy Act With Respect to North Korea," Proclamation 8271 (June 26, 2008; 73 F.R. 36785). On December 16, 1950, President Truman invoked authority granted his office under the Trading With the Enemy Act (TWEA) to declare that a U.S. national emergency existed because of the outbreak of the Korean War (and events elsewhere, as "world conquest by communist imperialism is a goal of the forces of aggression that have been loosed upon the world") (Proclamation 2914; 15 F.R. 9029). A few days later, the Department of the Treasury issued Foreign Assets Control Regulations (FACR; 31 CFR Part 500; 15 F.R. 9040, December 19, 1950, and subsequently amended) to forbid any financial transactions involving, or on behalf of, North Korea and China, including transactions related to travel or the access to North Korean assets that were subject to U.S. jurisdiction. Korea-related FACR have been modified on numerous occasions to take into consideration new circumstances (i.e., transactions relating to technology not in existence at the time the regulations were issued) or to ease restrictions in response to changing conditions (i.e., signing of the Agreed Framework, emerging reports of famine, North Korea's announced moratorium on missile testing).

[40] Executive Order 13466, "Continuing Certain Restrictions With Respect to North Korea and North Korean Nationals," 73 F.R. 36787, June 26, 2008. 31 CFR Part 510, November 4, 2010.

[41] In 1999, President Clinton announced he would lift many restrictions on U.S. exports to and imports from North Korea in areas other than those controlled for national security concerns; the Departments of Commerce, Treasury, and Transportation issued new regulations a year later, effective June 16, 2000, to implement the new policy.

[42] OFAC made add to this list at any time. The Specially Designated Nationals list may be searched online at http://www.treasury.gov/resource-center/sanctions/SDN-List/Pages/default.aspx

[43] OFAC, on January 2, 2015, designated three entities and 10 individuals under this executive order: Reconnaissance General Bureau, Korea Mining Development Trading Corporation, and Korea Tangun Trading Corporation; and Kil Jong Hun, Kim Kwang Yon, Jang Song Chol, Yu Kwang Ho, Kim Yong Chol, Jang Yong Son, Kim Kyu, Ryu Jin, Kang Ryong, Kim Kwang Chun—all officers of either the government or the sanctioned entities. Department of the Treasury. "Treasury Imposes Sanctions Against the Government of the Democratic People's Republic of Korea," press release, January 2, 2015.

[44] Executive Order 12735 of November 16, 1990. On the same day, the President announced his intention to pocket veto H.R. 4653—the Omnibus Export Amendments Act of 1990—with which Congress intended to reauthorize the then-expired Export Administration Act of 1979. In his announcement, President Bush stated his intentions to curtail significantly trade in goods and services that lent themselves to the proliferation of weapons of mass destruction. See "Memorandum of Disapproval for the Omnibus Export Amendments Act of 1990," Public Papers of the President, November 16, 1990. 26 Weekly Comp. Pres. Doc. 1839. E.O. 12735 was subsequently overhauled by President Clinton with the issuance of Executive Order 12938 (November 14, 1994; 59 F.R. 59099; 50 U.S.C. 1701 note). The national emergency therein is renewed annually.

[45] Executive Order 13382, Blocking Property of Weapons of Mass Destruction Proliferators and Their Supporters (June 28, 2005; 70 F.R. 38567).

[46] See Department of the Treasury. Office of Foreign Assets Control. "Nonproliferation: What You Need to Know About Treasury Restrictions." Information Bulletin, most recently updated September 19, 2012, http://www.treasury.gov/resource-center/sanctions/Programs/Documents/wmd.pdf. See also testimony of Robert W. Werner, Director of the Office of Foreign Assets Control, Department of the Treasury, before the House Committee on Financial Services, February 16, 2006.

On January 9, 2007, the Department of the Treasury announced that it had designated Bank Sepah, a state-owned Iranian financial institution, as an entity materially contributing to Iran's proliferation activities. Bank Sepah, coincidentally, according to Treasury, is credited with transferring more than $500,000 for an associate of the Korean Mining Development Corporation. That entity was cited on December 28, 2006, under the Iran, North Korea, and Syria Nonproliferation Act of 2000, for exporting missile technology to Iran. Department of the Treasury. Press release. Iran's Bank Sepah Designated by Treasury: Sepah Facilitating Iran's Weapons Program. January 9, 2007. HP-219; Weisman, Steven. "U.S. Prohibits All Transactions with a Major Iranian Bank," The New York Times. January 10, 2007. p. 3. Korean Mining Development Corporation is cited multiple times under Executive Order 13882.

[47] Pursuant to 31 U.S.C. 5318A, as enacted by the USA PATRIOT Act (Section 311 of P.L. 107-56; 115 Stat. 298). Effective September 12, 2005, the Treasury Department's Financial Crimes Enforcement Network issued a finding (70 F.R. 55214) and a notice of proposed rulemaking (to amend 31 CFR Part 103; 70 F.R. 55217). Documentation on the use of this authority may be found at http://www.fincen.gov/ statutes_regs/patriot/section311.html

[48] 31 U.S.C. 5318A(b) defines "special measures" as (1) record keeping and reporting of certain financial transactions; (2) collection of information relating to beneficial ownership; (3) collection of information relating to certain payable-through accounts; (4) collection of information relating to certain correspondent accounts; and (5) prohibitions or conditions on opening or maintaining in the United States correspondent accounts or payable-through accounts.

[49] Department of the Treasury. "Financial Crimes Enforcement Network; Amendment to the Bank Secrecy Act Regulations—Imposition of Special Measure Against Banco Delta Asia, Including Its Subsidiaries Delta Asia Credit Limited and Delta Asia Insurance Limited, as a Financial Institution of Primary Money Laundering Concern," Final Rule, 31 CFR Part 103 (72 F.R. 12730).

[50] Senate Committee on Banking, Housing and Urban Affairs hearings, September 12, 2006, testimony of Treasury Deputy Under Secretary Daniel Glaser. Congressional Quarterly.

[51] Executive Order 13551, "Blocking Property of Certain Persons With Respect to North Korea," 75 F.R. 53837, September 1, 2010.

In: The Sanctions Way
Editor: Brian Fields

ISBN: 978-1-63482-679-2

Chapter 5

BURMA'S POLITICAL PRISONERS AND U.S. SANCTIONS*

Michael F. Martin

SUMMARY

The release of all Burma's political prisoners is one of the fundamental goals of U.S. policy. Several of the laws imposing sanctions on Burma—including the Burmese Freedom and Democracy Act of 2003 (P.L. 108-61) and the Tom Lantos Block Burmese JADE (Junta's Anti-Democratic Efforts) Act of 2008 (P.L. 110-286)—require the release of all political prisoners before the sanctions can be terminated. The Consolidated Appropriations Act of 2014 (P.L. 113- 76) requires the Department of State and the U.S. Agency for International Development (USAID) to "support programs for former political prisoners" in Burma, as well as "monitor the number of political prisoners in Burma."

Burma's President Thein Sein pledged during a July 2013 trip to the United Kingdom to release all "prisoners of conscience" in his country by the end of the year. Since his announcement, he granted amnesties or pardons on seven occasions. While President Thein Sein has asserted that all political prisoners have been freed, several Burmese organizations maintain that dozens of political prisoners remain in jail and that new political prisoners continue to be arrested and sentenced.

* This is an edited, reformatted and augmented version of a Congressional Research Service publication R42363, prepared for Members and Committees of Congress, dated September 15, 2014.

Hopes for a democratic government and national reconciliation in Burma depend on the release of prisoners, including those associated with the country's ethnic groups. Several ethnic-based political parties have stated they will not participate in parliamentary elections until their members are released. Also, prospects for stable ceasefires and lasting peace with various ethnic-based militias may depend on the release of their members currently in detention.

Estimates of how many political prisoners are being detained in Burma vary. According to the Assistance Association for Political Prisoners (Burma), or AAPP(B), a nonprofit organization dedicated to identifying and locating political prisoners in Burma, the Burmese government was incarcerating 84 political prisoners as of the end of August.

Differences in estimates of the number of political prisoners in Burma can be attributed to two main factors. First, Burma's prison and judicial system is not transparent, making it difficult to obtain accurate information. Second, there is no consensus on the definition of a "political prisoner." Some limit the definition of "political prisoner" to "prisoners of conscience"; others include members of the ethnic militias as political prisoners. President Thein Sein established the Political Prisoner Review Committee (PPRC) in February 2013 to identify all political prisoners in Burma, but the committee reportedly has been unable to agree on a common definition.

The State Department is actively discussing the political prisoner issue with the Burmese government, opposition political parties, and representatives of some ethnic groups. In these discussions, U.S. officials emphasize the importance of the release of all political prisoners for the further easing or removal of U.S. sanctions on Burma.

The status of Burma's political prisoners is likely to figure prominently in any future congressional consideration of U.S. policy in Burma. Congress may choose to examine the political prisoner issue in Burma either separately or as part of a broader review of U.S. policy towards Burma. Congress may also consider inserting in legislation—such as the FY2015 appropriations bills for the State Department (H.R. 5013 and S. 2499)—language pertaining to the political prisoner issue in Burma.

INTRODUCTION

On July 15, 2013, Burma's President Thein Sein gave a speech at Chatham House in London in which he raised the issue of political prisoners, stating:

> Thousands of prisoners have been freed. A special committee, comprised in part of former prisoners, is working diligently to ensure that no one remains in prison due to his or her political beliefs or actions. We are reviewing all cases. I guarantee to you that by the end of this year there will be no prisoners of conscience in Myanmar.[1]

Since making this pledge, President Thein Sein has granted pardons or amnesties to a total of 258 political prisoners on seven separate occasions, the last taking place on January 2, 2014. That same day, in a radio address, President Thein Sein said, "I would also like to inform all of you that with the aim of national reconciliation together with the hard work of the Political Prisoner Review Committee, and in keeping with my promise, *all political prisoners have been freed by the end of last year* [emphasis added].[2]

However, several individuals and organizations quickly disputed the president's assessment. Ye Aung, a member of the Political Prisoners Review Committee (PPRC)[3] created by President Thein Sein, stated on December 31, 2013, that 35 political prisoners remained in prison because of other charges than those included in the presidential pardon.[4] Three weeks later, Ye Aung claimed the number of remaining political prisoners to be 33.[5] On January 3, 2014, the Kachin National Organization (KIO) issued a statement calling for the release of two of its members still in jail, and criticizing the Thein Sein government for "continuing to arrest and sentence fellow Kachins for their political belief."[6] The European Burma Network, a coalition of Burmese political action organizations in Europe, released a statement on January 16, 2014, indicating that "around 33 political prisoners" remain in prison, more than 100 people are awaiting trial for their political activities, and several hundred Rohingyas are being illegally detained.[7]

The status of Burma's political prisoners is a critical issue for U.S. policy. The full removal of many of the U.S. sanctions on Burma is contingent on certain conditions being met by the Thein Sein government and the Burmese military, including the unconditional release of all political prisoners. Moreover, no single issue may play a more pivotal role in Burma's possible transition to a free and democratic country than the release of its political prisoners. Several opposition parties and organizations have stated that they will not participate in parliamentary elections or agree to a national ceasefire until their members are unconditionally freed from detention.

At present, there is no consensus on how many political prisoners there are in Burma. One major reason is the lack of transparency of the records of Burma's 42 prisons and 109 labor camps. Another major reason for variation in estimates is the use of different definitions of political prisoners. Moreover, reports of new political prisoners being arrested and detained periodically appear in the press suggesting the number of political prisoners is a moving target.

State Department officials have held talks with senior officials of the Burmese government, representatives of Burma's leading opposition parties, and major ethnic groups in an effort to move towards a shared understanding of the scope of the political prisoner situation in Burma. Neither the White House nor the State Department has issued a comment on President Thein Sein's claimed fulfilment of his promise to release all political prisoners by the end of 2013.

The 113th Congress has demonstrated a continuing concern about Burma's political prisoners. The Consolidated Appropriations Act of 2014 (H.R. 3547, P.L. 113-76), enacted on January 17, 2014, requires the Department of State and the U.S. Agency for International Development (USAID) to "support programs for former political prisoners" in Burma, as well as "monitor the number of political prisoners in Burma." The political prisoner issue was also raised in hearings held by the House Committee on Foreign Affairs Subcommittee on Asia and the Pacific in September and December 2013.[8]

DEFINING POLITICAL PRISONERS

As noted above, one major factor complicating the determination of the number of political prisoners in Burma is a lack of agreement on the definition of a political prisoner. While the concept of political prisoner has a long history, there is no international standard for defining political prisoners. Prisoners detained for political reasons are afforded some protection by international agreements, such as the Universal Declaration of Human Rights and the International Covenant on Civil and Political Rights. The State Department has a general definition of political prisoner that it uses, but the Thein Sein government and other interested parties have their own, differing definitions.

For Burma, one of the more critical issues in defining political prisoners is whether or not to include individuals who have been detained for their alleged association with Burma's ethnic-based militias or their associated political parties. Because these militias periodically have been involved in armed conflict with the Burmese military, some analysts exclude detainees allegedly associated with the militias from their estimates of Burma's political prisoners.

In addition, certain groups being detained or subjected to serious oppression by the Thein Sein government or officials may also be considered "political prisoners."

President Thein Sein has consistently confined his definition to only include "prisoners of conscience," and has generally used that phrase when discussing the issue. He has repeatedly stated that individuals who have committed criminal acts are not considered "prisoners of conscience," and are expected the serve out their prison sentences. However, in announcing a prisoner amnesty in July 2013, he stated that individuals were released on "humanitarian grounds and encouraging them to be able to serve the national interest."[9] This may indicate a willingness to accept a broader definition in practice, especially if it serves to facilitate negotiations with ethnic minority organizations seeking a nation-wide peace agreement and progress toward national reconciliation.

The Assistance Association for Political Prisoners (Burma), or AAPP(B), an independent organization founded in 2000 by ex-political prisoners,[10] and Human Rights Watch (HRW) use a relatively broad definition of political prisoners. The AAPP(B) defines a political prisoner as "anyone who is arrested because of his or her perceived or real involvement in or supporting role in opposition movements with peaceful or resistance means."[11] Other groups, such as Amnesty International (AI) and the International Crisis Group (ICG), seemingly prefer a narrower definition that only includes so-called "prisoners of conscience."

The State Department's Bureau of Democracy, Human Rights, and Labor considers someone a political prisoner if:

1. the person is incarcerated in accordance with a law that is, on its face, illegitimate; the law may be illegitimate if the defined offense either impermissibly restricts the exercise of a human right; or is based on race, religion, nationality, political opinion, or membership in a particular group;
2. the person is incarcerated pursuant to a law that is on its face legitimate, where the incarceration is based on false charges where the underlying motivation is based on race, religion, nationality, political opinion, or membership in a particular group; or
3. the person is incarcerated for politically motivated acts, pursuant to a law that is on its face legitimate, but who receives unduly harsh and disproportionate treatment or punishment because of race, religion, nationality, political opinion, or membership in a particular group; this

> definition generally does not include those who, regardless of their motivation, have gone beyond advocacy and dissent to commit acts of violence.[12]

In applying this definition, the State Department recognizes that being accused of violent acts and committing violent acts are two different matters, and considers the circumstances pertaining to a particular person when determining if she or he is to be considered a political prisoner.

The AAPP(B) rejects the limitation of political prisoners to "prisoners of conscience" for several reasons. First, the AAPP(B) maintains that the Burmese government frequently detains political dissidents with false allegations that they committed violent or nonpolitical crimes. Restricting the definition to "prisoners of conscience" would exclude many political prisoners. Second, the AAPP(B) maintains that the decision to participate in armed resistance against the Burmese government should be "viewed with the backdrop of violent crimes committed by the state, particularly against ethnic minorities."[13] In short, the AAPP(B) views armed struggle as a reasonable form of political opposition given the severity of the violence perpetrated by the Burmese military and police.

The distinction between "prisoners of conscience" and a broader definition of political prisoners was highlighted by the sentence suspension of January 13, 2012. Only a few of the prisoners released on that date were associated with the ethnic militias or their affiliated political parties. Following his release, Min Ko Naing, a pro-democracy activist, stated that many political activists associated with ethnic armed groups remained in custody.[14] However, Home Affairs Minister Lieutenant General Ko Ko told reporters that some dissidents remained in detention because they had committed criminal acts or have links with the Taliban.[15]

The Political Prisoners Review Committee (PPRC, also known as the Political Prisoner Scrutiny Committee) reportedly attempted to develop a consensus definition of political prisoners. Bo Kyi, the Committee's AAPP(B) representative, told the press in May 2013 that the 19 members have agreed to a definition, but that the Thein Sein government had not formally adopted the definition.[16]

On August 17 and 18, 2014, AAPP(B) and the FPPS held a workshop in Rangoon to discuss a common definition of political prisoners and to open a discussion with the Thein Sein government and Burma's Union Parliament on the topic.[17] Representatives of various Burmese organizations and political parties, as well as the International Committee of the Red Cross, attended the workshop. According to press accounts, the draft definition would include anyone arrested, detained, or imprisoned for their direct or indirect activities to promote human rights, freedom, equality for minorities, and civil liberties, and/or were involved in anti-government protests, demonstrations, assemblies, or publications.[18] Following the workshop, a Member of Parliament from Aung San Suu Kyi's National League for Democracy (NLD) reportedly said that the NLD would submit a proposed definition of political prisoner to the Union Parliament.[19]

The plight of two segments of Burmese society has also been raised in association with the issue of political prisoners. First, local Burmese officials are notorious for corruption, and reportedly frequently use their official power to detain people on falsified charges in order to confiscate property or otherwise exact revenge on their opponents. In addition, officials have reportedly used provisions in old and new laws to arrest and detain people protesting alleged violations of their legal rights. These abuses of power by officials have been portrayed as creating a special group of "political prisoners." Second, the Burmese government continues to single out the Rohingyas, a predominately Muslim ethnic minority residing in northern Rakhine State along the border with Bangladesh, and subject them to more extensive and invasive political repression. According to the Burmese government, the Rohingyas are not Burmese citizens, but illegal immigrants from Bangladesh and India. The Rohingyas are subjected to severe oppression, including restrictions on movement, employment, education, and marriage.

CURRENT ESTIMATES

Different groups provide varying estimates of the number of political prisoners being detained in Burma. AAPP(B)'s August 2014 report on political prisoners states, "By the end of August, 84 political prisoners were incarcerated in Burma, while approximately 122 individuals have been charged for politically motivated actions and await trial."[20] Tun Kyi of the FPPS told reporters on August 24, 2014, that more than 100 activists, including a number of farmers protesting land seizures, have been recognized as political prisoners.[21] The International Federation for Human Rights (*Federation Internationale des Ligues des Droits de L'Homme*, or FIDH), and the Alternative ASEAN Network on Burma (ALTSEAN-Burma) published a list of eight political prisoners on July 15, 2014,[22] and in a separate press statement reported that there were 69 political prisoners in Burmese jails as of

July 10, 2014.[23] The State Department's "Burma 2013 Human Rights Report"[24] states:

> By year's end [2013] one prominent group assisting political prisoners estimated that between 34 and 70 political prisoners remained in detention. This number did not include detainees in Rakhine State, whose numbers were estimated to be in the hundreds.

Amnesty International released a public statement on July 15, 2014, indicating that after a year, President Thein Sein's pledge to release all "prisoners of conscience in Myanmar" remained unfulfilled.[25] While the press statement does not provide a precise number of prisoners of conscience in detention, it did state, "So far in 2014, at least 59 individuals have been charged and 17 of them imprisoned under a range of laws which restrict the rights to freedom of expression and peaceful assembly."

The Thein Sein government has never publicly released an official estimate of the number of political prisoners. Aung Thein, Deputy Minister of the President's Office, told the *Myanmar Times* on August 18, 2014, that 29 alleged political prisoners that were in prison before December 31, 2013, remain incarcerated because they "were found to have broken other penal codes."[26]

Obtaining an accurate and current tally of the number of political prisoners in Burma is complicated by the lack of transparency of Burma's judicial and prison system. Burma has 42 prisons and 109 labor camps scattered across the country, with no publicly accessible records of who is being detained and where they are being detained. To estimate the number of political prisoners, groups rely on a network of sources to provide information concerning each of the prisons and labor camps. The AAPP(B), for example, reports that it uses inside networks, confidential sources, court trial files, recently released prisoners, and families of prisoners to compile its list of political prisoners.[27]

Maintaining an accurate tally of the number of political prisoners is also difficult because the Burmese government and military allegedly continue to arrest and detain new political prisoners, or otherwise infringe on their civil liberties. According to the AAPP(B), the Thein Sein government arrested 12 political activists, sentenced 21 other activists, and released two political prisoners in July 2014.[28]

POLITICAL PRISONERS REVIEW COMMITTEE

On February 6, 2013, President Thein Sein announced plans to form a committee "to scrutinize the remaining political prisoners serving their terms in prisons throughout the country so as to grant them liberty."[29] The original 16-member Political Prisoners Review Committee (PPRC, also known as the Political Prisoners Scrutiny Committee) was chaired by Union Minister Soe Thein, and included representatives from opposition groups with a history of supporting the release of political prisoners, such as the 1988 Generation Students Group, AAPP(B), and the National League for Democracy (NLD). The committee met several times, but significant differences emerged regarding the definition to be used and, by extension, the estimates of the number of political prisoners in Burma. On May 8, 2013, President Thein Sein reconstituted the committee with 19 members and Soe Thein remaining as chair. The committee reportedly continued to disagree about the proper definition and number of political prisoners in detention in Burma.

Reports indicate that its members struggled to reach agreement on critical aspects of their committee's mandate. In addition, it is unclear what influence the committee's recommendations have had with President Thein Sein or Burma's National Defence and Security Council (NDSC), which has the constitutional authority to recommend prisoner amnesties to the President.[30]

In his announcement to form the PPRC, President Thein Sein indicated that Union Minister Soe Thane would be the committee chair, and that the other members of the committee would be "representatives from government ministries, civil society organizations and some political parties." The other 15 members are notable for the inclusion of representatives of three organizations known for their work to free Burma's political prisoners.

The State Department welcomed the formation of the committee and pointed to its creation as evidence that the Thein Sein government is taking serious steps to address the political prisoner problem.[31] Domestic and international human rights organizations also supported the creation of the committee, although in some cases with some skepticism.

The committee first met on February 13, 2013, at the Myanmar Peace Center in Rangoon. It met several times since then, working on developing a common definition of political prisoners, compiling a list of possible political prisoners in detention, and drafting recommendations for President Thein Sein on how to expedite the release of political prisoners identified by the PPRC.

Members of Political Prisoners Scrutiny Committee
(members added on May 8, 2013, in italics)

- Soe Thane (aka Soe Thein) (Chair), Pyidaungzu Minister, President Office
- Brigadier General Kyaw Kyaw Tun, Police Chief, Deputy Minister, Ministry of Home Affairs
- Tun Tun Oo, Deputy Chief Justice, Supreme Court of Burma
- Aung Saw Win, Director General, Bureau of Special Investigation
- Than Htay, Director General, Correctional Department
- Sit Myaing, Myanmar National Human Rights Commission
- U Kyi, Myanmar Red Cross
- Bo Kyi, Assistance Association for Political Prisoners (Burma) (AAPP)
- Nyo Tun, League of Former Political Prisoners (LFPP)
- Ye Aung, Former Political Prisoners Society (FPPS)
- Thura (Zarganar), House of Media Entertainment
- Khun Tun Oo, Shan Nationalities Democratic Party (SNLD)
- Ko Ko Gyi, 88 Generation Students Group
- Nyan Win, National League for Democracy Party (NLD)
- Hla Maung Shwe, Myanmar Egress
- *Win Naing, National Democratic Forces*
- *Thein Nyunt, New National Democracy Party*
- *Kaung Myint Htut, Myanmar National Congress Party*
- *Aung Thein, Deputy Minister, President's Office*

On May 8, 2013, President Thein Sein reconstituted the PPRC, expanding its membership to 19 people (see text box, "Members of Political Prisoners Scrutiny Committee").[32] The decision to augment the membership of the committee reportedly was not discussed with the original 16 members before the President's announcement.[33]

Among the difficulties the group has faced is developing a common definition of political prisoners. Sources indicate that some committee members prefer a narrow definition that would only include prisoners of conscience, while other members support a broader definition (see "Defining Political Prisoners"). On March 14, 2013, the FPPS gathered a group of Burmese political activists and lawyers to discuss the definition of political prisoner. A similar event was held in August 2014.

Another issue for the committee is its ability to work as a group. According to an FPPS spokesperson, his organization had submitted a longer list of people to be released prior to the April 23, 2013, amnesty, but the committee chose to ignore some of those on the list, and to include a number of people not considered political prisoners by the FPPS.[34] Prior to announcing the amnesty, the committee members were reportedly asked to endorse the committee's recommendations, but several refused to do. The FPPS spokesperson stated that the committee's leadership was not interested in the views of the civil society organizations, and was using the committee for political purposes, such as fostering better relations with the European Union.[35]

On December 31, 2013, the PPRC released a statement on its work to date that was printed in the *New Light of Myanmar* on January 1, 2014.[36] The statement recounts that the PPRC had met a total of 12 times between its creation and December 21, 2013, and had submitted the names of 354 people to receive presidential amnesty—which is 33 more than the number of political prisoner released during that time period (see *Table 1* below). On January 14, 2014, the PPRC announced that it would continue to meet because, in the words of one of its members, "there are still political prisoners in Burma."[37] However, it has reportedly met twice since the beginning of 2014, despite repeated requests from AAPP(B) and FPPS for more meetings.

PRISONER RELEASES

Since his appointment in April 2011, President Thein Sein has granted amnesty to selected prisoners on 17 separate occasions, the latest occurring on January 2, 2014 (see *Table 1*). In total, the Thein Sein government has released an estimated 36,761 prisoners, of whom at least 1,165 were political prisoners, according to the AAPP(B).

Several of the prisoner releases have occurred near the time of a major political development between Burma and the United States (see *Appendix* for details). In some cases, President Thein Sein may have released prisoners in an effort to obtain a desired response from the U.S. government or the international community. In other cases, the prisoners may have been released in response to an action by the U.S. government. This pattern is reportedly causing some concern at the State Department and by other observers as it may imply that the prisoners are being used as political pawns.[38]

Table 1. Burma's Announced Prisoner Releases
(In reverse chronological order)

Government	Date	Prisoners Released	Political Prisoners Released	Percentage of Political Prisoners
Union Government	January 2, 2014	13,274	3	negligible
	December 30, 2013	5	5	100.0%
	(amnesty)			
	December 30, 2013	—100	16	—16.0%
	(pardon)			
	December 11, 2013	44	41	93.2%
	November 15, 2013	69	66	95.7%
	October 8, 2013	56	56	100.0%
	July 23, 2013	73	68	93.2%
	May 17, 2013	23	21	91.3%
	April 23, 2013	93	69	74.2%
	November 19, 2012	66	51	77.3%
	November 15-16, 2012	452	0	0.0%
	September 17, 2012	514	88	17.1%
	July 3, 2012	46	25	54.3%
	January 13, 2012	336	302	89.9%
	January 2, 2012	651	34	5.2%
	October 11, 2011	6,359	247	3.9%
	May 16, 2011	14,600	73	0.5%
State Peace and	September 17, 2009	7,114	128	1.8%
Development Council				
	February 20, 2009	6,313	24	0.4%
	September 23, 2008	9,002	10	0.1%
	January 3, 2007	2,831	50	1.7%
	July 6, 2005	334	253	75.7%
	January 3, 2005	5,588	26	0.5%
	December 13, 2004	5,070	21	0.4%
	November 29, 2004	5,311	12	0.2%
	November 18, 2004	3,937	28	0.7%

Sources: AAPP(B); Alternative ASEAN Network on Burma (Altsean), Burma Bulletin, Issue 79, July 2013.

Most Recent Releases

On December 30, 2013, President Thein Sein granted amnesty for five prisoners "on humanitarian grounds" who were reportedly on the PPRC list of political prisoners,[39] and issued Order No. 51/2013, pardoning all persons who had been convicted, awaiting trial, or under investigation as of December 31, 2013, for the following crimes:

- Violations of the Unlawful Association Act;
- Treason (Code of Criminal Procedure Article 122);
- Sedition (Code of Criminal Procedure Article 124(a));
- Violations of the Law to Safeguard the State from Danger of Subversive Elements;
- Violations of the Peaceful Gathering and Peaceful Procession Law;
- "Harming public interests" (Code of Criminal Procedure Article 505); and
- Violations of the 1950 Emergency Act.[40]

An estimated 100 prisoners were released under Order No. 51/2013, of which 16 have been identified as political prisoners by the AAPP(B).

On January 2, 2014, President Thein Sein issued Order No. 1/2014, commuting all death sentences to life in prison, cutting all sentences of over 40 years to no more than 40 years, and reducing all sentences of under 40 years by one-fourth of the proscribed term "with the aim of honouring the 66th Anniversary Independence Day."[41] On January 6, 2014, the government-run newspaper, *The New Light of Myanmar*, reported that 13,274 prisoners had been released under Order No. 1/2014.[42] According to the AAPP(B) and the FPPS, only 3 of the released prisoners were political prisoners.[43]

Conditional or Not?

The use of Section 401 authority for some of the recent prisoner releases raises the issue of possible conditions on the prisoners' sentence suspension. Section 401 of Burma's Code of Criminal Procedure grants the president authority to suspend or remit sentences, with or without conditions, as well as cancel the suspension or remission if the person in question fails to fulfill the conditions for her or his release. As a result, a person released from detention under Section 401 may be required to serve out the rest of his or her suspended sentence if she or he is convicted of another crime or fails to fulfill the conditions of her or his release. At least one pardoned political prisoner, Nay Myo Zin, had been sentenced to serve the rest of his previous sentence (six years) after being convicted of a crime after his release, until he was granted a second pardon in May 2013.[44]

Following their release on January 13, 2012, several former political prisoners indicated that they had been provided unconditional pardons, but a few said that they were instructed to limit their political activities. None of the prisoners released were placed under house arrest. However, Sithu Zeya said to reporters that he was told that if he committed any crime, he would have to serve the remainder of his 18-year sentence. "It is like we are being freed with leashes still attached to our necks," he reportedly said.[45]

The use of Section 401 may also suggest the possibility of some opposition to the release of political prisoners within the Thein Sein government and/or within the Burmese military. Because President Thein Sein based the sentence suspensions on Section 401, he did not need to obtain the approval of Burma's National Defence and Security Council (NDSC), a constitutional body with significant power, consisting of Burma's president; its two vice presidents; the speakers for each chamber of its parliament; the commander-in-chief and deputy commander-in-chief of defense services; and the ministers of border affairs, defence, foreign affairs, and home affairs.[46] President Thein Sein may have decided to use Section 401 authority to avoid NDSC review, given the reported fate of a previous proposed prisoner release.[47]

Continuing Arrest of Political Prisoners

While President Thein Sein claims that there are no political prisoners in Burma, his government reportedly continues to arrest and detain new political prisoners for alleged illegal activities. As previously mentioned, the AAPP(B) reports that as of the end of July around 114 people have been detained and are awaiting trial for what it considers to be political actions. The Asian Human Rights Commission (AHRC), a nonprofit nongovernmental organization located in Hong Kong, is also tracking the detention of political prisoners in Burma. According to the AAPP(B) and AHRC, many have been detained for violations of Section 505 of Burma's Penal Code and/or Section 18 of the Peaceful Assembly and Peaceful Procession Law of 2011—two of the laws

President Thein Sein identified in his pardon of December 30, 2013. To many observers, the Union Government's response to popular protests, as well as its arrest of several journalists, have raised questions about the sincerity of its support of basic human rights, such as freedom of speech and freedom of the press.

As the year 2013 ended, several prominent voices of opposition where arrested, detained and/or sentenced for what were seemingly political reasons. For example, three people released under the December 11, 2013, presidential amnesty – Aye Thein, Htin Kyaw, and Thein San—were reportedly re-arrested within hours of their release for alleged violations of local offenses.[48] The *Democratic Voice of Burma* reported on November 29, 2013, that six activists were convicted for violating Article 18 of the Peaceful Gathering and Peaceful Procession Law for organizing unauthorized demonstrations in Pegu and Rangoon.[49] *Mizzima* reported on December 2, 2013, that nine activists against a copper mine in Letpadaung were also charged for violating Article 18 of the Peaceful Gathering and Peaceful Procession Law.[50]

Another prominent case is that of Naw Ohn Hla, who was sentenced in August 2013 to two years in prison for organizing a demonstration without a permit, but was granted amnesty on November 15, 2013. Naw Ohn Hla is one of the leaders of the anti-copper mine demonstration Sagaing Division. On December 11, 2013, lawyers for Naw Ohn Hla said that she was re-arrested on November 29, 2013, for organizing another demonstration, and has subsequently been charged with disturbing the peace in 2007 by publicly praying for the release of Aung San Suu Kyi.[51]

In 2014, the pattern of arresting, detaining, and trying demonstration organizers and journalists continued. For example, *Eleven Myanmar* reported that Sein Than was sentenced by a court in Latha Township in Yangon Division to four months in prison with hard labor on August 19, 2014, for violating the Peaceful Assembly and Peaceful Procession Act.[52] Sein Than helped organize a march in March 2014 to protest what was considered inadequate compensation for land seized by the Burmese military.

Htin Kyaw, the leader of the community-based Movement for Democracy Current Force, according to *Mizzima*, was sentenced to one year with hard labor by a court in Dagon Seikkan Township in Yangon Division on August 19, 2014, for the Peaceful Assembly and Peaceful Procession Act.[53] The land rights activist has already been sentenced to seven and a half years in prison by other courts for organizing demonstrations. He reportedly is awaiting trials in three other townships on similar charges.

The Thein Sein government arrested and detained four journalists and the chief executive officer (CEO) of the Burmese-language *Unity Journal* at the end of January 2014 for publishing a story alleging that the Burmese military was constructing a secret chemical weapons facility in the mountains of Magway Division.[54] On July 10, 2014, the four journalists—Aung Thura, Lu Maw Naing, Sithu Soe, and The Yazar Oo—and CEO Tin Hsan were sentenced to 10 years with hard labor for violating the State Secrets Act. On July 12, Burmese police reportedly arrested about 50 journalists protesting the *Unity Journal* sentences for violating the Peaceful Assembly and Peaceful Procession Act.[55] The charges against the 50 journalists were supposedly dropped and the Speakers of the two chambers of the Union Parliament have reportedly agreed to revise the penal code to address the treatment of journalists.[56]

Political Prisoners, Parliamentary Elections, and National Reconciliation

The release of political prisoners has potentially important implications for future parliamentary elections and prospects for national reconciliation. The NLD's decision to participate in the April 2012 parliamentary by-elections was apparently based in part on the October 11, 2011, amnesty, which included 39 NLD members, according to the AAPP(B).[57] At the same time, several political parties (including the Chin National Party, the Mon National Democratic Front, the Rakhine National Democratic Party, the Shan Nationalities League for Democracy (SNLD), and the Zomi National Congress) said they would not participate in the 2012 by-elections because some of their members remained in detention.[58] While the January 2012 and July 2013 prisoner releases included a significant number of NLD members and people associated with ethnic organizations, neither amnesty included members of political parties boycotting or barred from the April by-election. Regardless of how the by-elections were conducted, some groups may argue that future parliamentary elections would not be free and fair so long as some political parties are unwilling to participate because of what they perceive to be the detention of their members for political reasons.

The NLD decision to participate in the by-election gave rise to some tension with some ethnic groups, who saw the move as an abandonment of solidarity among opposition groups. One of the reasons the NLD and several ethnic political parties did not participate in the November 2010 elections that brought the Union Government into power was the continued detention of some of their party leaders and members. Some ethnic groups who still had members in detention at the time were unhappy with the NLD's decision to participate in the by-elections. As such, Aung San Suu Kyi and the NLD may be less able to play the role of intermediary in discussions between the Burmese government and various ethnic groups to forge a path towards national reconciliation.

It is unclear how committed the Thein Sein government and Burma's military, the Tatmadaw, are pursuing national reconciliation at this time. According to some observers, the Thein Sein government has made the signing of a nationwide ceasefire agreement (NCA) with the ethnic militias a top priority, and may pardon some prisoners associated with the ethnic organizations to obtain their support for the NCA. Other observers, however, contend that the talks could be designed to provide the Tatmadaw with time to redeploy and rearm troops in the field and resume a military campaign against the militias if the negotiations fail to result in an NCA. As such, it is uncertain if the Thein Sein government would be willing to release alleged ethnic militia members and supporters as part of the ceasefire negotiations.

U.S. Sanctions, Laws, and Political Prisoners

Burma's detention of political prisoners was a major reason for the United States to impose sanctions on Burma between 1988 and 2008.[59] The Customs and Trade Act of 1990 (P.L. 101- 382), which required the President to impose "such economic sanctions upon Burma as the President determines appropriate," was passed after Burma's ruling military junta, the State Peace and Development Council (SPDC), refused to honor the results of May 1990 parliamentary elections and detained Aung San Suu Kyi and many other opposition leaders. Similarly, the Burmese Freedom and Democracy Act of 2003 (BFDA) (P.L. 108-61) was passed after the SPDC cracked down on opposition parties, and once again detained Aung San Suu Kyi and other opposition leaders. The Tom Lantos Block Burmese JADE (Junta's Anti-Democratic Efforts) Act of 2008 (JADE Act) (P.L. 110-286) was passed after the violent suppression of the autumn 2007 popular protests and the subsequent arrest and imprisonment of many of the protest leaders, including a number of Buddhist monks.

The release of *all* political prisoners is also one of the preconditions for the removal of many of the U.S. sanctions on Burma (see *Table 2*).[60]

Table 2. Specified Conditions for the Removal of U.S. Sanctions on Burma (Text extracted from relevant legislation unless otherwise noted; emphasis added)

Law	Conditions
Section 138 of the Customs and Trade Act of 1990	(1) Burma meets the certification requirements listed in Section 802(b) of the Narcotics Control Act of 1986 (2) The national government legal authority has been transferred to a civilian government (3) Martial law has been lifted in Burma (4) Prisoners held for political reasons in Burma have been released.
Section 570 of the Foreign Operations, Export Financing, and Related Programs Appropriations Act of 1997	President determines and certifies to Congress that the Government of Burma has not physically harmed, rearrested for political acts, or exiled Daw Aung San Suu Kyi, and has not committed large-scale repression of or violence against the Democratic Opposition.[a]
Burmese Freedom and Democracy Act of 2003	(A) The SPDC has made substantial and measurable progress to end violations of internationally recognized human rights including rape, and the Secretary of State, after consultation with the ILO Secretary General and relevant nongovernmental organizations, reports to the appropriate congressional committees[b] that the SPDC no longer systematically violates workers' rights, including the use of forced and child labor, and conscription of child-soldiers. (B) The SPDC has made measurable and substantial progress toward implementing a democratic government, including— (i) releasing all political prisoners; (ii) allowing freedom of speech and the press; (iii) allowing freedom of association; (iv) permitting the peaceful exercise of religion; and (v) bringing to a conclusion an agreement between the SPEC and the democratic forces led by the NLD and Burma's ethnic nationalities on the transfer of power to a civilian government accountable to the Burmese people through democratic elections under the rule of law. (C) Pursuant to Section 706(20 of the Foreign Relations Authorization Act, Fiscal Year 2003 (P.L. 107-228), Burma has not been designated as a country that has failed demonstrably to make substantial efforts to adhere to its obligations under

Law	Conditions
	international counternarcotics agreements and to take other effective counternarcotics measures…
The Tom Lantos Block Burmese JADE (Junta's Anti-Democratic Efforts) Act of 2008	(T)he President determines and certifies to the appropriate congressional committees[c] that the SPDC has— (1) Unconditionally released all political prisoners, including Aung San Suu Kyi and other members of the National League for Democracy; (2) Entered into a substantive dialogue with democratic forces led by the National League for Democracy and the ethnic minorities of Burma on transitioning to democratic government under the rule of law; and (3) Allowed humanitarian access to populations affected by armed conflict in all regions of Burma.

Notes:

[a] The law required the imposition of sanctions if the President determines and certifies to Congress that the Government of Burma has committed these acts. It is assumed that removal requires a presidential determination that the Government of Burma no longer commits these acts.

[b] "Appropriate congressional committees" are Senate Appropriations Committee, Senate Foreign Relations Committee, House Appropriations Committee, and House Foreign Affairs Committee.

[c] "Appropriate congressional committees" are Senate Finance Committee, Senate Foreign Relations Committee, House Ways and Means Committee, and House Foreign Affairs Committee.

The economic sanctions required by Section 138 of the Customs and Trade Act of 1990 are to remain in place until the President certifies to Congress that certain conditions have been met, including "[p]risoners held for political reasons in Burma have been released." Section 570 of the Foreign Operations, Export Financing, and Related Programs Appropriations Act of 1997 (Section 570, P.L. 104-208) authorizes the President to ban new investments in Burma if "the Government of Burma has physically harmed, *rearrested for political acts* [emphasis added] or exiled Daw Aung Suu Kyi or has committed large-scale repression of or violence against the Democratic opposition." The BFDA requires a ban on all imports from Burma (including a ban on the products of certain Burmese companies), a freeze of the assets of certain Burmese officials and U.S. opposition to "any loan or financial or technical assistance to Burma" until certain conditions are met, including the release of "all political prisoners."[61] Finally, the JADE Act bans the issuance of visas to certain Burmese officials and their supporters, freezes the assets of certain Burmese officials and their supporters, and prohibits the provision of financial services to certain Burmese officials and their supporters until specific conditions have been met, including the unconditional release of all political prisoners.

The Burmese sanction laws, however, generally include provisions that allow for a presidential waiver if the President determines that it is in the national interest of the United States. The ban on new U.S. investments in Burma was waived on July 11, 2012. The BFDA import ban was waived on November 15, 2012, by the State Department using presidential authority granted in the BFDA. President Obama waived the financial sanctions in the JADE Act on August 6, 2013, as part of Presidential Executive Order 13651. As a consequence, most of the sanctions tied to political prisoners have been waived.

Beyond the laws imposing sanctions on Burma, Congress has also enacted legislation addressing the issue of political prisoners in Burma. Section 7043(b)(3)(A) of the Consolidated Appropriations Act of 2014 (H.R. 3547, P.L. 113-76) stipulates:

> Not later than 60 days after enactment of this Act, the Secretary of State, in consultation with the USAID Administrator, shall submit to the appropriate congressional committees a comprehensive strategy for the promotion of democracy and human rights in Burma, which shall include support for civil society, *former prisoners*, monks, students, and democratic parliamentarians [emphasis added].

The explanatory statement by the Chairman of the House Committee on Appropriations regarding the law elaborates further on the required support for former prisoners, stating:

> In addition to programs specified in section 7043(b)(2) of this Act, the Department of State and USAID shall support programs for former political prisoners (including health, education, and vocational training activities); ... and programs to monitor the number of political prisoners in Burma.[62]

U.S. Efforts Regarding Political Prisoners

U.S. officials have consistently called for the release of all political prisoners in Burma. As previously mentioned, President Obama spoke of the continued detention of prisoners of conscience during his speech at the

University of Yangon in November 2012. National Security Advisor Tom Donilon stated in a presentation in Washington prior to the President's trip to Burma that

> The President's meetings—as well as his speech to the people of Burma—will also be an opportunity to reaffirm the progress that still must be made. This includes *the unconditional release of remaining political prisoners* [emphasis added], an end to ethnic conflicts, steps to establish the rule of law, ending the use of child soldiers, and expanded access for humanitarian assistance providers and human rights observers in conflict areas.[63]

In her testimony at a December 4, 2013, hearing on U.S. policy in Burma, held by the House Committee on Foreign Affairs Subcommittee on Asia and the Pacific, then-State Department Senior Advisor on Burma Judith Cefkin stated:

> We are committed to working with the government, Aung San Suu Kyi and political opposition, and with civil society to fully implement commitments announced before President Obama's visit just a year ago. In particular, we are watching closely the commitment to release all political prisoners by the end of the year.... We are committed to assisting the reintegration of these heroic individuals back into society and ensuring that they are released without conditions.[64]

In its report to Congress required by section 7043(b)(3)(A) of the Consolidated Appropriations Act of 2014, the State Department indicated that it intends to continue to work with the PPRC "to resolve remaining cases of prisoners convicted under repressive laws or for political activism."[65] The report also stated that the technical assistance programs would be established to "rehabilitate released political prisoners so they can effectively resume their role promoting democratic transition and human rights."

Secretary Kerry reportedly raised the case of the five *Unity Journal* staffers in his meetings with President Thein Sein and other senior Burmese officials during his August 2014 trip to Burma.[66]

The State Department has also raised the issue of political prisoners in Burma with other governments. U.S. Ambassador to Burma Derek Mitchell traveled to China, Japan, and South Korea following Secretary Clinton's 2011 trip to Burma to discuss the status of U.S. policy towards Burma during his time as U.S. Special Representative and Policy Coordinator for Burma. The issue of political prisoners was reportedly raised during his meetings on that trip. Similar discussions have been held with other governments and the European Union. Following his visit to Burma, British Foreign Secretary William Hague told reporters that EU sanctions on Burma should not be lifted while political prisoners remain in detention.[67]

In addition to leading an international effort to press for the release of all political prisoners in Burma, senior U.S. officials indicate that the State Department has also had talks with senior Burmese officials, Aung San Suu Kyi and other NLD leaders, several opposition parties, and representatives of some ethnic groups about compiling a complete and accurate list of political prisoners currently in custody.[68] One of the key factors in these discussions is finding a common understanding of who is to be considered a political prisoner. Such discussions are reportedly ongoing.

ISSUES FOR CONGRESS

The continued detention of political prisoners in Burma—as well as the state of human rights in general—are likely to figure prominently in congressional consideration of U.S. policy towards Burma. In the coming months, Congress may decide to examine the status of the implementation of existing U.S. sanctions on Burma. It may also assess the political prisoner issue, either in isolation or as part of a broader consideration of human rights in Burma and sanctions policy. Congress may take up legislation to amend or alter U.S. sanctions on Burma, depending on the evolving conditions in the country. In addition, the Obama Administration may ask Congress for additional funding for humanitarian programs in Burma to address the serious humanitarian needs of Burma's internally displaced people (IDPs), refugees, and other vulnerable populations.

Existing U.S. sanctions on Burma are based on several laws specifically focused on Burma, as well as other laws that sanction nations that fail to comply with U.S. standards of conduct related to specific issues. The changing political situation in Burma, including the status of political prisoners, may warrant congressional consideration of whether existing sanctions should be altered or removed. Similarly, the President has the authority—which he has used several times— to waive or suspend some of the existing sanctions on Burma if he determines that the necessary conditions have been met, or if he determines that doing so is in the national interest of the United States. If the

President were once again to exercise this executive authority, Congress may choose to review the President's determination.

Congress may also choose to monitor and evaluate the Obama Administration's efforts to address the political prisoner and human rights situation in Burma. As previously mentioned, the Consolidated Appropriations Act of 2014 (H.R. 3547, P.L. 113-76) requires the Department of State and the U.S. Agency for International Development (USAID) "support programs for former political prisoners," as well as "monitor the number of political prisoners in Burma." A State Department "Fact Sheet" on U.S. assistance to Burma released on August 8, 2014, specially mentioned "rehabilitation and reintegration programs for released political prisoners."[69] Congress may decide to use its oversight authority to check the Obama Administration's compliance with its legal obligations.

Taken together, information available to CRS suggests that the level of detail provided by the Obama Administration to Congress about the conduct of U.S. policy toward Burma, including its efforts to address the political prisoner problem, falls short of some Members' expectations.[70] The JADE Act explicitly requires that the Special Representative and Policy Coordinator for Burma "consult with Congress on policies relevant to Burma and the future and welfare of all the Burmese people, including refugees."[71] However, the post of Special Representative and Policy Coordinator has been vacant since June 2013.[72] The nomination of a new Special Representative and Policy Coordinator could provide Congress with an additional point of contact through which to communicate with the Obama Administration on the conduct of U.S. policy in Burma. Congress may choose to press President Obama to nominate a Special Representative and Policy Coordinator. In addition, Congress may decide to consult with non-Administration sources and/or hold hearings to ascertain the human rights situation in Burma, including the issue of political prisoners.

Prior to Secretary Kerry's August trip to Asia, which included two days in Burma, Members of the House of Representatives and the Senate sent letters to Secretary Kerry expressing concern about the conduct of U.S. policy toward Burma and indicating dissatisfaction with recent trends in the country. The House letter to Secretary Kerry, which was signed by 72 members, observed, among other things:

> Political prisoners remain behind bars and those released still have sentences hanging over their heads, despite President Thein Sein's

explicit commitment to President Obama and the United States Congress that all such prisoner would be released.[73]

The letter also cites the "jailing and harsh sentences of 10 years of imprisonment with hard labor" of the five *Unity Journal* journalists as evidence that "press freedoms have gone awry." The letter to Secretary Kerry from Senator Marco Rubio and Senator Mark Kirk also indicates that "[f]resh arrests of journalists for simply doing their jobs ... have sent a chill through the press corps."[74] Congress as a whole, the two chambers separately, or Members individually or collectively, may decide to continue to press the Obama Administration and the State Department to address the political prisoner issue with Burmese officials, as well as its implications for further political reform in Burma.

Beyond its oversight function, Congress may decide that circumstances warrant consideration of new legislation related to U.S. policy towards Burma. Section 7043(b) of P.L. 113-76 places new requirements and restrictions on State Department Economic Support Funds in Burma, including support for former political prisoners. It is also possible that the Obama Administration may request Congress consider legislation to amend existing laws to facilitate adjustments in U.S. policy.[75]

Congress may also be called upon to consider additional funding for assistance to Burma. For FY2015, the Obama Administration requested $58.7 million for various projects inside Burma "to promote national reconciliation, democracy, human rights, and the rule of law; foster economic opportunity; increase food security; and meet other basic human needs to enable Burma's population to contribute to and sustain reforms."[76]

If it chooses, Congress could place conditions on the availability of assistance to Burma, including requirements related to the identification and release of political prisoners. Neither the House version of the FY2015 appropriations bill for the Department of State and foreign operations, H.R. 5013, nor the Senate version, S. 2499, contain restrictions and conditions on the use of appropriated funds for Burma, but none explicitly related to political prisoners.

APPENDIX. REVERSE CHRONOLOGY OF PRISONER RELEASES BY THEIN SEIN GOVERNMENT

Since his appointment in March 2011, President Thein Sein has granted pardons or amnesties to prisoners in Burma on 17 separate occasions, resulting in the release of 36,761 prisoners, of whom at least 1,165 were political prisoners, according to the AAPP(B). The following table provides a quick summary of each of those prisoner releases in reverse chronological order.

Table A-1. Summary of Prisoner Releases by Thein Sein Government (in reverse chronological order)

Date and Type	Description
January 2, 2014 Pardon	President Thein Sein issues Order No. 1/2014, commuting all death sentences to life imprisonment, reducing all sentences of over 40 years to 40 years, and reducing all sentences under 40 years by 25%. The pardon results in the release of a reported 13, 274 prisoners, of which only 3 are considered political prisoners by the AAPP(B).
December 30, 2013 Amnesty	Using authority granted by Section 204(a) of Burma's 2008 constitution and Section 401(i) of Burma's Criminal Procedure, President Thein Sein granted amnesty to five people, all of which are considered political prisoners by the AAPP(B).
December 30, 2013 Pardon	President Thein Sein issues Order No. 51/2013, pardoning all prisoners sentenced on or before December 31, 2013, under seven specific laws (see "Most Recent Releases" above). An estimated 100 prisoners are released under the pardon, of which 16 have been identified as political prisoners by the AAPP(B).
December 11, 2013 Amnesty	President Thein Sein granted amnesty to "41 prisoners who were in the list of the committee for scrutinizing remaining political prisoners." The amnesty was granted using authority provided by Section 204(a) of Burma's 2008 constitution and Section 401(i) of Burma's Criminal Procedure. Two of those released, however, were reportedly rearrested within hours of their release. In addition to the 41 prisoners included in the official amnesty announcement, three child soldiers were reportedly released from prison on the same day. The amnesty announcement coincided with the opening of the 27th Southeast Asian Games, which were being held in Burma.
November 15, 2013 Amnesty	Using authority granted by Section 204(a) of Burma's 2008 constitution and Section 401(i) of Burma's Criminal Procedure, President Thein Sein granted amnesty to 69 people. Among the

Table A-1. (Continued)

Date and Type	Description
	released were nine activists who had organized demonstrations in support of the Rohingyas in Rakhine State and an activist who had organized protests against the expansion of the Letpadaung copper mine in Sagaing Division.
October 8, 2013 Amnesty	President Thein Sein granted amnesty to 56 prisoners using authority granted by Section 204(a) of Burma's 2008 constitution and Section 401(i) of Burma's Criminal Procedure. Nearly half of those released—27 people—were reportedly alleged members of the Kachin Independence Army (KIA), the militia associated with the Kachin Independence Organization (KIO). Another 24 people were either alleged members of the Restorative Council of the Shan State (RCSS) or its affiliated militia, the Shan State Army (SSA). Most of the people granted amnesty had been convicted of violating Section 17(1) of Burma's Unlawful Associations Act, among other charges. Some observers think the release was designed to promote progress in ongoing ceasefire talks with the KIO and the RCSS. The amnesty announcement came just before Brunei formally transferred the chair of the Association of Southeast Asian Nations (ASEAN) to Burma during the 23rd ASEAN Summit held on October 8-10, 2013.
July 23, 2013 Amnesty	President Thein Sein granted amnesty to 73 prisoners using authority granted by Section 204(a) of Burma's 2008 constitution and Section 401(a) of Burma's Criminal Procedure. Some sources considered all 73 of the released prisoners as political prisoners. According to AAPP(B) and the FPPS, however, only 68 of those released were political prisoners, including at least 30 people associated with Kachin Independence Army and the Shan State Army–South. A week after the release, Deputy Minister of Home Affairs Brigadier General Kyaw Zan Myint reportedly told the Union Parliament that the prisoners had been granted a conditional release, and that they may have to serve out the remainder of the sentence if they break the law in the future.
May 17, 2013 Amnesty	Four days before his historic trip to the United States in May 2013, President Thein Sein granted amnesty to 23 prisoners, of whom 21 were considered political prisoners by the AAPP(B). Among those released was Nay Myo Zin, who had been previously released, but subsequently returned to prison to serve out the remaining six years of his sentence after his arrest for insulting a police officer. Nay Myo Zin was the first ex-political prisoner re-imprisoned after being granted amnesty.
April 23, 2013 Amnesty	President Thein Sein granted amnesty to 93 prisoners. According to AAPP(B), 69 of those released were political prisoners. Also

Date and Type	Description
	included among the 69 political prisoners were 40 "Shan rebel soldiers," according to the opposition publication, Irrawaddy. The prisoner release was announced the day after the European Union voted to terminate all its sanctions on Burma, except for the arms embargo. In addition, the Political Prisoners Review Committee reportedly recommended a number of people to be released, but President Thein Sein apparently chose to release other individuals, raising questions about the influence of the committee.
November 19, 2012 Amnesty	Using authority granted by section 204(a) of Burma's 2008 constitution and Section 401(a) of Burma's Criminal Procedure, President Thein Sein granted amnesty to 66 prisoners on November 19, 2012, during President Obama's visit to Burma. The AAPP(B) identified 51 of those released as being political prisoners.
November 15-16, 2012 Amnesty	President Thein Sein granted amnesty to 452 prisoners using authority granted by section 204(a) of Burma's 2008 constitution and Section 401(a) of Burma's Criminal Procedure. None of the prisoners released were identified as political prisoners by AAPP(B).
September 17, 2012 Amnesty	Shortly before President Thein Sein was scheduled to visit the United States to speak before the United Nations General Assembly, he granted amnesty to 514 people. The AAPP(B) identified 88 political prisoners among those released. According to some observers, the prisoner release was intended to bolster the chances that the Obama Administration would announce a further easing of sanctions during President Thein Sein's visit to the United States.
July 3, 2012 Amnesty	Using authority granted by section 204(a) of Burma's 2008 Constitution, President Thein Sein granted amnesty to 46 domestic prisoners and 34 foreign nationals. The AAPP(B) identified 25 of the domestic prisoners as political prisoners.
January 13, 2012 Amnesty	President Thein Sein suspended the sentences of 651 prisoners "who were serving their appropriate prison terms" using authority granted by Section 401 of Burma's Code of Criminal Procedure. The AAPP(B) identified 302 political prisoners among the 336 people released. The release came at the tail end of the fourth visit by U.S. Special Representative and Policy Coordinator for Burma Derek Mitchell and a week after British Foreign Minister William Hague's first trip to Burma.
January 2, 2012 Amnesty	President Thein Sein issued Presidential Order No. 1/2012, granting a partial amnesty to all existing Burmese prisoners "[a]s a gesture of hailing the 64th Anniversary Independence Day and for the sake of State peace and stability." The AAPP(B) considered 34 of the 651 people released as political prisoners.

Table A-1. (Continued)

Date and Type	Description
October 11, 2011 Amnesty	President Thein Sein issued Order No. 49/2011, terminating the prisoner sentence for 6,359 individually named persons, including 247 political prisoners.
May 16, 2011 Amnesty	President Thein Sein issued Order No. 28/2011, commuting all death sentences to life in prison, and reduced all other sentences by one year in duration (exclusive of remission days). As a result, 14,600 prisoners are released, but only 73 are identified as political prisoners by the AAPP(B).

Source: CRS.

End Notes

[1] Thein Sein, "Myanmar's Complex Transformation: Prospects and Challenges," speech given at Chatham House, London, United Kingdom, July 15, 2013.

[2] President Office, "Committee for Scrutinizing the Remaining Political Prisoners Healthy Constitution Must Be Amended from Time to Time to Address National, Economic, Social Needs of Society," press release, January 2, 2014, http://www.president-office.gov.mm/en/?q=briefing-room/news/2014/01/02/id-3135.

[3] The committee is also frequently referred to as the Political Prisoner Scrutiny Committee, or PPSC.

[4] "Thirty-five Political Prisoners Still in Jail Despite Amnesty for 'Other Offenses,'" Eleven Myanmar, January 2, 2014.

[5] Aye Myint San, "33 Political Prisoners Still in Jail, Says Committee," Mizzima, January 21, 2014.

[6] Kachin National Organization, "Kachin National Organization Demand Unconditional Release of All Kachin Political Prisoners," press release, January 3, 2014.

[7] European Burma Network, "No End in Sight for Political Prisoners in Burma—Permanent Review Mechanism Needed," press release, January 16, 2014.

[8] U.S. Congress, House Committee on Foreign Affairs, Subcommittee on Asia and the Pacific, An Unclear Roadmap: Burma's Fragile Political Reforms and Growing Ethnic Strife, 113th Cong., 1st sess., September 19, 2013; and U.S. Congress, House Committee on Foreign Affairs, Subcommittee on Asia and the Pacific, Oversight of U.S. Policy Toward Burma, 113th Cong., 1st sess., December 4, 2013.

[9] "Amnesty Granted to 73 Prisoners," New Light of Myanmar, July 24, 2013.

[10] The AAPP(B) describes itself as being dedicated to identifying and locating political prisoners in Burma, and providing support for the prisoners and their families.

[11] AAPP(B), "The Recognition of Political Prisoners: Essential to Democratic and National Reconciliation Process," press release, November 9, 2011.

[12] Definition provided to CRS by the State Department

[13] AAPP(B), "The Recognition of Political Prisoners: Essential to Democratic and National Reconciliation Process," press release, November 9, 2011.

[14] "Burma's Remaining Jailed Dissidents," Irrawaddy, January 17, 2012.

[15] Aye Aye Win, "Praise for Myanmar Release of Political Prisoners," Associated Press, January 15, 2012.

[16] "Burma Releases Political Prisoners Ahead of US State Visit," Irrawaddy, May 17, 2013.

[17] "Myanmar Still Seeks Definition of Political Prisoner," Eleven Myanmar, August 18, 2014.

[18] San Yamin Aung, "Definition of Political Prisoner Sought with Govt, Activists at Odds," Irrawaddy, August 21, 2014.

[19] "NLD Moving to Recognise Myanmar's 'Political Prisoners,'" Eleven Myanmar, August 20, 2014.

[20] Assistance Association for Political Prisoners (Burma), Monthly Chronology of July 2014, August 8, 2014.

[21] "Protesting Farmers among over 100 Activists Recognised as Political Prisoners," Eleven Myanmar, August 24, 2014.

[22] International Federation for Human Rights, Who Are Burma's Political Prisoners?, July 15, 2014.

[23] International Federation for Human Rights, "Burma: Increased Number of Political Prisoners Calls for Renewed International Presure," press release, July 15, 2014.

[24] Department of State, Burma 2013 Human Rights Report, February 27, 2014, http://www.state.gov/j/drl/rls/hrrpt/ humanrightsreport/index.htm?year=2013&dlid=220182#wrapper.

[25] Amnesty International, Myanmar: One Year On, President's Promise to Rele ase All Prisoners of Conscience Remains Unfulfilled, ASA 16/014/2014, July 15, 2014.

[26] Ye Mon and Lum Min Mang, "Government Denies Political Prisoners Remain Behind Bars," Myanmar Times, August 18, 2014.

[27] AAPP(B), "Political Prisoner List is Now 1,572—Location of 918 Confirmed and Documented," press release, December 23, 2011.

[28] Assistance Association for Political Prisoners (Burma), Monthly Chronology of Burma's Political Prisoners for July, 2014, August 8, 2014.

[29] President Office, Republic of the Union of Myanmar, "Committee to be Formed to Grant Liberty to Remaining Political Prisoners," press release, February 6, 2013.

[30] Section 204 of the constitution grants the NDSC the authority to recommend prisoner amnesties to the President.

[31] On February 11, 2013, the State Department issued a statement welcoming the formation of the committee, stating that the Union Government "has taken an important step towards national reconciliation," and that the State Department looked forward "to supporting the implementation of this process." (State Department, "Progress on Political Prisoners in Burma," press release, February 11, 2013.)

[32] President Office, "Committee for Scrutinizing the Remaining Prisoners of Conscience Reconstituted," Notification No. 43/2013, May 8, 2013.

[33] Naw Say Phaw Waa, "Activists Slam Reshuffle of Prisoner Body," Myanmar Times, May 13, 2013.

[34] "Prisoner Release Draws Criticism from Activists," Myanmar Times, April 24, 2013.

[35] Ibid.

[36] "Press Release on Work Progress Report of Committee for Scrutinizing the Remaining Political Prisoners," New Light of Myanmar, January 1, 2014.

[37] Feliz Solomon, "'Not Finished Yet—Political Prisoner Committee to Continue," Democratic Voice of Burma, January 14, 2014.

[38] For example, see "Myanmar Uses Prisoners as Pawns," Bangkok Post, May 6, 2013; or Hanna Hindstrom, "Thein Sein Using Political Prisoners as 'Pawns,'" Democratic Voice of Burma, September 19, 2012.

[39] "Amnesty Granted for Five Prisoners," New Light of Myanmar, December 31, 2013.

[40] "Order No. 51/2013—Pardon," New Light of Myanmar, December 31, 2013.

[41] President Office, "Order No. (1/2014)—Presidential Pardon," January 2, 2014, published in the New Light of Myanmar, January 3, 2014.

[42] "13,274 Prisoners Released Under Pardon," New Light of Myanmar, January 6, 2014.

[43] Ei Ei Toe Lwin, "Activists Say Political Prisoners Remain in Jail," Myanmar Times, January 6, 2014.

[44] Nay Moe Zin was released in January 2012, with six more years to serve on his sentence. He was originally sentenced to 10 years in prison in August 2011 for breaking the Electronic Transactions Act, a law that is highly criticized by free speech advocates. In May 2013, he chose to serve a three-month sentence for allegedly defaming a police officer. The Ministry of Home Affairs subsequently decided to reinstate his previous sentence. ("Burma Cancels Amnesty for Former Political Prisoner," Irrawaddy, May 8, 2013)

[45] "Burma Frees High-Profile Dissidents in Amnesty," BBC, January 13, 2012.

[46] Hla Hla Htay, "Myanmar Prisoner Release Delayed," Agence France Press, November 14, 2011.

[47] On January 2, 2012, President Thein Sein issued Presidential Order No. 1/2012, granting a partial amnesty to all existing Burmese prisoners using authority granted by section 204(a) of Burma's 2008 Constitution. Amnesties granted under section 204(a) are subject to the approval of the NDSC. That amnesty was reportedly delayed by NDSC for nearly three months.

[48] "Pardoned Prisoners Re-arrested within Hours, Says Activist Group," Mizzima, December 11, 2013.

[49] Shwe Aung, "Activists Convicted Under Article 18 in Rangoon, Pegu," Democratic Voice of Burma, December 3, 2013.

[50] Assistance Association for Political Prisoners (Burma), Monthly Chronology of Burma's Political Prisoners for December, 2013, January 13, 2014, http://www.aappb.org/ AAPP_December_chronology_2013..pdf.

[51] Kyaw Hsu Mon, "Burma Activist Naw Ohn Hla Faces 'Religious Disturbance" Complaint," Irrawaddy, December 11, 2013.

[52] "Protest Leader Sentenced to Four Months with Hard Labour," Mizzima, August 20, 2014.

[53] "MDCF's Founder Geta Another Year in Prison," Eleven Myanmar, August 19, 2014.

[54] Committee to Protect Journalists, "Burma Holds 4 Journalists for Chemical Weapons Report," February 3, 2014. The Thein Sein government and the Burmese military deny that they are constructing a chemical weapons factory.

[55] Front Line Defenders, Burma - More than 50 Journalists Charged for Protesting the 10-year Prison Sentence of Unity Weekly Journalists, July 15, 2014.

[56] Yen Snaing, "Parliament Speakers Consider Revision of Penal Code for Journalists," August 21, 2014.

[57] Another factor in the NLD decision was the amendment of election laws to allow Aung San Suu Kyi and other NLD members to run for office.

[58] Tun Tun, "Newly Formed Parties to Contest in Burmese By-Election," Mizzima, November 17, 2011; and Wai Moe, "NLD Decides to Re-Register, Compete in Coming Elections," Irrawaddy, November 18, 2011. In June 2103, the Chin National Party, Rakhine National Democratic Party, the Shan Nationalities League for Democracy (SNLD), and 12 other ethnic parties agreed to form a united Federal Union Party for the 2015 elections. The Mon National Democratic Front (renamed the Mon Democracy Party) and the Zomi National Congress also decided to participate in the 2015 elections, but as individual parties.

[59] For more about the history of U.S. sanctions on Burma, see CRS Report R41336, U.S. Sanctions on Burma, by Michael F. Martin.

[60] For a description of the waiver provisions of U.S. sanctions on Burma, see CRS Report R41336, U.S. Sanctions on Burma, by Michael F. Martin.

[61] The general import ban and company-specific import ban in the BFDA lapsed in July 2013, when Congress did not pass the required annual resolution to renew the trade restrictions. The other sanctions specified in the law remain in effect.

[62] "Explanatory Statement by Mr. Rogers of Kentucky, Chairman of the House Committee on Appropriations regarding the House Amendment to the Senate Amendment on H.R. 3547, Consolidated Appropriations Act, 2014," Congressional Record, daily edition, vol. 160, No. 9 - Book II (January 15, 2014), p. H1169.

[63] Office of the Press Secretary, The White House, "President Obama's Asia Policy and Upcoming Trip to Asia," press release, November 15, 2012.

[64] Department of State, "Oversight of U.S. Policy Toward Burma: Testimony of Judith Beth Cefkin," press release, December 4, 2013.

[65] Department of State, Strategy for the Promotion of Democracy and Human Rights in Burma, Ref: Sec. 7043(b)(3)(A) of H.R. 3547, "Consolidated Appropriations Act, 2014," April 21, 2014.

[66] Michael R. Gordon, "Kerry Urges Myanmar to Stay on Path to Democracy, Despite Stumbles," New York Times, August 10, 2014.

[67] Ba Kaung, "EU Sanctions Remain Until Burmese Prisoner Release: Hague," Irrawaddy, January 6, 2012.

[68] Interview with CRS, January 2012.

[69] Department of State, U.S. Assistance to Burma, August 8, 2014.

[70] Based on CRS communications with Members of Congress and their staff.

[71] JADE Act, Section 7(c)(4).

[72] While the Special Representative position has been vacant, the State Department created the position of Senior Advisor for Burma in March 2013. The first Senior Advisor was W. Patrick Murphy, and his successor in August 2013 was Judith Cefkin.

[73] Letter from 72 Members of the House of Representatives to John Kerry, Secretary of State, July 31, 2014.

[74] Letter from Marco Rubio, Senator, and Mark Kirk, Senator, to John Kerry, Secretary of State, August 7, 2014.

[75] The Obama Administration has previously asked Congress to amend Burmese sanctions law. The 112th Congress passed P.L. 112-192, at the request of the Obama Administration. The law grants the President the authority to waive U.S. opposition to international financial institution assistance to Burma required under Section 5 of the 2003 BFDA if the President determines to do so is in the national interest of the United States.

[76] Department of State, Congressional Budget Justification, Volume 32: Foreign Operations—Fiscal Year 2015, June 18, 2014.

INDEX

D

E

F

G

H

I

J

K

L

O

P

Q

R

S

T

Y